GREAT ZULU COMMANDERS 1838–1906

GREAT ZULU COMMANDERS

IAN KNIGHT

ARMS AND
ARMOUR

Arms and Armour
An Imprint of the Cassell Group
Wellington House, 125 Strand, London WC2R 0BB

British Library Cataloguing-in-Publication Data:
a catalogue record for this book is available from the
British Library

ISBN 1-85409-390-8

Distributed in the USA by Sterling Publishing Co. Inc.,
387 Park Avenue South, New York, NY 10016-8810.

Designed and edited by DAG Publications Ltd.
Designed by David Gibbons; layout by Anthony A. Evans;
edited by John Gilbert; printed and bound
in Great Britain by MPG Books, Bodmin, Cornwall.

CONTENTS

To Alexander:
lightning at dawn

INTRODUCTION

In 1964, a feature film, based upon the battle of Rorke's Drift, one of the most famous incidents in the Anglo-Zulu War of 1879, was released under the simple title *Zulu*. The producers no doubt hoped that that one word would be sufficient to a strike a chord with the potential audience in Europe and America, and that it would sell the film on the exciting image of 'savage, untamed' Africa it conjured up. Indeed, the film itself went further, portraying the Zulu people as part of the African landscape itself, incomprehensible, alien and utterly hostile to the group of British redcoats who provide the film's dramatic focus. Zulu warriors appear mysteriously over the crest of a hill, their presence announced by a mysterious drubbing sound as they rattle their spears on their shields, or rise up from the very grass itself, threatening to swallow up the soldiers who have strayed too far from home, and in a bad cause.

They were right, of course, for the film has an enduring appeal, particularly in Britain. *Zulu* provides an interesting critique of colonial adventurism through the jaundiced eyes of the 1960s, yet the very terms in which it does so are part of the colonial legacy. Despite it's title, there is no Zulu perspective to the story presented in *Zulu*; nor could there be, for the sense of menace and tension which pervades the Zulu presence is dependent upon the audience identifying with the redcoats' isolation. Indeed, much of the dramatic power of the film comes from the way it exploits a popular view of the Zulu as the archetypal African warrior society, a view which has lingered since the time of the war itself. In that regard, the film accurately reflects a genuine nineteenth-century paranoia; the vulnerability experienced by generations of white settlers and soldiers trying to colonise Africa, surrounded by strange and inevitably hostile cultures, and impossibly outnumbered. Surrounded, indeed, by 'savage and untamed' Africa, which they will 'civilise' and 'tame', according to their very different value systems. The role of the Zulu in this particular vision is deep-rooted, for the Zulu were one of the most robust African societies encountered by white colonial groups, and they resisted European penetration stoutly. The image of the Zulu as an overwhelming warrior horde - impersonal, faceless, brave, remorseless and brutal - so effectively conjured up in the film, can be traced directly to some of the events described in this book. The Zulu people have never escaped the impact of their military successes against the Boer Trekkers in 1838, or against the British at Isandlwana in 1879, and the image of them which survives today owes much to the sense of shock experienced by their enemies on those occasions. The Zulu attacks on the Boer camps along the Bushmans and Bloukrans rivers helped shape the Afrikaner view of the *swart gevaar* - the black threat - for generations to come, and was one of the psychological roots of apartheid, while Isandlwana became part of a different British mythology, that of hopeless courage and sacrifice on the far distant frontiers of Empire.

Yet all of these views remain those of outsiders, couched in the loaded terms of the Imperial past. They have helped to obscure not only the fact that in their conflicts with whites the Zulu were more often on the defensive than offensive, but also the true nature and role of the Zulu army, and the individual achievements of the men who functioned within it. The stereotype of the Zulu as the ultimate warrior society was deliberately fostered by the British as part of a propaganda war on the eve of the 1879 campaign, but is profoundly misleading. Unlike European armies, the Zulu military system was composed not of full-time professional soldiers, but of armed citizens, whose role as 'warriors' was only one of many they fulfilled within Zulu society. While every Zulu man was enrolled in an *ibutho* - a regiment, raised according to the common age of its members - he only served with that regiment for a few months each year, and for the rest lived at home with his family, tending cattle, guarding crops and hunting.

This was true as much for each of the famous men described in this book, as for the most ordinary warrior, whose name is recalled today only in the lineages of his family. While the strong sense of group identity and morale possessed by the Zulu army, which was encouraged by pre-combat rituals which bound the warriors together into a spiritual whole, created the impression of the great threatening mass among their enemies, the conduct of the army in the field - and therefore the course of the great battles, like Blood River, Isandlwana or Msebe - nevertheless reflected the skills and shortcomings of its individual commanders.

It is not always easy to draw out the details of the lives of some of the men who led the Zulu army into battle. Much of what has come down to us was recorded by literate observers who, by definition, were often on the other side. The surviving evidence is often therefore hostile, ill-informed, and marred by cultural misconceptions. While evidence from Zulu sources fills some of the gaps, gulfs inevitably remain, and the accelerating erosion of the chain of oral tradition today makes the gathering of such evidence increasingly difficult. Nevertheless, by studying the careers of individual Zulu commanders, it has been possible to set the great dramatic incidents of Zulu history within a specific and very human framework; to see the impact of decisions made by individuals who were sometimes inspired, often flawed, who had their good days and bad days, but were always real people, and never stereotypes.

A word of explanation is perhaps needed for the criteria of selection, since several of the men studied herein might fairly be said to have been neither 'great commanders', nor even 'Zulu'. Certainly, Mbilini waMswati, while undoubtedly the greatest guerrilla leader to emerge from the war of 1879, was actually a Swazi prince, while Prince Dabulamanzi kaMpande, who became the Zulu general best-known to the British, had a military career marked more by heroic failure than anything else. Not all were always loyal to the Zulu Royal House; Zibhebhu kaMaphitha fought gallantly in the cause of the Zulu kingdom in 1879, but after the war fiercely rejected the authority of the Zulu kings, and proved their most ruthless opponent in the civil wars of the 1880s. Bambatha kaMancinza was the chief of the Zondi people, whose territory lay in colonial Natal, and who had no great links with the Zulu kingdom.

Yet all of these men were played an important part in the one great struggle which underpins the history of the Zulu kingdom in the nineteenth and early twentieth century; the struggle to create the kingdom, and to hold it together in the face of external threats and internal tensions. King Shaka, undoubtedly the greatest warrior produced by the Royal House, waged war to extend his control over neighbouring groups, and to establish the fabric of the kingdom itself. His successors - from Dingane, through Cetshwayo to Dinuzulu - fought desperately and ultimately without success to defend that kingdom against white intrusion, and the lives of all the men considered in this book were part of that struggle in one respect or another. If Bambatha is unusual in that he was not part of the establishment of the old kingdom, his dilemma brings the story into the twentieth century, for he had grown up in a world dominated by the realities of colonial rule, and he was drawn to the mystique of the Zulu kingdom, which had achieved a potency no less powerful among African communities than among the whites. In the face of desperate and intolerable pressure from an unsympathetic colonial administration, Bambatha took up arms to restore a kingdom of which he had been no part, and gambled everything upon the nostalgic appeal of the heroic traditions of a golden age which, in truth, had already been broken.

It is worth remembering that the rise and fall of the old kingdom covered a remarkably short time - less than three generations. In the close-knit world of the Zulu ruling elite, this can often be charted in the lives of a single family. The family of Ndlela kaSompisi, for example, reflected the fortunes of the Royal House itself. Ndlela fought under Shaka as a warrior, and rose to become Dingane's great general in his war against the Boers - the first against the successive waves of white encroachment. Ndlela's sons, Godide and Mavu-mengwana, both held important command in the Anglo-Zulu War, while

INTRODUCTION

Ndlela's grandson, Mangathi kaGodide, joined Bambatha in that last hopeless struggle. Moreover, the pace of events, and shifting political allegiances, over that period meant that many of the men described in this book not only knew each other, and fought alongside one another, but lived to fight again later on opposite sides. Thus Zibhebhu had fought under the command of Ntshingwayo kaMahole in the great Isandlwana and Khambula campaigns, but in the divided post-war years actually commanded the force which killed Ntshingwayo, together with scores of other royalist dignitaries, in the attack on oNdini in 1883. That the ultimate destruction of the old Zulu kingdom was wrought by Zulus who had once fought bravely in its defence is brutal proof of the success of the policy of 'divide and rule' adopted by the British after the 1879 war. For this reason, it has sometimes been necessary here to consider some battles more than once, from the different perspectives of the individuals concerned.

There is more, then, to the lives of these great Zulu commanders than their victories and defeats. Their lives were the very stuff of which the history of the old kingdom was made, and it is their achievements and failures which have moulded the image of their people which survives to this day.

ACKNOWLEDGEMENTS

My greatest debt remains to *Makhandakhanda*, 'SB' Bourquin, that great repository of Zulu history and culture, who started me on a journey into Zululand and its past long before the advent there of tourist lodges and guided tours. Many people have helped in my researches in the years since, too many to mention here; among those who deserve particular note this time, Gillian and Grant Scott-Berning have proved generous hosts in Durban, while Graeme and Cynthia Smythe have allowed me free rein of their home in Dundee, the base for many of my travels. I have spent many happy hours exploring Zululand with Eric Boswell, who introduced me to Paul Cebekhulu, a grandson of Zibhebhu kaMaphitha, who in turn provided perceptive insights into the life of that most dynamic of the Zulu commanders. I have drawn great inspiration, too, from the traditional histories of Mdiceni Gumede and Prince Gilenja Biyela, while L.B.Z. Buthelezi, one of Zululand's finest Zulu-language poets, took great pains to answer my questions about the history of the Buthelezi people. John Laband generously allowed me access to his own ground-breaking research into the Zulu kingdom, while in the UK Ian Castle has consistently allowed himself to be used as a sounding-board with good humour, and also drew the maps. Rai England, as ever, proved a source of fresh illustrations, and John Devenport deserves especial thanks for drawing my attention to the remarkable photo of Mehlokazulu under guard.

KING SHAKA kaSENZANGAKHONA
'What kind of king has now arisen?'

Of all the great men who rose to prominence in the old Zulu kingdom, King Shaka kaSenzangakhona remains perhaps the most discussed, and the least understood. The image perpetuated of him in the European world was created during his life by a handful of white adventurers, whose letters and memoirs deliberately blackened his reputation for their own ends, and did lasting damage to his name. After the triumph of colonialism, white historians justified their control over the Zulu by using that image to damn as cruel and corrupt the independent political systems they had displaced. Yet among African groups, too, Shaka was the subject of fervent mythologising, cast either in the mould of a heroic warrior of almost classical proportions, or as a ruthless tyrant and oppressor. Shaka has come down to us as a glowering stereotype, frozen in time on the misty hillsides of a long-vanished Zululand, clutching his fabled stabbing spear and great hide war-shield, the very embodiment of every European concept of the ultimate African warrior-king.

In attempting to unravel the strands of fact and myth, it must be acknowledged that Shaka was very much a product of his time and culture, and his actions were the result of a very specific historical context. Yet Shaka's legacy cannot ultimately be denied, for he stamped his character on a political and military system which survived him by more than 50 years, and influenced our perception of his people into modern times. More than any other single individual, he gave shape to the Zulu kingdom.

Shaka was born into an African society on the verge of crisis. At the end of the eighteenth century the eastern coast of southern Africa, between the Kahlamba (Drakensberg) mountains and the Indian Ocean, and framed by the Mzimkhulu river in the south, and the Phongolo to the north – the area later known to whites as Natal and Zululand – was settled by a patchwork quilt of chiefdoms who spoke broadly the same language, and followed basically the same customs. They were pastoralists, who were dependent for their survival on a range of good grasses to sustain their cattle. Cattle provided not only the staples of their everyday existence – milk products for food, and hides for cloaks and shields – but also a means of assessing wealth and status, and, since the slaughter of a beast was an essential part of all important religious ritual, a bridge with the spirit world itself. They were a polygamous people, and each man might marry as many wives as he could support, which in practice meant three or four for a commoner, and more for a chief. They lived in homesteads (sing. *umuzi*, pl. *imizi*) consisting of dome-shaped huts, made from thatch fastened over a framework of saplings, which were arranged in a circle around the all-important cattle-pen, and were surrounded by a palisade to keep out predators. Each *umuzi* was home to an extended family unit – a married man, his wives, unmarried children, and their dependants. Families who traced their descent to a common ancestor, real or mythical, considered themselves part of the same group, and were ruled over by a hereditary chief.

Before the nineteenth century, European penetration of this region was limited. Whites were known as *abelungu*, strange pallid sea-creatures who were occasionally washed up, sometimes alive, often dead, by the pounding breakers and deposited among the sand-dunes, for the coast was wild and treacherous, and venturesome seafarers often came to grief on hidden reefs and shoals offshore. Little was known in Zululand of the white toehold at the Cape before at least the eighteenth century, although both Arab traders and the Portuguese were more familiar from the closer enclave at Delagoa Bay, in Mozambique.

Indeed, the activities of Portuguese traders may have been responsible for the great upheaval which shook African society on the eastern seaboard at the end of the eighteenth century. For the most part, the Portuguese did not themselves venture extensively into the interior, but had established trading lines through intermediaries which stretched for hundreds of miles. Through these they extracted ivory and hides – and sometimes slaves – and in return supplied exotic goods such as brass and beads. To the Africans, possession of these goods had an important political dimension; since the chiefs maintained a monopoly of trade, which they distributed as rewards to their favourites, European goods tended to reinforce existing political structures. As some chiefdoms grew rich at the expense of others, competition to control trade routes grew. This tendency to conflict was probably exaggerated by a drought known as the *Madlathule* – 'let him eat what he can and say nothing' – which devastated the region at the turn of the century, withering crops and killing cattle. Hard pressed by natural disaster, unsettled by an undercurrent of European economic penetration, the chiefdoms of Zululand began to grate against one another.

It was into this world that Shaka was born about 1787. His father was Senzangakhona kaJama, the young and handsome chief of the Zulu people, who lived along the valley of the Mkhumbane stream on the southern banks of the White Mfolozi river. His mother, Nandi, was a member of the Langeni people, who lived further south, along the upper reaches of the Mhlatuze. The two had met one day while Senzangakhona was herding cattle, and Nandi and her companions fetching water; such meetings were often contrived to allow lovers to indulge in a little boisterous foreplay, but on this occasion Senzan-gakhona failed to show proper restraint, and within a couple of months representatives of the Langeni arrived at Senzangakhona's homestead with the disconcerting news that Nandi was pregnant. At first, the Zulu indignantly denied any complicity, and went so far as to suggest that Nandi was suffering from an intestinal parasite which produced much the same symptoms, and was known as *ishaka*. When she was later delivered of a baby boy, the Langeni ironically called him Shaka.

Senzangakhona accepted his responsibilities and Nandi became his first wife. Yet the marriage was by all accounts an unhappy one, as Nandi was a domineering woman with a fierce temper, and the two frequently quarrelled. Moreover, Shaka could never hope to succeed to his father's estate, as in Zulu culture the role of first wife was a junior one, and a man nominated his heirs from the house of his 'great wife', who was carefully selected from among those he married later. Shaka was still a child when Senzangakhona lost patience, and sent Nandi back to her family in disgrace. This marked the beginning of a formative period in Shaka's life when he grew to manhood having little contact with his father. Instead, Senzangakhona's role seems to have been filled by Chief Dingiswayo kaJobe of the Mthethwa.

The Mthethwa were one of two groups who were already rising to prominence in central and northern Zululand. Their traditional territory lay along the lower Mhlatuze river, but Dingiswayo had extended his influence over a number of chiefdoms as far north as the White Mfolozi. As such, the Langeni came under his control, and when Shaka reached the age at which he was expected to serve his chief, it was to Dingiswayo's regiments that he reported. Dingiswayo is remembered in Zulu tradition as a compassionate and just ruler, who built his power base by offering greater military security in return for the allegiance of his neighbours. It is also said that he possessed a number of European trade goods, which is as good an indication of his motives as any.

Dingiswayo's main rival, Chief Zwide kaLanga of the Ndwandwe people, lived north of the Mfolozi river complex. The groups living along the southern bank of the White Mfolozi therefore had an important strategic significance to the Mthethwa, and this had momentous consequences for Shaka when, about 1816, Senzangakhona died. Senzangakhona's 'great wife' was Bhibhi, and his legitimate heir was their son Sigujana. But Dingiswayo was keen to extend his control over the Zulu, and the presence of Shaka in his ranks was too good an opportunity to miss. Sigujana was murdered in a carefully orchestrated quarrel, and Shaka arrived one day at the Zulu royal homestead at the head of one of Dingiswayo's regiments.

Shaka had already by this time begun to establish the awesome reputation as a warrior by which he is still remembered. There is little in contemporary accounts to support the view, widespread in European literature, that Shaka's rise was actually due to a new military technology, which he invented – a broad-bladed spear used exclusively for stabbing. It is probably true that battles at that time were largely fought with light throwing spears, and were less dangerous and destructive as a result, but Shaka, who had an aggressive and ruthless personality, preferred to fight at close quarters. Since the conventional throwing spears were not designed to withstand the stresses of hand-to-hand combat, Shaka selected a much heavier weapon. He may indeed have commissioned this from a specialist smith himself, but stabbing weapons were by no means unknown, and his prototype weapon was simply a variation on existing types. It had a long blade, 18 inches long and 1.5 inches wide, and a short, strong haft. With grim humour, he called this after the sucking sound that it made on being withdrawn from a deep body-thrust – *ikwa*. What was new about Shaka's methods was not so much the concept of the weapon itself, but the extent to which he developed new fighting techniques around it. He practised its use in combination with a large cow-hide war-shield, using the shield to batter his enemy off-guard, then catching him with an underarm thrust of the spear, aimed at the rib-cage or stomach. It was brutal, terrifying and effective, and his unconventional and very conspicuous behaviour soon drew him to the attention of Dingiswayo himself, who dubbed him 'Tshaka who is not beaten, the axe that surpasses other axes, the impetuous one who disregards warnings'. Dingiswayo recognised his prowess by appointing him as *induna* in charge of one of his homesteads.

Dingiswayo needed a reliable ally on the White Mfolozi because that area was rapidly developing into a dangerous frontier with Zwide's Ndwandwe. Like the Mthethwa, the Ndwandwe had extended their control over a number of chiefdoms in northern Zululand, spreading out from their heartland around modern Nongoma. Zwide's methods are remembered as being rather more ruthless than Dingiswayo's, however, and he regularly raided groups who did not submit. Moreover, Zwide's mother, Queen Nthombazi, was a *sangoma* – diviner – of awesome reputation, who kept the skulls of Zwide's fallen enemies in her hut, and used them to harness their spiritual power to her son's ambitions.

By 1816, Zwide controlled much of the area between the Phongolo and the White Mfolozi, and had driven out a number of groups on the periphery. Events were steadily bringing him towards a confrontation with Dingiswayo, at precisely the same time that Shaka assumed control of the Zulu. The result was a series of violent and dramatic events which reshaped the political structure of Zululand in just three short years.

Sometime about 1816, Dingiswayo attacked Zwide. Queen Nthombazi's *itonya* – the mystical power which gave one individual supernatural superiority over another in battle – was too much for him, however, and Dingiswayo was captured by the Ndwandwe, and put to death. Zwide then attempted to move south of the White Mfolozi, hoping to reap rich pickings from the former allies of the Mthethwa as Dingiswayo's hegemony fell apart.

He was brought up short beneath a rocky knoll known as kwaGqokli, in the Zulu territory, just south of the White Mfolozi.

KwaGqokli was destined to be one of Shaka's most important battles. Events had contrived to free him of his responsibilities to Dingiswayo, and he was now not only pursuing his own ambitions, but fighting for survival. Unfortunately, details of the battle remain sketchy, and have been obscured by a deliberate attempt on the part of European writers to invest it with all the mythic quality of an Arthurian epic. Nevertheless, those details which have survived suggest that Shaka met the challenge in characteristic manner.

Once news of the Ndwandwe approach had reached him, he assembled his army. There is no evidence as to its size, but it was undoubtedly just a fraction of the size of the forces he later commanded. The warriors were ritually prepared for war, and Shaka, typically, called on volunteers who might distinguish themselves, offering rewards to those who survived. Where the names of some who accepted the challenge – like Manyosi kaDlekezele – have come down to us, it is interesting to note that they did indeed later rise to positions of power and prominence within the kingdom.

Once the army was ready, Shaka drew it up on the lower slopes of kwaGqokli, a rocky knoll which rises from a low ridge running down to the White Mfolozi river. There is very little direct contemporary evidence regarding the tactics employed by Shaka, although there are suggestions that he did indeed employ a formation known as *impondo zankomo* – the horns of the beast – which was later so associated with the Zulu army. Whether he invented it or not is another matter; probably it was a refinement of existing concepts, developed to meet the need of bringing large numbers of men into close combat with the enemy. The formation required four tactical groups – the *izimpondo*, or horns, the *isifuba*, or chest, and the *umuva*, or loins. The horns, usually composed of young, fit warriors, rushed out to surround the enemy on either side, while the chest, made up of steady, experienced warriors, pinned the enemy in place with a direct frontal assault. The loins acted as a reserve, and were sent forward to plug any gaps in the attack. The formation was simple but effective, the more so when one of the horns masked its attack by careful use of the terrain, and could take up a position in the enemy's rear without being detected. It did, however, require careful co-ordination on the part of the Zulu commanders, and both discipline and courage on the part of the warriors who made up the respective elements. Its success or failure over the years was more-or-less dependent on the success of these factors.

At kwaGqokli, the Ndwandwe, who were in overwhelming numbers, began with a determined attack on Shaka's right. Despite stiff resistance, the right horn was driven back, but Shaka's left managed to push forward successfully on its front, with the result that the fighting seems to have pivoted around the crest of the knoll itself. At one point Shaka, who directed the fight from the high ground close to his men, was in danger of being cut off and surrounded, but his warriors rallied and drove the Ndwandwe back. The fighting was fierce and bloody, and no less than five of Zwide's sons were killed, leading their men. Nevertheless, the battle was essentially a stalemate, and the Ndwandwe withdrew carrying off large numbers of Zulu cattle.

Yet the battle must be counted a Zulu victory, as Shaka had survived the first great challenge of his career, and he immediately set about consolidating his position. Several smaller groups who had formerly been under Dingiswayo's shield (as the Zulu expression has it) promptly joined him, rather than face possible Ndwandwe attacks themselves. Some, like the Qwabe of Chief Phakathwayo kaKhondlo, who lived to the south-east, between the lower Mhlatuze and the Mzinyathi, refused. The Qwabe believed that they and the Zulu were descended from two brothers, and that the Qwabe were the senior line; they therefore considered any alliance on Zulu terms to be beneath them. Shaka promptly attacked them, overthrew Phakathwayo, and raised up his junior brother instead. As one early black historian put it, 'And there was wild confusion among the people, who began to lift their ears and say, "What sort of king has now arisen?" And he conquered everywhere.'

All of this took place over the space of less than a year. Perhaps Shaka was a great opportunist rather than a master of grand strategy, but if he was reacting to events as they unfolded, he certainly did so swiftly and surely. In a very short time, he had effectively assumed control of almost the entire area of former Mthethwa influence.

These developments begged a number of important military questions. How did Shaka expand, train and infuse his army with a common sense of identity and purpose over so short a period? The answers, sadly, remain obscure. Certainly, once the period of rapid expansion was over, Shaka relied upon the *amabutho* system, in which young men of a common age were formed into regiments (sing. *ibutho*, pl. *amabutho*) to give service to the king, regardless of their local origins and affiliations. This was a powerful tool for central control, but it can hardly have been introduced in a matter of months. In fact, it seems that as groups joined Shaka, he assumed control of their existing military units, and these were later either incorporated with Zulu *amabutho*, or had Zulu *amabutho* grafted to them. It seems likely, therefore, that these early armies consisted of a core of Zulu regiments, supported by contingents supplied by newly won-over groups. Moreover, Shaka followed Dingiswayo's practice of interfering in the line of succession of freshly incorporated groups, raising up inferior candidates, with the result that such new groups could be more easily controlled.

As a general, Shaka displayed classic leadership qualities. For the most part, until the very end of his reign, he commanded his armies in person, and his conspicuous presence greatly encouraged his men. Although he often kept his exact objectives secret until the last moment, to prevent the intelligence reaching the enemy, he understood the value of delegation, and regularly gave important tasks to his most trusted *izinduna*. Indeed, he had the knack of mixing freely with ordinary warriors, and of catching their imagination with appropriate incentives, whether it was recognising an individual's bravery by bestowing a line from his own praises, or offering as a reward a herd of cattle so large that a stick, placed across their backs, would not fall off in the press. On more than one occasion, when an ill omen threatened to dishearten his men, his quick retort turned the situation to his advantage.

Once new elements had been incorporated into his army, Shaka trained them in the close-quarter techniques he had himself pioneered. He forbade his men to carry throwing spears, arguing that it would encourage cowardly behaviour, since it allowed warriors to stand off rather than rush in hand-to-hand. To demonstrate the effectiveness of his new system, he had two *amabutho* line up facing one another, armed with reeds instead of spears. While one lot threw their reeds, and soon ran out of ammunition, the others crouched behind their shields, then rushed down as if they were carrying stabbing spears. The point was effectively made. After a campaign, Shaka would review his regiments, and any warrior who could not show his stabbing spear was liable to be executed as a coward, on the grounds that he had clearly thrown it aside and run. In battle, his men did not advance packed shoulder to shoulder, but openly spaced, to give them room to move with their weapons. They could cover large distances at an easy jogging pace, but the final assault was made very rapidly, with the men crouching low to avoid spears thrown at them. One source suggests that Shaka insisted his men kept their shields tucked up under their arms, face inwards, and only turned them to the front as they struck the enemy. The psychological effect of such a display must have been electric.

Shaka's rise inevitably intensified the Zulu–Ndwandwe rivalry, and before the end of 1819, Zwide had mounted two major raids into Zulu territory. It has become almost impossible to disentangle the chronology of these campaigns, so closely have they become entwined in Zulu folklore. Nevertheless, it seems that in both cases Zwide's forces considerably outnumbered the Zulu, and Shaka fell back before the Ndwandwe advance.

The first expedition was apparently repulsed by guerrilla tactics. When the Ndwandwe were deep in Zulu territory, camped on the heights near modern Melmoth, Shaka called for volunteers to infiltrate the Ndwandwe army after dark. Since the two armies spoke the same language and were dressed in similar fashion, it was almost impossible to tell them apart at night, especially as Shaka had directed his men to crawl among the enemy on their bellies, like snakes. They then struck out at the nearest Ndwandwe warriors, and made their escape under cover of the ensuing chaos. On the same occasion, one of Shaka's most famous warriors, Mvundlana kaMenziwa, chief of the Biyela, accepted Shaka's challenge to kill the Ndwandwe commander. According to Biyela tradition, Mvundlana passed himself off as an Ndwandwe, and was taken unarmed into the presence of the Ndwandwe commander. As he squatted on the ground, together with the Ndwandwe councillors, Mvundlana suddenly snatched up an Ndwandwe spear and drove it into the commander's chest, before making a dash for a nearby forest. The Ndwandwe were so taken by surprise that Mvundlana managed to escape, but an armed patrol was sent into the forest to find him. He hid in a narrow defile, and as the Ndwandwe worked their way through it in single file, he stabbed first one man, then another, as they passed, all the time remaining hidden. This was such an unsettling experience that the Ndwandwe concluded that Mvundlana was a particularly powerful *sangoma*, and abandoned their pursuit. The Biyela explain their close association with the Zulu Royal House by suggesting that Shaka rewarded Mvundlana for this heroic deed with a status almost equal to his own. In all events, Shaka's effective harassing tactics were sufficient to persuade the Ndwandwe to abandon their expedition and retire.

The second Ndwandwe raid was a more serious affair. Once again Shaka, heavily outnumbered, avoided contact with the Ndwandwe as they crossed the White Mfolozi. He knew that Zwide's army, like his own, must survive by foraging when operating in enemy territory. To prevent them feeding themselves at his expense, Shaka ordered that the grain pits of the principal Zulu settlements be emptied, and the contents carefully hidden. His army then retired, accompanied by a huge herd of cattle, and by their women and children, whom they could not leave behind. The Ndwandwe inevitably gave chase. Shaka moved south, across the headwaters of the Mhlatuze below Babanango mountain, and towards the high ground of the great Nkandla forest. Here, he led his men down a steep spur near the Mome gorge – a spot destined to play an equally significant role in later Zulu history – following the Nsuze river towards its junction with the Thukela.

It was in the Thukela valley that the Ndwandwe gave up the chase, winding up the heights and moving eastwards. Shaka's scouts kept them under constant observation, and his army turned about to follow them. That night, the Ndwandwe bivouacked on the Mvuzane stream, not far from its confluence with the Mhlatuze. The Zulu camped a few miles to the south, near the site of modern Eshowe. The tables had been neatly turned; the pursuers had become the pursued, and the Ndwandwe, tired and hungry, were beginning to lose heart.

Shaka attacked them at first light – 'in the horns of the morning', the favourite Zulu time of attack, when the horns of the cattle are first visible against the dawn sky. His army moved rapidly down from Eshowe, advancing up the Mvuzane valley. Here, as he stood on a knoll issuing orders, a gust of wind lifted the crane feather he wore at the front of his head-dress, and cast in on the ground. His men were dumbstruck; it was a dreadful omen, and several of his attendants bent nervously down to pick the feather up. With typical quick thinking, Shaka called out, 'Let it stand! This one will not fall. There is another that will fall!'

The battle which followed was of the greatest importance for the emerging Zulu kingdom, but while stories of individual courage have survived in oral tradition, the broader details of the fighting remain obscure. It seems that Shaka launched his centre against the Ndwandwe first, driving them down the Mvuzane until they reached the Mhlatuze. The Ndwandwe retired across the river, but then turned to make a stand. The Zulu could not secure a toehold on the far bank, and the fighting raged along a number of fiercely contested drifts. The combatants slipped and stumbled over piles of corpses along the banks, and the water was soon red with blood. With the chest thus stalled, Shaka apparently threw out his left horn, which swung across the Mvuzane, then crossed the Mhlatuze further upstream, rushing down to roll up the Ndwandwe flank. The Ndwandwe stood their ground for as long as they could, and the fighting is remembered as bitter and bloody; then they suddenly collapsed, and streamed away from the river. With nothing to oppose them, the remainder of Shaka's army crossed the Mhlatuze and harried them as they fled.

The Ndwandwe army disintegrated after the battle of Mhlatuze. Some elements made their way back to Zwide, while others rallied around surviving commanders, such as Soshangane kaZikode and Zwagendaba kaHlatshwayo, and retired up the coast, crossing into modern Mozambique. These groups later formed the nucleus of new kingdoms to the north, the Gaza and Ngoni.

Zwide had not commanded his army in person, and Shaka was determined to follow up his spectacular victory by capturing him. He advanced rapidly north, outpacing the Ndwandwe survivors, and closed in on Zwide's royal homestead. In some versions of the story he had his men sing a Ndwandwe victory song as they approached; certainly the women of Zwide's homestead mistook the Zulu for the returning Ndwandwe army, and hurried out to greet them, singing *'Halala! abuy' amabandla' akaLanga!'* – 'Hurray! The assemblies of Langa are coming!' They discovered their mistake only when it was too late. The Zulu rushed among them, killing some and capturing the rest, spreading out to surround Zwide's homestead. The commotion had alerted Zwide, however, who managed to slip out of his hut and take refuge in a nearby reed bed. Shaka's warriors swept through Ndwandwe territory, burning homesteads and carrying off cattle. It is said that Shaka directed them to 'eat up' Zwide so thoroughly that not even the grindstones remained, and even today broken grindstones can be found across the former Ndwandwe districts.

In fact, of course, it was neither possible nor politic to destroy the Ndwandwe entirely. Zwide managed to collect several thousand of his followers together, and to retire north across the Phongolo river, where he was able to re-establish something of his old influence, beyond the range of Shaka's armies. Those Ndwandwe who remained in their traditional lands submitted to Shaka, who raised up Zwide's son, Somaphunga, to rule over them.

The battle of Mhlatuze arguably marks the point at which the Zulu kingdom came truly into being. Shaka's control extended from the Phongolo in the north to the Thukela in the south. True, his control was patchy, and there were many groups in that area who resisted being brought tightly under his control. Even among those who had submitted there were some who had joined as allies rather than subjects, a status that afforded them a greater degree of autonomy, which Shaka ignored at his peril. Even some of those who had been defeated, and were squarely under Shaka's thumb, such as the Qwabe, continued to resent their position, and provided a focus for clandestine opposition to his rule.

Nonetheless, however, after Mhlatuze the last major rival to Shaka's supremacy had been driven out, and the power of the Zulu had become fact. Shaka had brought dozens of formerly independent chiefdoms under his control, and his authority over them far outstripped anything that Dingiswayo or Zwide had been able to achieve. His praises celebrated him as *inkhosi y'amakhosi* – the chief over the chiefs. Before Shaka, it is said, there were only chiefs – then Shaka became king.

The extent of this revolution should not be underestimated. Much of the old order had been overturned; chiefs who ruled with the weight of centuries of legitimate succession had been cast down, and a new generation raised up in their place. At the centre of the new elite was Shaka, himself an outsider, and his core of personal favourites and advisers, who were often newcomers like himself. All of this had happened within the space of three or four years, and a whole new infrastructure had to be created to legitimise Zulu control, and to bind the nation more fully under Shaka's control.

This was achieved through an effective mix of religious and political structures. It should not be thought that Shaka invented these mechanisms, but he certainly extended and refined them beyond anything that had existed previously. Chiefs had always been regarded as the spiritual head of their followers, for example, the medium through which the chiefdom as a whole communicated with the most important ancestral spirits. Shaka simply expanded the role of the Zulu Royal House in this capacity, recasting it as the spiritual head of the greater extended kingdom, and limiting the influence of regional chiefs to their immediate districts. Thus the ancestors of the Zulu Royal House were elevated to the supreme position among the spirits, and it was their blessing which was held to be necessary at the start of great national occasions, including a new military campaign. The king himself was the central figure in the great umKhosi ceremony, which ushered in the new harvest every year, and which representatives from all groups within the kingdom were expected to attend. Shaka created new religious paraphernalia, which was considered more powerful than anything belonging to regional chiefs, simply by virtue of the fact that it bound the chiefs together. The most important of these was the *inkatha yesizwe ya'kwaZulu* – the 'sacred coil of the nation'. This was a grass rope, bound into a coil, which contained items of great spiritual importance and was believed to symbolise the unity of the kingdom. It formed part of the great national rituals, and it was said that the nation would stand so long as the *inkatha* survived; curiously enough, the British destroyed it when they set fire to King Cetshwayo's esiKlebheni homestead a fortnight before the battle of Ulundi in 1879.

The most powerful administrative tool which united the nation was the *amabutho* system. The practice of binding youths of a common age together to serve their chief pre-dated Shaka; both Zwide and Dingiswayo had *amabutho*, and indeed Shaka had been enrolled as a member of Dingiswayo's iziCwe *ibutho*. On the whole, however, the evidence suggests that these remained essentially local units. Where Shaka's system was significantly different was that his *amabutho* were drawn from right across the kingdom. Every few years, youths who had reached a certain age – eighteen or nineteen – were called together to be formed into a regiment, regardless of their local loyalties. As such, they were required to give a period of service directly to the king, until such time as they assumed the full responsibilities of manhood. This meant that they were effectively lost as a resource to the regional chiefs throughout the most productive – and militarily powerful – period of their lives, and placed directly under the king's command instead. The transition from youth to man had little to do with age, but was represented by their first marriage. In pre-Shakan times the consent of a man's chief was a prerequisite of marriage, and under the new system Shaka assumed a monopoly over the right to grant or withhold that consent. By keeping an *ibutho* unmarried as long as possible, he maximised the period of national service, and as a result he seldom allowed regiments to marry until the men were nearly 40. When an *ibutho* did marry, the men were allowed to disperse to build their own homesteads, and only mustered as a regiment for the great public ceremonies, or at times of national emergency.

The *amabutho* performed many tasks for the king besides their role as battlefield tactical units. They built and repaired his homesteads, tended his fields, herded the great national cattle herd, took part in the king's hunts, and acted as his police force. Contrary to popular belief, however, they were not permanently mustered for service. After an *ibutho* was formed, and the king had appointed it a specific ceremonial uniform of feathers, furs and shield colour, it would spend perhaps a year in training, learning how to manoeuvre and fight as a unit. After that, it would disperse, the young men returning to their family homes until the king had need of them again. Most regiments were probably only assembled for three or four months of the year, partly because it was difficult to provision a large number of men for any length of time, and partly because they were needed to fulfil their civilian functions at home.

When the *amabutho* were assembled, they lived in royal homesteads, known as *amakhanda* (sing. *ikhanda*) – *heads*, literally of the king's authority. These were built in the manner of ordinary Zulu homesteads, but on a grand scale; a large circle of huts surrounding a central parade ground, and surrounded in turn by a stout palisade. The *amakhanda* were established strategically about the kingdom, to serve as local centres of royal administration. In the north of the kingdom, for example, Shaka established the ebaQulusini *ikhanda*, near the Hlobane mountain, as a bastion against the Ndwandwe. Most *amakhanda* consisted of no more than 300–400 huts – enough to house a regiment – but those particularly favoured by the king could be much larger.

Sometime after Zwide's defeat, for example, Shaka moved his principal capital out of the Mkhumbane valley, the place of his ancestors, and built a new one on a ridge overlooking the misty Mhlatuze valley, the site of his great victory. He called it variously kwaGibixhegu – *take out the old man*, a reference to Zwide – or kwaBulawayo, *the place of he who was killed*, an ironic reference to the humiliations he had suffered as a youth. It contained over a thousand huts, a seething metropolis of warriors in residence, court advisers and functionaries, and female attendants. Shaka lived in some seclusion in the *isigodlo*, a private area at the top of the complex, which he shared only with his girls (also called *isigodlo*). The *isigodlo*, indeed, was another characteristic of the enlarged Zulu state, and it comprised daughters of important chiefs who had been given as tribute to Shaka. While a few of these served as his personal harem, most merely acted as servants, and the king enjoyed the right of bestowing them in marriage. To be given one of the king's *isigodlo* girls as a bride was a great honour, and was another of the means by which the king allied himself to important men within the kingdom, and rewarded his favourites.

Personal patronage, indeed, was a prop of royal power. Although service in the king's *amabutho* could be onerous, it had its excitements, and Shaka was famous for his generosity in rewarding successful warriors. The Zulu kingdom became extremely rich at this time, due to the thousands of cattle which were captured in Shaka's wars. These cattle were the property of the state, and administered by the king. After each campaign they were carefully sorted into herds according to the colour of their hides, and distributed about the kingdom. Shaka always reserved some, however, to give to warriors who particularly distinguished themselves, and these were especially prized as young men had few other opportunities to establish their own herds. More-over, the king had the right to distribute various tokens as a mark of royal favour. These included *iziqu* – necklaces made of interlocking wooden beads – which were given to warriors whose regiments had distinguished them-selves in a particular battle, and European trade goods. In particular, Shaka maintained a monopoly of beads from European sources, which he distrib-uted to his *isigodlo* girls as a mark of favour. Heavy, rich red beads were espe-cially highly prized.

If Shaka could be generous to those he approved, however, he could be deadly to those he did not. It was, of course, crucially important that an army so recently forged from former enemies should be infused with a common sense of values. Shaka despised cowardice above anything, and after a major campaign would sit beneath a tree which still grows near kwaBulawayo, and is known as the *isihlahla samagwala* – 'the bush of the cowards'. Here the *amabutho* would parade before him, and each regimental commander would report on the conduct of his men. Those who had misbehaved before the enemy would be brought forward to be punished. They would be pinioned and their left arm raised; Shaka would ask, 'Is this, then, the thing you fear?' and they would be stabbed in the side with a small-bladed spear used for killing sheep and goats.

Such tough treatment naturally helped stiffen the army's resolve in battle, but Shaka is also remembered as regularly executing men on the flimsiest of charges. Although early white travellers exaggerated stories of his killings to add local colour to their reminiscences, there is no doubt that Shaka did kill people. Even though he reacted to their deaths with a carefully calculated insouciance, he did not enjoy inflicting pain himself, but understood the value

23

of terror as a political tool. The atmosphere of awe which surrounded his person and court was highly effective as a means of stifling internal opposition.

Physically, only one portrait of Shaka has survived, and that is clearly romanticised. Descriptions suggest that he was of medium height, with a dark brown complexion, and the muscular physique of the habitual warrior. By all accounts, however, he was not particularly handsome, for he had a broad nose and forehead, and a problem with his front teeth which may have given him a slight speech impediment. In later life he wore the *isicoco* – the gum headring which indicated the married state – though he never formally married, and a light beard. He took snuff a good deal, and his favourite conversation was always about military matters. One of the first white traders in Zululand has left a striking description of Shaka in his war dress:

> Round his head he wore a [headband] of otter skin with a feather of the crane erect in front, fully two feet long, and a wreath of scarlet feathers, formerly worn, only, by men of high rank. Ear ornaments made from dried sugar cane, carved round the edge, with white ends, an inch in diameter, were let into the lobes of the ears, which had been cut to admit them. From shoulder to shoulder, he wore bunches, five inches in length, of the skins of monkeys and genets, twisted like the tails of these animals. These hung half down the body. Round the ring on his head, were a dozen tastefully arranged bunches of loury feathers, neatly tied to thorns which were stuck into the hair. Round his arms were white ox-tail tufts, cut down the middle so as to allow the hair to hang about the arm, to the number of four for each arm. Round the waist, there was a kilt or petticoat, made of skins of monkeys and genets, and twisted as before described, having small tassels around the top. The kilt reached to the knees, below which were white ox-tails fitted to the legs so as to hang down to the ankles. He had a white shield with a single black spot, and one assegai. When thus equipped he certainly presented a fine and most martial appearance.

The destruction of the Ndwandwe challenge allowed Shaka to consolidate. Freed from a major external threat, he could concentrate on reducing those groups within the kingdom – such as the Khumalo in the Ngome forest, north of the Black Mfolozi – or on the borders who continued to resist him. In the early 1820s he launched a series of campaigns against the most powerful of these, driving out the amaNgwane from the Kahlamba foothills, and pushing the amaChunu across the Thukela and further south. By 1824, he had extended his influence almost to the Mzimkhulu river, and was threatening the powerful amaMpondo kingdom beyond.

Yet the area south of the Thukela was never fully incorporated into the Zulu kingdom. True, about 1826, Shaka moved his capital again, abandoning kwaBulawayo for a new residence, kwaDukuza, which lay in the humid coastal downland south of the Thukela. Nevertheless, large areas inland from there were controlled only through the agency of client chiefdoms, such as the Cele, while some groups had simply removed themselves rather than submit, leaving parts of the country only thinly populated. Here and there, some groups – usually with the benefit of an unassailable natural stronghold – continued to resist Zulu rule entirely.

From 1824, however, Shaka had been able to add a new and exotic element to his military capabilities, and this had undoubtedly helped reduce some of his more stubborn opponents. In July of that year the first permanent European trading settlement was established in the bay at Port Natal.

The settlement was the product of a global expansion in world trading routes which had followed the end of the Napoleonic wars in Europe. Britain, in particular, was suddenly awash with adventurous young men, whose promising military and naval careers had been cut short by the unexpected outbreak of peace, and who were keen to turn their military skills to good effect by taking advantage of the removal of Britain's greatest imperial rival, and carrying the flag – and trade – into hitherto unexploited regions. Thus an ex-Royal Navy lieutenant, Francis Farewell, had secured the backing of a syndicate of Cape Town merchants to open trade with the Zulu kingdom. The Zululand coast was notoriously short of good harbours, but Farewell's party braved the sand-bar which almost sealed the bay at Port Natal, and built a ramshackle settlement on the shores of the lagoon. Here, for an idyllic decade, they lived a Robinson Crusoe existence, gloriously free of the restraints of European law and morality, hunting, trading and setting themselves up as white African chiefs. From this unlikely beginning did all subsequent British claims to the region develop.

Farewell and his party existed only by sufferance of Shaka, who treated them as if they were one of his client chiefdoms. Their presence brought him more direct access to the world of prestige trade goods, and the traders themselves proved willing to serve in his armies as mercenaries. At that stage, neither the Zulu or their enemies had any direct experience of firearms. Shaka was fascinated by them, and demanded demonstrations, arguing their pros and cons with the traders and his councillors. He immediately spotted that the old smooth-bore Brown Bess muskets carried by the British party rendered their owners vulnerable during the cumbersome process of reloading. He suggested that his warriors might rush down and overwhelm European troops while they were thus engaged, and the whites responded by explaining the British techniques of volleying by ranks, which maintained a constant round of fire. Curiously enough, the issue would be put to the test in exactly those terms many times before the century was out.

The presence of the traders with Shaka's armies gives an insight, not only into their own military value, but into the great events of the latter part of his reign. In 1825, Zwide of the Ndwandwe had died, and was succeeded by his son Sikhunyana. For reasons that remain obscure, Sikhunyana attempted to return to Zululand to recapture the traditional Ndwandwe lands, from which Shaka had driven them. When the news reached Shaka in August 1826, he immediately assembled his army, and marched north to confront them. He was accompanied by a small party of Natal traders and some of their armed retainers. Contrary to popular myth, his army did not advance rapidly, but took its time, to ensure that the men were in good condition when they encountered the enemy. Shaka was camped on the flanks of a hill known as *inqaba kaHawana* – Hawana's stronghold, near the 1879 battlefield of Khambula – when his scouts brought the news that the Ndwandwe were camped further north on the inDolowane hill. While his army prepared for battle, Shaka went forward to examine the enemy position from a nearby hilltop.

The battle of inDolowane is particularly interesting, because it is one of the few of Shaka's great battles which were witnessed by a literate observer. One of the traders, Henry Francis Fynn, left a vivid account of the action, which suggests something of the reality of early Zulu warfare. The Ndwandwe were camped on the slope of the hill, with their warriors below and the non-combatants and cattle behind. After a cursory discussion with his commanders, Shaka ordered his army to be formed into a circle – *umkhumbi* – to receive orders, and last-minute ritual preparation. Then they were deployed in the traditional chest-and-horns attack formation. Indeed, in Zulu accounts of the battle it is the horns which played a decisive role in the engagement, sweeping round across such a wide range of country that, when they met behind inDolowane, each thought the other was an Ndwandwe force, and they had actually attacked one another before the mistake was recognised. Nevertheless, the horns effectively encircled the main Ndwandwe force, which was broken by a direct assault from the chest. Fynn, however, could see nothing of such tactical complexity, and witnessed only the frontal attack:

Shaka's forces marched slowly and with much caution, in regiments, each regiment divided into companies, till within 20 yards of the enemy, when they made a halt. Although Shaka's troops had taken up a position so near, the enemy seemed disinclined to move, until Jacob [one of Fynn's attendants] had fired at them three times. The first and second shots seem to make no impression on them, for they only hissed and cried in reply, 'That is a dog.' At the third shot, both parties, with a tumultuous yell, clashed together, and continued stabbing each other for about three minutes, when both fell back a few paces.

Seeing their losses were about equal, both enemies raised a cry and this was followed by another rush, and they continued closely engaged for about twice as long as in the first onset, when both parties again drew off. But the enemy's loss had now been the more severe. This urged the Zulus to a final charge. The shrieks now became terrific. The remnants of the enemy's army sought shelter in the adjoining wood, out of which they were soon driven. Then began a slaughter of the women and children. They were all put to death ... The battle, from the commencement to the close, did not last more than an hour and a half.

Once the fighting was over, Fynn noticed, the Zulu rounded up the Ndwandwe cattle, killing some to feast upon, and cutting off their tails for use as war-dress. Wounded Zulu were given treatment by the Zulu *izinyanga* – doctors – although the enemy wounded were usually killed. Those warriors who had taken part in the battle were cleansed of the ritual pollution caused by the shedding of blood, and Shaka inevitably paraded his army to seek out the heroes and the cowards. As Fynn commented, 'Many of these, no doubt, forfeited their lives only because their chiefs were in fear that, if they did not condemn some as being guilty, they would be suspected of seeking a pretext to save them and would incur the wrath of Shaka.'

In Fynn's estimation, no less than 40,000 Ndwandwe had been killed or captured in the battle. This is without doubt an exaggeration, but in fact inDolowane did mark the final end of the Ndwandwe chiefdom. With his northern border rather more secure, Shaka looked increasingly south.

It is possible that Shaka's policies in southern Natal were influenced both by the activities of the traders, and by a growing opposition to his rule inside the kingdom. Certainly, when Shaka's mother died in August 1827, there was a period of public mourning, and anyone who failed to observe it was ruthlessly punished. Although the traders cited this as an example of Shaka's increasingly psychotic behaviour, modern research suggests that underlying his action was the need to purge dissidents, particularly among the Qwabe. As early as 1824 there had been an attempt on Shaka's life – an assassin had stabbed him one evening when he was dancing by torchlight, but the blade had stuck in his arm, and the wound was not serious – and the Qwabe were widely thought to be responsible. It may be that by 1828 Shaka's need for military activity was twofold; it demonstrated his power, and intimidated his opposition, while at the same time acquiring cattle with which to bolster his supporters.

In May 1828, Shaka led a major expedition against the amaMpondo, at the extreme southern limit of his military range. His motives for this remain obscure. Certainly, there was no possibility of him establishing any permanent control over the Mpondo, although he had raided there before, in 1824, and it appears that their cattle were his primary objective. Nevertheless, he may also have been influenced by the white traders, some of whom accompanied the expedition. Quite what the traders hoped to achieve is debatable; the amaMpondo territory lay just beyond the growing British sphere of influence on the Eastern Cape Frontier, and it may be that they hoped somehow to sway British policy towards the Zulu. At the same time as the expedition was under way, Shaka also sent a diplomatic mission to open negotiations with the British. This was the first official contact between two peoples whose destinies in southern Africa would become increasingly entwined, and typically, it proved a disaster. In the light of Shaka's expedition, the British officials on the frontier regarded Shaka's envoys as spies, and turned them away.

Indeed, Shaka's raid had a curious sequel. The British, fearing the Zulu were about to attack the frontier, despatched an expedition to halt their advance. Shaka's army had long since withdrawn by the time it arrived at the front, but instead the British blundered into the followers of Matiwane kaMasumpa, the Ngwane chief who had been driven away from Zululand a few years previously. Convinced the amaNgwane were Zulu, the British forces attacked and dispersed them, and returned triumphantly to the frontier under the impression that they had defeated the mighty Shaka.

In fact, the Mpondo campaign was only a limited success. Shaka divided his army in two, remaining near the Mzimkhulu with one party while the other, under Mdlaka kaNcidi, swept through Mpondoland. But it proved difficult to bring the Mpondo to battle, and the haul in terms of cattle was not large.

After such a major campaign the army expected to rest, but Shaka immediately despatched it on a fresh campaign. This time it was to go north to attack Soshangane kaZikode, Zwide's erstwhile general, who was beginning to build up a following of his own along the lower Oliphants river, north of Delagoa Bay.

There is an air of desperation about this last campaign of Shaka's. He did not accompany it himself, and it is difficult to see what threat from Soshangane could have made it so urgent. Perhaps the failure of the Mpondo campaign to secure sufficient cattle to appease his followers was a factor; perhaps Shaka was just beginning to lose his grip over the extremely complex political situation he himself had created. In the event, the campaign was a disaster. Soshangane's followers wisely avoided battle, and the army procured so little forage that the warriors were reduced to eating their shields. On their return, weak and emaciated, many fell victim to malaria or dysentery. The army, when it finally returned home, had every appearance of being thoroughly defeated.

Yet Shaka was not there to berate them. He had been left almost defence-less by the army's departure, and had fallen victim to a palace coup carried out by members of his own family. His aunt, Senzangakhona's sister Mnkabayi, a powerful and domineering woman who held considerable influence within the Royal House, had apparently become convinced that Shaka's policies were damaging to the country at large, and she had hatched a plot with Shaka's younger brothers, Dingane and Mhlangana, to assassinate him. Unlike his successors, Shaka had always shown a marked reluctance to acknowledge any threat from his father's sons, and he showed no suspicion when both men, who belonged to *amabutho* attached to the Soshangane expedition, pleaded illness and returned home.

On the evening of 24 September 1828, a party of Mpondo representatives arrived at kwaDukuza. They were bearing rare pelts and feathers which had been sent as a gift to Shaka following the end of the recent hostilities. Shaka received them in kwaNyakamubi, a small homestead just outside the top of the great complex of kwaDukuza, to which he sometimes retired for privacy. He was inspecting the pelts when, all of a sudden, his personal attendant, Mbopha kaSithayi, suddenly rushed upon the envoys, beating them with a stick. The Mpondo were naturally terrified, and promptly fled, leaving the astonished Shaka to admonish Mbopha. Yet the reason for Mbopha's behav-iour became apparent a moment later when Dingane and Mhlangana burst through a reed fence which sheltered the huts, and produced spears from under their cloaks. In some versions of the story, the assassins could not dare to look upon Shaka's face, and one of them threw a spear which passed through the cloak of skins Shaka was wearing, and lodged in his body. While Shaka stood stunned and shocked, Mbopha ran forward and stabbed him in the back. Shaka promptly cast aside his cloak, and started to run towards the gate of the homestead. He had just passed through it, however, when he stumbled, and Dingane, who was closest to him, stabbed him again. There was now no hope of escape, and the assassins speared him to death as he lay on the ground.

While Shaka's last words will never be known for certain, it was widely believed, even during the kingdom's heyday, that he turned on his tormentors and prophesied 'Your country, children of my father, will be ruled by the white people who come from the sea.'

Given his history, it is perhaps not surprising that Shaka had seen the writing on the wall earlier than most.

The conspirators disposed of what remained of Shaka and his administra-tion with remarkable speed and efficiency. His body was buried at kwaDukuza, which was soon deserted, and fell into ruin; today the founder of the Zulu kingdom lies under the pavement of the high-street in the modern town of Stanger. Shaka's most ardent supporters were isolated and purged, and when the army returned it was only too grateful to escape his wrath. Dingane then adroitly outmanoeuvred Mhlangana, had him killed, and established himself as the second of Senzangakhona's sons to rule the Zulu.

Yet Shaka's legacy has survived into modern times. The political and military system which he created survived, with modifications, until the British destroyed the kingdom in 1879. As a commander, Shaka's reputation remained the benchmark by which his successors were judged. And as a powerful symbol of an independent and powerful pre-colonial Africa, his image still shapes contemporary political perceptions in South Africa to this day.

'He wiped out all the nations,' sang his warriors in praise, 'where will he wage war? He worsted enemies. He conquered nations.'

— 2 —

NDLELA kaSOMPISI

'Daily they stab the Rattler, but he retaliates ...'

Ndlela kaSompisi remains a shadowy figure, much of his early history lost to oral tradition, while his later reputation suffered at the hands of literate observers for the part he played in the first great campaigns against European encroachment. Nevertheless, his career is of the greatest importance, since it spanned not only the formation and consolidation of the kingdom, but also the first major challenge from the colonial world. Indeed, the threat posed to the Zulu kingdom by the Boer Voortrekkers and their British allies in 1838 was almost as great as that presented by the British in 1879; indeed, the challenge was perhaps greater, since the Zulu were facing for the first time a new military technology. Although it is not always possible to chart Ndlela's path through these events with certainty, there can be no doubt that he was involved at the highest level in the prosecution of this war, and that his influence helped to prevent the complete collapse of the kingdom.

Ndlela's family had connections with the Zulu Royal House which stretched back before Shaka's time. Ndlela's father, Sompisi, had been one of Chief Senzangakhona's attendants, and had been given the trusted position of grinder of his mealies and preparer of his food. Indeed, Senzangakhona had married one of Sompisi's daughters, Ndlela's sister, Bhibhi, and had appointed her his 'great wife'; her son was Senzangakhona's legitimate heir, the unfortunate Sigujana. Ndlela was a member of the Bele people, who are more usually known by their *izitakazelo*, or name of respect, *Ntuli*. The Ntuli lived south of the central Mzinyathi river, in what is now the Msinga district. This was an area that had suffered early in the wars which marked Shaka's rise to power, and the Ntuli had been so badly dislocated that some of their members took to surviving by cannibalism, living out among the inaccessible caves along the upper Mzinyathi valley.

It was probably because of these connections between the two families that Ndlela escaped these degradations, entered Shaka's service, and was raised up by him. As a young man, Ndlela showed extraordinary daring as a warrior, and this drew him to the attention of Mdlaka kaNcidi, Shaka's senior military adviser. In due course, both Ndlela and his colleague Nzobo kaSobadli – who would together become Dingane's senior councillors – rose to become high-ranking officers under Mdlaka's patronage. One anecdote survives which suggests something of Ndlela's prowess, and of how highly he was regarded by Shaka. During Shaka's decisive campaign against the Ndwandwe, which culminated in the battle of Mhlatuze, Ndlela was in the thick of the fighting:

[Ndlela] fought fiercely with the enemy. As the enemy began to give way ... [he] fell, severely wounded ... as if dead. The enemy retreated, then broke and fled ... Ndwandwe and Zulu corpses were lying across one another where the armies had met.

Those who could do so returned to Shaka. They said 'Hlati fought fiercely, until at last he fell. Ndhlela too fought fiercely, until at last he fell.' The king asked, 'Are they dead?' His men replied, 'They are still groaning; they are not yet dead.' The king sent out his [praise singers] with oxen to call on the ancestors with praises so that the two men should recover. 'For if they die then I too am as if dead'... They were lifted up by the arms; they vomited blood ... Blood came from their mouths ... The king sent doctors to treat them with medicines ... They eventually recovered. On the king's orders they went to him at his home; they did not go to their own homes.

According to this story, Shaka directed that the principal homestead of the Ntuli be renamed *eManxebeni*, after the wounds (*amanxebe*) endured by Ndlela. His praises honoured him as 'Rattler of Spears! ... Daily they stab the Rattler, but he retaliates!' Shaka rewarded Ndlela with cattle, and directed him to establish his own homestead, which he did on the slopes of Macala mountain. Later, Shaka appointed Ndlela as his *induna* to administer on his behalf the Ntuli and other broken groups who lived along the middle Thukela.

Nevertheless, when Shaka was assassinated in 1828, Ndlela survived Dingane's purge of the survivors of the old regime. Mdlaka, Shaka's commander, was among those killed, and it may be that both Ndlela and Nzobo, who were clearly ambitious men, thought it an opportune moment to give wholehearted support to Dingane. As Shaka had once raised up men to create his own establishment, so too did Dingane create a new order, and men like Ndlela brought a weight of experience to the new administration.

Ndlela and Nzobo soon established themselves as the most powerful of Dingane's new councillors. Although they usually worked together, they are remembered as having very different personalities, for Nzobo (who was also known as Dambuza) was a harsh man with an autocratic manner, who regularly urged the king to kill off rivals and criminals to inspire a proper degree of respect among the kingdom at large, while Ndlela had a kindlier disposition. Descriptions of Ndlela at his prime reveal that he was a tall man, over 6 feet, with thin legs and a big chest, a dark complexion, high forehead, and light beard. He wore the *isicoco*, and on ceremonial and military occasions, he carried a white war-shield with two black spots in the centre. During Dingane's reign he spent much of his time at the king's principal homestead, uMgungundlovu. Dingane had abandoned kwaDukuza after Shaka's death, and in 1829 had established a magnificent new homestead on the Mkhumbane, in the heart of the old Zulu territory. It was perhaps the largest such complex ever built, and at its height may have contained as many as 1700 huts. A special hut was reserved for Ndlela on the immediate right of the *isigodlo*, the king's private enclosure. The great arc of huts on that side of the enclosure housed four regiments, which were under Ndlela's direct command. Nzobo held a corresponding position on the other side and, indeed, Ndlela and Nzobo were a feature of life at the capital, since the king rarely appeared in public without one or the other of them, and they regularly entered his private quarters to discuss matters of state with him.

As such, Ndlela would have been at the heart of many of the important events for nearly ten years of King Dingane's reign: the elimination of Shaka's supporters, rivalry with the royal family, the problems of containing the aspirations of regional chiefs and consolidating the administration established by Shaka, foreign policy, and growing tension with the settler community at Port Natal. All of these were as nothing, however, compared with the threat posed by a new group of whites, who appeared from beyond the Kahlamba mountains in 1837.

By that time, whites were, of course, no longer a novelty to the Zulu. The first white settlement had been established at Port Natal in 1824, and although their numbers had not grown hugely by the 1830s, the whites were more sure of themselves, and the anarchic little settlement had become increasingly difficult to control. But if friction between the traders and Dingane had increased, the traders posed little or no threat to the security of the kingdom.

The Boers, however, were a different matter. Since 1806, when the British had assumed control of the Cape, the descendants of the original Dutch inhabitants, living along the troubled Eastern Cape frontier, had become increasingly disenchanted with British rule. In 1834 several hundred Boer families had packed their possessions into their ox-wagons, and trekked beyond the British boundaries in the hope of establishing new independent territories. This was the beginning of an exodus which lasted into 1840, and is remembered in South Africa as the Great Trek. The route of their progress took them through the interior, and was marked by a series of bitter conflicts with the African inhabitants they encountered along the way. In particular, the Trekkers had clashed with the followers of one Mzilikazi kaMashobane, and had defeated his *impis* and driven him north of the Limpopo river. Mzilikazi was well known to Dingane's administration, for he had been the chief of a lineage of the Khumalo people, whose territory lay in northern Zululand. Mzilikazi had fled across the Kahlamba mountains rather than accept Shaka's authority, and the Zulu Royal House still harboured hopes of recovering some of the cattle Mzilikazi took with him. Indeed, when the first news of Mzilikazi's troubles with the Boers reached uMgundundlovu, Dingane despatched an army under Ndlela's command to try to take advantage of his discomfort. Mzilikazi's territory, in the region of modern Pretoria, was at the far end of the Zulu's effective raiding range, however, but while the fighting was inconclusive, Ndlela's army returned with a large herd of captured cattle.

Dingane had, therefore, already formed an impression of the threat posed by the Boers when, in late 1837, a party led by Piet Retief crossed the Kahlamba. Gazing over Natal and Zululand from the mountains, Retief believed he was looking out upon the promised land, dreams of which had sustained the Trekkers throughout their wanderings. At the beginning of November, therefore, Retief visited Dingane to ask him for permission to settle in Natal.

From the first, Dingane clearly understood that the Boers were different in their outlook to the British traders at Port Natal. They were not interested in trade; their entire history had been characterised by an insatiable hunger for land, and they had been prepared to go to war more than once to obtain it. Although the Zulu had experience of the firearms used by the British traders, the large numbers of armed Boers, on their terrifying horses, seemed more intimidating. Moreover, Retief's habit of punctuating his dealings with veiled threats, underlined by Biblical scripture, must have suggested a disconcerting lack of respect to Dingane.

At first, the king and his councillors could not decide how best to meet the threat. They prevaricated, suggesting that Retief might recover some cattle looted from Dingane's outposts by a Sotho chief, as a gesture of goodwill before negotiations began. Retief did not return until February 1838; by that time Dingane and his councillors – including Ndlela – had probably decided on a number of options. The course they eventually embarked upon was perhaps dictated by Retief's subsequent behaviour.

Retief arrived at uMgungundlovu on 3 February 1838, at the head of 69 Boers and 30 of their mixed-race servants. Only men were present; the women and children remained in camps in the Kahlamba foothills, poised to spill out over Dingane's territory and stake their claim to it. Retief's party were all armed with firearms, and looked for all the world like a military force; nor was this impression dispelled when Retief's men staged a martial display as they arrived, riding into the great enclosure and firing their guns in the air. More-over, the king was unimpressed with Retief's report of his expedition to recover the cattle. He had apparently tricked the Sotho chief in a manner which smacked of witchcraft, and had then, most unwisely, kept some of Dingane's cattle for himself, as a commission. For two days, Dingane enter-tained the Boers with dancing displays staged by his assembled *amabutho*, while his councillors discussed their next move; then, suddenly and without warning on 6 February, he killed them all.

The final decision to attack the Boers was probably only taken over those two days. By that time, the Zulu were thoroughly alarmed by the Boers' over-bearing manner, and feared their intentions. Their suspicions were apparently confirmed when, on their last night at the capital, some of the Boers tried to enter the *isigodlo* under cover of darkness; the tracks of their horses were clearly visible the following morning. It may well be that some of the young, unmarried Boers had their own reasons for trying to sneak in to the king's private enclave, where several hundred of his young female attendants lived; to the Zulu mind, however, this was a heinous crime, which could only be seen as an attempt on the king's personage, and, through him, the nation as a whole.

Yet the Boers' all too obvious firearms presented particular difficulties; any attack on them in the open was bound to lead to enormous casualties. Instead, probably at Nzobo's suggestion, the council opted to destroy them by guile. When, on the morning of the 6th, Retief arrived to formally agree a treaty with Dingane, the Boers were reminded that it was not etiquette to take weapons into the presence of the king. They duly piled their arms at the main gate of uMgungundlovu, and sat down near the top of the great enclosure. Here Dingane had marshalled several of his *amabutho*, ostensibly to perform a dance to entertain them. As the warriors shuffled back and forth, like waves on the beach, however, Dingane suddenly called out, 'Seize them!', and the regiments rushed forward to overpower the astonished Boers. They were dragged out of the main gate, across to a rocky knoll opposite known as kwaMatiwane, the hill of execution, and done to death. They were killed with sticks, like common Zulu criminals.

In Zulu custom, the families of condemned men were also considered guilty by association, and it was usual practice to 'eat them up' – to destroy them utterly, kill the victim's family, burn his huts and carry off his cattle, so that nothing remained. Having embarked on such a brutal programme, it was particularly necessary that this was done with the Boers, as they were clearly a vengeful people, and the main Zulu hope of discouraging further groups from crossing the Kahlamba was to discourage them by completely destroying

Retief's party. Within a few hours of Retief's death, the assembled *amabutho* had been prepared for war, and marched out towards the Boer camps along the headwaters of the Bushman's and Bloukrans rivers.

The story of the ensuing campaign is usually told from the perspective of the Trekkers, whose ultimate victory is generally portrayed both as just retribution for the horrors inflicted that February upon the unsuspecting Boer families, and as the inevitable triumph of sophisticated European military systems. Yet the Boer victory at the end of 1838 was by no means as comprehensive as it first seems, while the apparently remorseless combination of the horse and gun was not always successful. Indeed, it seems that the Zulu were well aware of the nature of Boer warfare, and had evolved stratagems to counter it. What is striking about the Zulu response is not that it was ineffectual, but that it was imaginative, flexible and very nearly succeeded. Ironically, while the struggle between Zulu and Boer fighting methods produced a military stalemate, it was a more traditional African conflict which ultimately brought the war to a close.

While it is not always possible to tie Ndlela to particular battles, his presence pervades the war. His voice undoubtedly carried the greatest weight in the council meetings which decided the Zulu strategy, he commanded the most important expeditions in person, and he probably planned those he did not.

The war fell into three broad phases. Firstly, in mid-February, the Zulu fell on the Trekker encampments in the foothills of the Kahlamba. Their attacks were timed to take place at night and in the early pre-dawn, possibly in the hope that this would reduce the effectiveness of the Trekker muskets. In this they were not entirely successful, although they did cause heavy casualties among the most exposed Boer groups, killing men, women and children. That they were not able to wipe them out entirely, however, is revealing; those Boer groups furthest from the assault, who received some warning from the sound of distant slaughter, were able to form defensive wagon laagers. Time and again throughout their history, the Zulu found to their cost that they had no answer to an effective all-round barricade, which negated their encircling tactics, and which kept them beyond the reach of their stabbing spears, where they might be shot down almost with impunity. The Zulu retired, leaving the survivors still in place.

In the second phase, in April 1838, the Trekkers, reinforced from the interior, tried to seize the initiative, with the support of the Port Natal traders. In this they were utterly unsuccessful. The Zulu army, still recognisably the same institution that Shaka had created, and led by men who had learned their trade under Shaka, was faced with a series of challenges which had been beyond Shaka's experience, but it rose to meet them head on, as Shaka would surely have wished.

At the end of the first week of April, a commando of 347 Trekkers set out from the beleaguered Boer laagers in the Kahlamba foothills. They were commanded by two experienced Trek leaders, Piet Uys and Hendrik Potgieter, who had crossed the mountains with their followers to support them. This was a formidable force, but Uys and Potgieter had not been able to agree a common strategy, and the commando was dangerously divided. Moreover, Dingane's spies had been watching for Boer movements, and was well aware of the enemy approach. The commando crossed the Mzinyathi at Rorke's Drift, and rode past Babanango mountain towards uMgungundlovu. They captured some Zulu scouts, who told them that the main Zulu army lay closer to the capital. Descending the heights towards the great valley of the White Mfolozi, the commando was within sight of uMgungundlovu when it spotted a herd of cattle being driven down the valley of the Mkhumbane, towards a nek between two stony hills.

In retrospect, the situation suggests all the classic elements of a Zulu ambush; the talkative scouts, difficult ground and a vulnerable herd of cattle. Indeed, a force of several thousand men had been carefully concealed on either side of the nek, hoping to use the broken ground to trap the Boer horses. The Zulu force consisted of the uMkhulutshane *ibutho*, supported by elements from a number of other regiments based at uMgungundlovu. There is some uncertainty about the identity of the commanders; Nzobo was present, and since the force was operating so close to the capital, Ndlela was probably with him. Yet the Trekkers seem to have had no suspicion of danger, and rode into the valley to round up the cattle. As they approached the nek, two large bodies of warriors came into view, sitting patiently on the hills on either side. Uys proposed attacking at once, and advanced towards the hill on the right. Potgieter's men were more cautious, and after a tentative advance against the other hill, began to fall back. Uys, however, rode close to the Zulu in front of him, and his men dismounted and opened a heavy fire. The Zulu promptly abandoned their position and retreated. As the Boers opened fire, an *induna* was heard to call out, 'As soon as the whites shoot, charge them!' Even then, the Boers did not guess the degree of planning which had gone into the Zulu trap, and Uys's followers gleefully gave chase. Beyond the hill they scattered into a grassy basin, seamed with dongas, on the far side. Here, suddenly, the Zulu turned and rallied, while fresh bodies of warriors rose up from among the dongas.

Uys's commando was now dangerously exposed, and tried to ride back the way it had come. They rode off among a hail of thrown spears, for the Zulu had abandoned Shaka's strictures, and had revived the practice of carrying throwing spears, no doubt anticipating that they would be a useful weapon against horses. They were right; several men were cut off and killed, including Uys's teenage son, Dirkie, who was overtaken and stabbed when his horse stumbled. Uys himself was struck by a thrown spear, which hit him in the back and stuck out through his loins. His followers tried to help him from the field, but he fainted from loss of blood, and fell from his horse. Potgieter's men, meanwhile, had fallen back before a determined charge launched by the Zulu party on the other hill. As they rode away, a third Zulu force appeared, and tried to cut them off. Potgieter's men were too quick for them, but the Zulu circled around to block the line of retreat for the Uys party. The Boers had to concentrate their fire on a particular section of the Zulu line, opening a gap through which they narrowly managed to escape.

Altogether ten Boers had been killed, and the expedition was ignominiously christened the *Vlugcommando* – the commando that ran away. Most of the commando's pack horses had also been captured. Although the losses were slight, the battle – which the Zulu called eThaleni – was deeply significant, because it was the first time the Zulu army had deliberately confronted a mounted Boer force in the open. The Zulu commanders had recognised the nature of the Boer threat – and similar techniques had utterly defeated Mzilikazi – and had chosen means to deal with it. As Shaka had predicted, they had been able to exploit the interruption to Boer fire which resulted from reloading, and they had chosen broken ground to neutralise the speed and manoeuvrability of the horses. In addition, when, a few days later near the coast, an army under the nominal command of Mpande kaSenzangakhona, utterly routed a force raised by the British settlers at Port Natal, the Zulu demonstrated that they were equally capable of exploiting weaknesses among an enemy consisting largely of infantrymen with guns, who were employing a variation of conventional European tactics.

Moreover, if the whites still harboured any lingering feelings that the Zulu were in awe of their white skins or supposedly superior technology, these two battles must have come as a rude awakening.

Nevertheless, the Zulu still could not find an answer to the problem posed by secure defensive positions. The Boers still maintained their fortified camps in the Kahlamba foothills, and Dingane needed to destroy these if he were to rid himself entirely of their presence. In August an army of 10,000 men, under Ndlela's direct command, assembled at uMgungundlovu, and marched out to attack the Boer camps. The subsequent fighting revealed both the strength of the laager technique, and the lengths the Zulu were prepared to go to overcome it.

The Boers had established a strong laager of over 290 wagons on top of a ridge known as the Gatsrand, in the Bushman's river valley. The Zulu had hoped to take them by surprise, but their advance was spotted by some of the Trekkers' herdsmen on 13 August. The Trekkers therefore had time to secure themselves behind their barricades, but had little choice but to abandon much of their livestock. The Zulu halted as they came within sight of the laager, then deployed in traditional style to surround it on all sides. They then made a rush for the face of the laager, only to be met with a hail of shot which drove them back. Several times Ndlela attempted to probe for weaknesses in the laager wall, but the presence of a large number of women and children inside – who loaded muskets for the men – helped to ensure a constant rate of fire, and each time the Zulu were repulsed. Nevertheless, the attacks went on throughout the entire day, and that night the Zulu retired to bivouac nearby. It was very unusual for a Zulu battle to spill over into a second day, and that it did so was an indication both of the importance the Zulu placed on the battle, and their determination to overrun the laager. They may also have hoped that the Trekkers would be unable to sustain their position inside the laager for any length of time, and be tempted out in search of food or water.

The following morning a Boer sortie rode out to investigate the Zulu position, and was met by the *impi*, already deploying to attack. This time the warriors rushed in close, and tossed spears, tied round with burning grass, at the wagon-tents. Fire was an obvious way of destroying the fabric of the laager, but the Zulu were unlucky; those who got close enough to aim their spears properly were shot down, and most fell short. Where some did strike home, the Boers quickly doused them. Instead, the Zulu set fire to the veld – no doubt hoping the wind would blow the flames through the Boer camp – but again without success. They finished the second day by rounding up the Trekkers' livestock. Once more, they camped in the vicinity overnight – a fact that must have severely strained the nerves of the defenders. When, however, the laager was still clearly intact in the morning, the Zulu withdrew. Whatever sense of frustration Ndlela must have felt would be echoed by the next generation of Zulu commanders, faced with similar problems in 1879.

The battle was disappointing to the Zulu. Moreover, with the *amabutho* needing to purify themselves, to disperse and rest, and with no new solutions to the conflict in mind, the Zulu high command became inactive, and let the initiative slip to the Boers. By late November, the Trekker groups in Natal had received further reinforcements from beyond the mountains, and a new leader, an experienced frontier fighter by the name of Andries Pretorius, revitalised their flagging morale. Pretorius, like Uys and Potgieter before him, was a civilian with no formal military training, but he planned a new expedition with military thoroughness. He assembled the strongest commando yet seen in Natal – 472 Trekkers, supported by three settlers from Port Natal, with 120 of their armed retainers, 330 grooms and wagon-drivers, 64 wagons and at least two small ships' cannon, mounted on improvised carriages. Since this was a fighting commando, no women and children were taken. A proper chain of command was established, and to stiffen their resolve the Trekkers' religious leader, Sarel Celliers, brought them together to vow before God that, if He granted them victory, the Trekkers would forever hold the day sacred in His name.

The commando advanced from the beleaguered camps at the beginning of December 1838. Dingane's scouts were watching for such an event, and the king was fully appraised of the Boer movements. An army was assembled from the *amakhanda* in the central part of Zululand. It was between 12,000 and 16,000 men strong, and commanded by Ndlela and Nzobo personally. Since the Trekker threat was a strong one, it was important that the king's most senior generals should supervise the national response.

The Boers were advancing from the north-west, and on the afternoon of 15 December the Zulu encountered a party of mounted Boer scouts east of the Ncome river. The Boers, however, made no move to attack that afternoon, while Ndlela must have been reluctant to open an engagement with evening coming on. Instead, the Zulu planned their attack for dawn the following morning.

Yet when the Zulu force advanced to take up position before daylight on the 16th, they found that Pretorius had anticipated them. The Zulu advance breasted a line of low hills before entering the flat, featureless valley of the Ncome. Pretorius had established his laager on the opposite – western – bank, on a spot which was protected on one side by the river, and on the other by a deep donga. Only one side of the laager, on the north-western side, faced open ground, and Pretorius correctly guessed that the Zulu would have little option but to concentrate their attacks from this direction. Moreover, the river was comparatively full, and could only be forded in two places, above and below the laager. Ndlela's ability to deploy properly had effectively been compromised, a problem that was compounded by the oblique line of the Zulu advance. The column which comprised the Zulu left had advanced somewhat ahead of the centre and right, and in any case was closest to the river. It struck the river before first light, long before the main body had come up, and crossed the Ncome downstream of the laager, spreading out to surround it, squatting down in the long grass to await the arrival of the main body. The Boer laager must have seemed an insignificant sight in the moonlight, a small European island in the enveloping landscape of Africa. Yet it was an unsettling

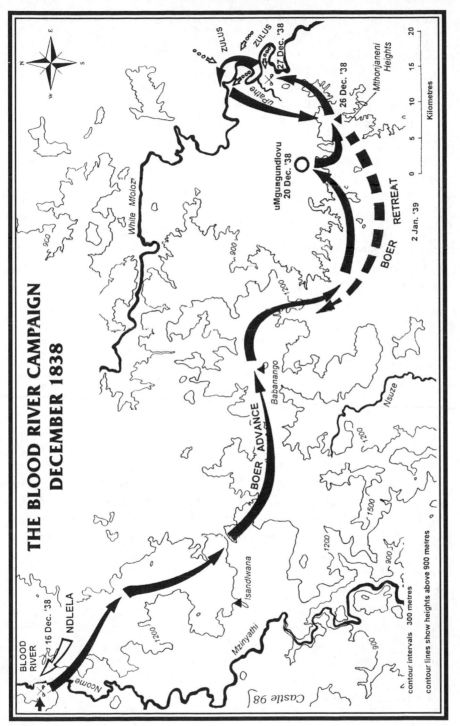

THE BLOOD RIVER CAMPAIGN
DECEMBER 1838

BLOOD RIVER
16 Dec. '38
NDLELA
Ncome

Castle 98

Mzinyathi

Isandlwana

BOER ADVANCE

Babanango

Nsuze

BOER RETREAT

2 Jan. '39

uMgungundlovu
20 Dec. '38

26 Dec. '38

Mthonjaneni
Heights

27 Dec. '38

uPathe

ZULUS

ZULUS

White Mfolozi

contour intervals   300 metres

contour lines show heights above 900 metres

Kilometres

sight, too, for the Trekkers had tied their lanterns to their whip-stocks, and hung them over the sides of their wagons, to cast a pool of light around the wagon-face in the event of a surprise attack. When a thick mist arose, just before dawn, the light hung there, a pale, ghostly circle, incomprehensible, alien and threatening.

The battle began at first light on the 16th. It seems likely that Ndlela was with the main body, and had not yet arrived on the field, and without him to restrain the warriors already in position, the battle immediately assumed a pattern that would become depressingly familiar over the next 50 years. As soon as it was light, the left wing rose to attack. This indiscipline would prove characteristic of the Zulu army, for time and again the young men, who habit-ually made up the encircling horns, and who were invariably in position before the rest of the army, began an attack prematurely. Buoyed up by confidence in their own aggressive spirit, they saw it as their duty to destroy the enemy as quickly as possible, and by doing so they made it impossible for the Zulu commander to co-ordinate his attacks properly.

And so it happened on the banks of the Ncome. The Boers held their fire until the Zulu were comfortably within range, then let fly with a devastating barrage. Although the Trekkers were renowned marksmen, there was no need now for careful long-range shooting; instead, many of the Boers fired *loopers*, small bags of shot which burst on leaving the barrel like a giant shotgun, cutting great lanes through the Zulu attack. The left horn pressed forward in the face of this fire until they had reached the wagons, but there was no way in, and they could not remain exposed to such a terrible fire. They fell back, only to regroup and try again, each time with the same results. After several attacks, some elements began to slip away from the open face of the laager, and into the donga which bordered the wagons to the south. This was dead ground from the laager, and the Zulu massed along the banks, many of them holding their shields above their heads to ward off Boer fire. Pretorius saw them gathered there, and ordered some of his men to ride out and line the bank of the donga. By that stage the Zulu were bunched too tightly to react quickly, and the Boers poured a heavy fire into them at close range. The donga became a death trap.

As the remainder of the left horn began to fall back in some confusion, Pretorius directed some of his men to harry them as they retired. Thus the left horn was largely spent before the rest of the army came into position. Nevertheless, the battle was by no means over, for the rest of the army was now approaching on the far side of the river. The right horn was somewhat in advance of the chest, and moved to cross the Ncome at a drift upstream of the laager. Pretorius realised that the Zulu would be vulnerable at the drift, and hurried some of his men to line the near bank ahead of them. As the right horn suddenly emerged from the low ground beyond the river and streamed down the bank and into the water, they were met with a heavy fire from close range. Seeing that there was little chance of them forcing a crossing, they retired, and moved downstream towards the lower drift, where the left horn had crossed before dawn. This they accomplished safely, but they were now compelled to advance over ground already strewn with the dead and dying from the earlier attack. Moreover, the chest, coming up behind, had little choice but to follow them, and once again Pretorius had succeeded in channelling all the Zulu assaults over the killing ground of his choosing.

For several hours, first the right horn, then the chest, continued to attack the laager in the same fruitless manner as before. Each time they were met with the same impenetrable fire, and forced back. After several assaults, the attacks became increasingly confused, with *amabutho* mixed up, jostling one another, and increasingly frustrated. The ground in front of them was carpeted with dead and dying warriors, and some elements, who had been particularly active, were beginning to show signs of exhaustion. At about 11.30 a.m. Ndlela called off the attacks.

The Zulu were not allowed to retire unmolested. At first, they fell back towards nearby hills and across the river in good order. But Pretorius ordered his men to ride out and fall upon them, and as the exhausted warriors bunched together on the river banks, trying to reach the drifts, the Boers shot them down almost without reply. Most of the warriors were so tired they could scarcely carry their weapons, let alone use them. The Boers pushed them clear across the river, and the Zulu discipline collapsed as they stumbled across the plain beyond, where the Boers shot them down without mercy. Almost as many were killed on the far bank of the Ncome as around the laager. When the main pursuit was spent, the Trekkers found many warriors had submerged themselves in the river, breathing through reeds, or with just their nostrils exposed, hoping to escape detection. But the Boers, with their hunters' instincts, stalked along the banks, and shot them where they found them. Soon the sluggish river was so full of corpses that it resembled a huge pool of blood; the Boers renamed the Ncome *Bloedrivier* – Blood River.

Certainly, the scale of the Boer victory appeared to be impressive. They estimated that as many as 3000 Zulu had been killed; this was probably an overestimate by a people unused to the scale of such slaughter, but the Zulu losses had been heavy. Many of those wounded in early attacks had been unable to get away, and had been killed during the pursuit. Ndlela himself is said to have had a narrow escape, the Zulu command group was clearly visible across the river, and one of Pretorius's guns lobbed a shell which exploded nearby. Several men were hurt.

In return for such a terrible loss of life, the Zulu had wounded just three Boers during the pursuit. One of them was Pretorius himself, who was stabbed through the hand. Small wonder that the Boers gave thanks to God in the belief that He had granted them the victory they had so earnestly prayed for.

Furthermore, the Zulu attack had utterly failed to stop the Boer advance. Pretorius broke up the laager, and advanced towards uMgungundlovu, hoping to catch the king himself, but by the time the Boers reached the emaKhosini valley, Dingane and his followers had retired. Rather than let his magnificent capital fall into Boer hands, Dingane had set it on fire. The Boers were left to poke about among the ruins, and to bury the remains of Retief and his followers.

Yet the Boer victory was by no means as decisive as it seemed. True, the king's main army, under his most experienced commander, had been scattered with heavy losses. But many of his *amabutho* had not taken part in the fight, while even those who had, like their counterparts in 1879, were still able to reassemble once they had recovered. The loss of uMgungundlovu was a blow, but the king merely selected a position further north, near Nongoma, to rebuild it, beyond the range of Trekker reprisals. Indeed, the true balance of power was revealed by an incident in the closing stages of the campaign.

From uMgungundlovu the Boers retired up onto the Mthonjaneni ridge, which commanded spectacular views over the greater White Mfolozi valley below. The heart of the Zulu kingdom lay spread out among the vista of rolling blue hills and glittering rivers, in all its aching beauty, and with all its promise of Dingane's fabulous herds of cattle. Yet the Trekkers soon found they could not plunder with impunity, as they might have hoped.

The Boers had captured in their perambulations a Zulu by the name of Bhongoza kaMefu. Bhongoza let slip that many of Dingane's cattle had been concealed in the Mfolozi valley, in the hope that this might distract the Trekkers from their pursuit of him, and Bhongoza offered to lead the Trekkers to them. On 27 December a commando of 300 mounted Boers, supported by one of the Port Natal settlers, Alexander Biggar, and 70 of his trained retainers, followed Bhongoza's lead down from Mthonjaneni heights. They descended a steep ridge flanking the uPathe stream, but just as they reached the spot where the uPathe flows into the White Mfolozi, a cry of *'Bapakathi!'* – 'They are inside!' – suddenly echoed around the hills. Instantly, several Zulu *amabutho* rose up from among the long grass and bush around them. Bhongoza had deliberately led the Boers into a trap; it was sprung so effectively that there was no hope of them returning the way they had come. Instead, the

Boers pressed forward, bursting through the Zulu screen in front of them, and splashing across the Mfolozi. The country on the other side was open and undulating, far more suited to mounted tactics, and the Boers managed to break free of their pursuers, trying to recross the Mfolozi upstream. One of the regiments which had ambushed them, the uDlambedlu, had anticipated this, however, and had shadowed them on the southern bank. As the Boers tried to find their way back through a new drift, the uDlambedlu rose to meet them. Alexander Biggar's musketmen, who were on foot, were by this time lagging behind, and Biggar chose to stand by them. He, and many of his men, were cut down and killed, together with four of the Boers. The rest managed to fight their way back to the camp on the heights.

The ambush on the uPathe had proved that the Zulu still retained the measure of mounted Boer commandos in open warfare. In the light of this, Blood River emerges not as the crushing victory of popular myth, but as something of a stalemate. By the end of December 1838, both sides had fought each other to a standstill, and neither possessed the means of bringing the war to a decisive conclusion. Instead, the Boers rounded up as many of Dingane's cattle as they could find, and returned to Natal.

The temporary end to the hostilities allowed the Boers to expand from their defensive positions in the Kahlamba foothills, and to stake their claim to much of the best grazing land south of the Thukela. Dingane, meanwhile, investigated the possibility of shifting the focus of his kingdom still further north. In 1839 he mounted a major expedition across the Phongolo river and into the Swazi kingdom, in an attempt to force the Swazi to abandon the southern part of their territory. Here Dingane hoped to establish himself instead. The Swazi realised the extent of this threat, however, and instead of retiring to their strongholds, as they usually did when pressed by the Zulu, they mounted a vigorous counter-attack, and after a ferocious battle on the Lubuye river, the Zulu were driven back. Dingane was forced to reconsider this policy, and consolidated his position near Nongoma instead.

It is interesting that the Swazi campaign was commanded not by Ndlela kaSompisi, but instead by Klwana kaNgqengelele of the Buthelezi, and it may be that Ndlela was already beginning to lose favour with Dingane. Certainly, Dingane had a suspicious nature, and must have found it difficult to forgive the man who lost Blood River. There are, moreover, suggestions that Ndlela, in turn, was beginning to make tentative approaches to establish himself with one of Dingane's rivals within the Royal House.

Dingane had begun his reign by purging a number of his brothers, who might have been inclined to press a claim as Shaka's successor which was stronger than his own. He had, however, always spared his younger brother

Mpande. Mpande scarcely appeared to be made of the stuff of warrior kings; he seemed to be slow-witted, and a leg injury had made him unfit for arduous duty in the *amabutho*. Mpande, however, had grown up among the Ntuli people, and had found an ally in Ndlela. Whenever the king expressed his exasperation with Mpande, Ndlela had urged the king to ignore him, saying that Mpande was a fool, and no danger. Moreover, Mpande, unlike Shaka and Dingane, had produced a number of heirs, and Ndlela had urged the royal council to allow him to live, as he, if no other, had provided the nation with a dynasty.

In 1838, however, Mpande's carefully cultivated facade of indolence and stupidity had slipped. He had been responsible for the assembly and ritual preparation of the force which had defeated the British settlers on the banks of the Thukela. Although the battlefield command had been exercised by others, Mpande had suddenly risen to public acclaim. Furthermore, when Dingane had ordered Mpande to bring the *amabutho* quartered in his district to join the army assembling for the Swazi campaign, Mpande had made his excuses. He had been assiduously building up a regional power-base, and to take part in such an expedition would have risked the dispersal of his following.

His refusal confirmed Dingane's suspicions that Mpande was pursuing his own agenda, and Dingane resolved to 'eat him up'. He sent Mpande a message accompanied by a gift of 100 head of cattle. Etiquette demanded that Mpande would have to visit Dingane to thank him personally for such a gift, and while in the royal capital Dingane intended to have him killed.

And here Ndlela's role became crucial. Ndlela had not been consulted about the plot, but when he heard of it, he directed one of the *izinduna* in charge of the cattle, whom he knew he could trust, to warn Mpande, and to urge him to flee. Mpande realised that his position within the kingdom had become impossible, and in September 1839 he crossed the Thukela river, out of Zululand, together with 17,000 of his supporters and 25,000 head of cattle. This defection was of such enormity that it is remembered as the 'breaking of the rope which bound the kingdom together'.

Interestingly enough, Ndlela did not join him in Natal. Whatever sympathy he might have had for Mpande, Ndlela seems to have felt tied by his personal history of loyalty to the established order. After all, Dingane at that point was still in effective control of much of the old Zulu kingdom: Mpande was now merely a fugitive.

That situation, however, did not last for long. Mpande was an obvious ally for the Boers, who were keen to find a means of finally ending their quarrel with Dingane. They offered to support Mpande's claim to kingship in return for recognition of their claims in Natal and Zululand, and in January 1840 they embarked together on a joint military expedition.

It is interesting to note, however, that this protracted and very destructive conflict was finally resolved by traditional means. Mpande's followers were camped along the lower Thongathi river, near the coast, while the main Boer settlements lay further inland. It was agreed that Mpande's troops would advance into Zululand up the coast, while the Boers would follow a more northerly track, passing the old battlefield of Blood River. Since Mpande himself accompanied the Boer party, as proof of his good faith, his troops were commanded by his senior *induna*, Nongalaza kaNondela.

Curiously, it seems that both the Boers and Mpande were content to let the bulk of the fighting fall to Nongalaza's army. As a general rule, the Boers preferred not to place themselves in the front line when fighting on behalf of African allies, while Mpande probably felt that the mere moral support of the Boers would cost him less in the long run. In any event, Nongalaza's army made rapid progress into enemy territory, and had confronted Dingane's army long before the Boers had been able to join it.

Dingane was well aware of the new invasion, and, rather than make a stand at his new uMgungundlovu, he had retired north-west, and taken up a position among a group of low kopjes known as the Maqongqo hills. He had perhaps 5000 warriors with him – about the same number as Nongalaza – and, as he always did when the future of the kingdom was at stake, he had given command of them to Ndlela. One can only speculate on Ndlela's feelings as he prepared to defend his king against an attack with which he had connived.

Details of Ndlela's last battle are sketchy. Nongalaza's army arrived at Maqongqo on 29 January, and attacked in traditional style. The battle was carried out at close quarters, in the manner of Shaka's day, great cow-hide shield and stabbing spear against shield and stabbing spear. At first it seemed that Ndlela's force would prevail, and the uDlambedlu *ibutho* steadily pushed back Nongalaza's men. One hero of the battle, Nozitshada kaMagoboza, an *induna* of the uDlambedlu, stabbed so many men that their corpses piled up in heaps around him, and his stabbing arm became so tired that he had to change to the other hand. Yet Nongalaza had secured the support of one of the great specialist war-doctors of the day, Mahlungwana kaTshoba, who had burnt a patch of grass and treated it with medicines which would ensure defeat for Dingane's warriors; and sure enough, Nongalaza's forces rallied. In some versions of the story his *izinduna* shouted out to their men that the Boers were about to reinforce them; Ndlela's men heard, and lost heart. They began to give ground, and some even defected to the enemy. The great Nozitshada refused to retreat, but was so exhausted he could fight no longer, and called upon Nongalaza's men to finish him, which they did. Suddenly Ndlela's army collapsed completely, and fled the field, with Mpande's men in pursuit. Many of Dingane's notables tried to hide in nearby bush, but were hunted down and killed. Queen Bhibhi, Senzangakhona's wife and Ndlela's sister, was among the killed, while Ndlela himself was speared through the thigh as he tried to escape.

It was the last of many wounds he suffered in the service of the Zulu kings. The battle of Maqongqo was decisive. The remnants of Dingane's army scattered, and the king, together with a few loyal members of his household, retired still further north. Here numbers of his *izinduna* and warriors, who had made their way across country, exhausted and harried by Nongalaza's men, caught up with him. Among them was Ndlela.

Yet Ndlela was to learn the bitter lesson of defeated generals across history. Dingane turned on him, angrily denouncing him, not only for losing the battle, but for causing Mpande to be spared in the first place. In his bitterness, Dingane ordered the man who had once been the most trusted of all his councillors to be taken out and executed. He was not killed with knobkerries, like most criminals, but was strangled with rawhide thongs, like a woman. To complete his humiliation, Dingane ordered that his body be not buried, but left out on the veld for the scavengers.

It was an act of ingratitude, terrible and unjust, and it marked the passing of an old order. Ndlela had been raised up and trained under Shaka, and he carried the Shakan tradition into a new era, waging war against the enemy whom Shaka never had to fight. On the whole, he had faced the challenge well; he had won as many victories as defeats, and it was a particular irony that in the end he had not lost to men armed with the terrible new engines of war, the horse and the gun, but to men who, like himself, had learned their trade under Shaka.

Yet the Zulu kingdom would never quite be the same again after 1840. The sense of grandeur and of military invincibility, of being all-powerful at the centre of the universe, which had characterised Shaka's later years and most of Dingane's reign, had received a desperate blow. Mpande would prove a patient and subtle ruler, adroitly exploiting tensions between the Boers and the British to free himself from his obligations to the Trekkers; and he spent much of his reign repairing the damage wrought by the civil war of 1840. But the arrival of the whites could not be undone, nor the menace of their military might denied, and their presence on the borders cast a long shadow over Zululand's subsequent history, until at last the European presence in Natal, which had once been a child succoured by Shaka himself, rose up, and ate its father.

Dingane's administration collapsed. Shortly before the battle of Maqongqo he had sent Nzobo kaSobadli, Ndlela's colleague and his other great councillor, to try to negotiate with the Boers. The Trekkers suspected Nzobo of being responsible for the death of Piet Retief, however, and promptly arrested him. After a parody of a trial, and sundry humiliations, he too was executed; the Boers shot him. Dingane himself tried to set up a new homestead in the territory of the Nyawo people in northern Zululand with the handful of supporters still loyal to him, but the Nyawo were fearful of having so dangerous a guest among them, and they conspired with the nearby Swazi to have him murdered.

When the last of Dingane's supporters trickled back to Zululand after his death, they were contemptuously dubbed *umdidi kaNdlela* – Ndlela's rectum – by those who had supported Mpande. Yet Mpande remembered the service Ndlela performed him. Anxious to heal the bitter wounds which divided the country, he banned such talk, and took Ndlela's sons, Godide and Mavumengwana, under his shield, so that they both rose to prominent positions in his kingdom.

Ironically, both Godide kaNdlela and Mavumengwana kaNdlela were to face similar military challenges to their father. Both men were appointed commanders by Cetshwayo during the Anglo-Zulu War; Godide commanded the forces which mustered in the coastal district, and attacked Colonel Pearson's column at Nyezane river on 22 January 1879, while Mavumengwana, together with Ntshingwayo kaMahole, commanded the great *impi* which, that same day, visited so much destruction upon the British camp at Isandlwana.

Clearly something of their father's spirit had passed to them.

3

KING CETSHWAYO kaMPANDE

'The Thunder that crashed above Isandlwana hill ...'

Cetshwayo kaMpande was born in 1832 at the emLambongwenya royal homestead of his father, King Mpande kaSenzangakhona, in southern Zululand, not far from the majestic Dlinza forest, which still grows on the outskirts of modern Eshowe. Cetshwayo's name is rich in unintended irony, for it means 'The Slandered One', and if ever a man's history came to suit his name, it is Cetshwayo. Quite why his name was chosen is a mystery, though it undoubtedly reflected one of the many intrigues and suspicions which characterised life in the Zulu Royal House at the time of his birth. Indeed, it was indicative of the insecurities which were to frame Cetshwayo's life.

Historical accident had contrived to deprive the Zulu kingdom of an established tradition of peaceful succession. King Shaka, who had ruled just twelve short years, had never formally married, and refused to raise children on the grounds that they would one day usurp his authority. Although rumours of illegitimate children born to Shaka's *isigodlo* girls, and smuggled out of harm's way before their father discovered their existence, were current in Zululand throughout the nineteenth century, no one arose to claim Shaka's patrimony, and there were certainly no recognised heirs when Shaka was assassinated in 1828. Instead, his brother, Dingane kaSenzangakhona, took the throne, only to produce no heirs in his turn. Indeed, while Shaka had remained remarkably tolerant towards potential rivals within his own family, King Dingane's reign was characterised by the progressive elimination of most of his father's surviving sons, so that only a handful remained alive when Dingane was overthrown in 1840.

One of those who survived was Dingane's younger brother, Mpande. Behind the facade of an indolent, harmless simpleton, Mpande was an astute politician, who carefully manipulated events through a network of subtle alliances, without ever truly arousing Dingane's suspicions. Because of his position as the king's closest relative, Mpande was only too aware that his own sons – who provided him with a secure line of succession – were just as much at risk as he himself. Indeed, it is said that Mpande's first-born son had been killed on Shaka's orders. Mpande therefore placed his next son, Cetshwayo, at a safe distance from the centres of royal power in Zululand, and Cetshwayo's early years were spent among the Sibiya people of Chief Sothobe, who had been an influential adviser to King Shaka. Nor were there any doubts about

Cetshwayo's status; in a polygamous society, the Zulu had strict rules regarding the seniority of sons born to different wives, and Cetshwayo fulfilled them all. He was the eldest son of Mpande's 'great wife', Ngqumbazi, who was herself related to the chiefly line of the important Zungu people. Moreover, when Mpande had married Ngqumbazi, it had been Shaka himself who had paid the *ilobolo* – the transfer of cattle to the bride's family which was necessary to seal the marriage contract – on his younger brother's behalf.

Mpande successfully managed to deflect Dingane's attention until the great crisis which faced the kingdom in 1838. During the war with the Boers he had aroused the king's suspicions by his part in the successful attack on the Port Natal settlers, and as Dingane came increasingly under pressure, both within and without the kingdom, Mpande stood out as the one alternative candidate within the legitimate Royal House who might replace Dingane. Dingane moved against him, but Mpande was warned of the plot, and fled with his followers to Natal.

The defection of Mpande was a turning point in the kingdom's history, for it permanently loosened the bonds which tied the great chiefs to the monarchy. During the civil war which resulted, many chiefs sold their support to the rival kings in return for a greater degree of local autonomy, and the internal stability of the kingdom could never again be taken for granted. Yet Mpande, with Boer support, defeated and drove out Dingane, and on 10 February 1840 the Boers proclaimed Mpande king of the Zulu. As a precaution, in case Mpande had been killed in the fighting, the Boers had marked out his heir, Cetshwayo, by cutting a notch in his ear, exactly as if he had been a prize heifer.

Mpande built a new royal homestead, kwaNodwengu – 'the place of the irresistible one' – on the Mahlabathini plain, north of the White Mfolozi river. From here he embarked on a career that would see him rule longer than any of the other kings in pre-colonial Zululand. He was, moreover, the only one of Senzangakhona's sons to die peacefully, of old age. His rule was dominated by the need to rebuild the kingdom in the aftermath of the civil war, and to cope with the growing pressures posed by the developing settler economies on Zululand's borders. That the kingdom was still substantially intact and largely economically self-sufficient at the time of his death in 1872 was the measure of his success.

With Mpande secure on the throne, Cetshwayo grew to manhood in confident expectation of his inheritance. Like every other Zulu youth, he became a cadet, serving periodically at one of the provincial *amakhanda*, and in 1850 he was enrolled in the newly formed uThulwana *ibutho*. The uThulwana included no less than seven of Mpande's sons, and the prestige which their presence conferred soon earned the regiment a reputation for unruly behaviour and arrogance. This became so pronounced that the king appointed one of his most trusted councillors, Chief Mnyamana kaNgqengelele of the Buthelezi, as the regiment's senior *induna*, since he proved to be one of the few who had the strength of character to control them.

In 1852 the uThulwana were blooded in action. Blocked to the south and west by European expansion, Mpande had looked to the north for his territorial ambitions. In particular, he was keen to establish his authority over the northern banks of the Phongolo river, and to force the Swazi king, Mswati Dlamini, to give his allegiance. Several times in the 1840s and 1850s Mpande launched his army into Swaziland, usually with mixed results; the Swazi, well aware that they could not match the Zulu in an open battle, retired to their traditional strongholds, and the Zulu were unable to drive them out. In July 1852, however, the Zulu attack caught the Swazi by surprise. The Swazi scattered, and the Zulu *amabutho* carried off huge herds of cattle. The uThulwana were the youngest of the Zulu regiments employed in action, but Prince Cetshwayo was said to have greatly distinguished himself in one skirmish when he found himself surrounded by a group of Swazis, and killed several in hand-to-hand combat before scattering the rest. Significantly, the campaign was remembered among the Zulu as the *ukufunda kuk'uThulwana* – the learning of the Thulwana.

Cetshwayo's success in the Swazi campaign undoubtedly added to his growing prestige within the country – a factor that was of increasing concern to Mpande. Whereas Shaka and Dingane had only to worry about potential rivals among their own brothers, Mpande – who fathered no less than 29 sons and 23 daughters – was acutely conscious that he was bringing his own rivals into the world himself. Cetshwayo's popularity made Mpande increasingly concerned for his own security, and within a few years of his accession he was working to keep Cetshwayo's ambitions in check. To prevent Cetshwayo building up a regional power-base, he first separated him from his mother. Mpande placed Ngqumbazi in charge of the kwaGqikazi homestead in northern Zululand, while he attached Cetshwayo to the ekuBazeni homestead in the south. Nevertheless, Cetshwayo frequently visited his mother, and the young prince soon had a following of young men of his own age at both sites. After the Swazi campaign, Mpande gave in to pressure to provide Cetshwayo with a homestead of his own – oNdini, not far from present-day Eshowe – and it proved impossible to prevent Cetshwayo cultivating supporters there.

To offset Cetshwayo's growing influence, Mpande deliberately let it be known that he was considering repudiating Cetshwayo's claim as his heir in favour of another of his sons, Prince Mbuyazi. While he had grown increasingly suspicious of Cetshwayo, Mpande had remained close to Mbuyazi, whose mother, Monase, had been given to him in marriage from among Shaka's own *isigodlo* girls. Mpande therefore let it be known that Mbuyazi was effectively the heir to Shaka's estate, a position that overruled Cetshwayo's otherwise impeccable claims. Moreover, he took the opportunity to show favour to Mbuyazi at public occasions, snubbing Cetshwayo in the hope that the nation would take its cue from him. In one instance, Mpande himself distributed shields to the uThulwana *ibutho*, in which both princes were enrolled. Holding two shields cut from the same hide, he was about to give Cetshwayo the shield bearing the wound where the animal was killed – which was considered to have special properties – when at the last minute he crossed them over and tossed it at Mbuyazi's feet instead. On another occasion he pointedly praised the efforts of Mbuyazi's supporters at a dancing competition, while ignoring the efforts of Cetshwayo and his followers.

Such behaviour drove Cetshwayo to a fury. Fiercely proud of his royal status, he railed at the insults which Mpande and Mbuyazi heaped upon him, and it soon became obvious that unless the king took direct steps to prevent it, the two princes were heading for a violent clash. Reluctant to act against Cetshwayo himself, for fear of alienating his supporters, Mpande could do little but comment meekly that 'two bulls cannot live in the same cattle kraal'. 'Our house did not gain the kingship by being appointed to sit on the mat,' he observed regretfully, 'our house gained the kingship by stabbing with the assegai.'

By the end of 1855 Cetshwayo, who had been assiduously courting the regional *izikhulu* and military commanders among his father's army, commanded wide support throughout the country. His followers had taken the name *uSuthu* – a reference to the huge herds of Sotho cattle which Mpande had taken in a raid through the northern Transvaal in 1851, and which implied both the military strength and size of Cetshwayo's followers. Thereafter, the term uSuthu was deeply associated with the Zulu Royal House, and would be used as a rallying cry by those who wished to associate themselves with it. By contrast, Mbuyazi's followers became known as the *iziGqoza*, a wry term reflecting the fact that he received a steady trickle of support; the word is derived from the verb meaning to drip down, as rain drops from a roof.

Cetshwayo's success in attracting supporters was not due alone to his superior claim. While Mbuyazi was a big, imposing man, he had an arrogant manner about him, and he irritated his superiors and intimidated his subjects. Cetshwayo, on the other hand, was careful always to give the nation's elders their due respect, and, while deeply conscious of his royal status, nonetheless took an interest in the lives of ordinary people. Moreover, Cetshwayo had a genuine passion for the traditions, history and language of his people, which added weight to his air of authority. Broad-chested, with a regal manner, and a pleasant, open face, he was more charismatic than his brother, despite bouts of moodiness and a temper which, on the rare occasions when he lost it, terrified even his councillors.

The first hint that the crisis was reaching a head came when both parties applied to the king to hold a hunt in the thorn-bush between the confluence of the White and Black Mfolozi rivers, an area traditionally set aside as a hunting ground for the kings. Such hunts were often an excuse for military display, and both sides turned out carrying war-shields rather than the smaller shields traditionally used for hunting. But if Mpande had hoped Mbuyazi might have out-manouvered Cetshwayo, he was disappointed, since the uSuthu turned out in far greater numbers than the iziGqoza, and the iziGqoza shied away from an open clash. Nevertheless, the song they composed on marching home suggested their true intentions: 'We almost got the buck, almost. We almost stabbed it.'

Worried by his failure to turn the tide of support in favour of Mbuyazi, Mpande decided to award his favourite a new tract of land, north of the Thukela river. This placed Mbuyazi in close proximity to the border with colonial Natal, and was a broad hint that Mbuyazi should follow his father's precedent and flee to the whites if he became too hard-pressed. It was nonetheless a risky strategy, since Cetshwayo's own homesteads were also in the south of the country, and Mbuyazi would be sandwiched between his rival and the border.

Furthermore, when Mbuyazi arrived to take over his new lands in the middle of 1856, he acted in a typically provocative manner. Many people already living there were supporters of Cetshwayo, and Mbuyazi demanded that they either give him allegiance or move away. He raided those who failed to comply, forcing them out, burning their homes and driving off their cattle. Cetshwayo responded by summoning his supporters to the oNdini homestead. Mpande, realising that a clash was imminent, sent out secret messages to influential chiefs and *izinduna* instructing them to support Mbuyazi, but most realised the likely consequences, and refused.

In November 1856 Cetshwayo completed his mobilisation, and moved to attack Mbuyazi. Ominously, most of the king's *amabutho* had declared for Cetshwayo in large numbers, while a number of influential chiefdoms had sent him their fighting men, regardless of regimental affiliations. Estimates of the total uSuthu strength vary, but Cetshwayo had between 15,000 and 20,000 men at his disposal. Many of his father's more important sons had also joined him, including Prince Ndabuko – his full brother – and the princes Dabulamanzi, Shingana and Ziwedu. Significantly, even Prince Hamu kaNzibe – who harboured his own designs on the throne, and lived far away from the centres of royal authority, in northern Zululand – supported Cetshwayo, as did the equally independent-minded Mandlakazi section. Nevertheless, some five of

Mpande's sons rallied to Mbuyazi, but the iziGqoza were heavily outnumbered, for Mbuyazi had succeeded in mustering only 7000 fighting men.

As soon as Cetshwayo's army advanced from oNdini at the end of November, Mbuyazi collected his followers together and tried to rush for the border. He had with him nearly 13,000 non-combatants, and many thousands of cattle. When he reached the Thukela, however, he found the river in flood with the seasonal summer rains, and almost impossible to cross. Indeed, a group of white traders who had been trading in Zululand, and who had attempted to flee before the fighting started, had been trapped midstream; they had managed to pick their way through the shallows, driving a big herd of cattle with them, to a large sandbank close to the Natal side, but had found the last stretch blocked by a fast, deep channel. Mbuyazi's followers camped in the valleys among the hills north of the Lower Drift, while Mbuyazi himself sent messages across the border appealing for help.

The Natal authorities, however, were not inclined to become involved in a purely internal Zulu affair, particularly one that threatened to engulf them in imminent bloodshed. They refused to offer either sanctuary or support, and the best that Mbuyazi could secure was the assistance of a group of trained African hunters, led by a young white adventurer, John Dunn, who had been acting as an assistant to the Natal border agent. Dunn crossed the river, ostensibly to negotiate with Cetshwayo, but in fact to support Mbuyazi.

It was, however, too late for talking; Cetshwayo and the uSuthu were only a few miles off, moving down the Mandeni valley from the north. Mbuyazi's followers were clustered in the valley of the Thambo and iNyoni streams, further south, and Mbuyazi placed his fighting men along a ridge which lay between them and Cetshwayo's approach. Nearby lay the site of a homestead called 'Ndondakusuka, which had belonged to one of Dingane's *izinduna*, and the Zulu would remember the coming fight by that name. On 1 December, the uSuthu approached within sight of the iziGqoza, then stopped to undergo their final pre-battle rituals. Dunn urged Mbuyazi either to seize the initiative and attack, or to find a way to get his women and children across the river, but Mbuyazi prevaricated. In doing so, he forfeited what little chance he had.

The battle, which began early the next morning, was the only battle which Cetshwayo ever commanded in person. The day broke cold and miserable, with mist and drizzle hanging on the green hills. The uSuthu moved down from their bivouac of the night before and deployed in battle formation, with the more formal *amabutho* on the right and centre, and the contingents supplied by the Zungu, Mandlakazi and abaQulusi sections on the left. Cetshwayo and his commanders took up a position on a ridge behind his men. The prince was wearing the uniform of the uThulwana at that time – a headband of otter-skin with a single crane feather, and carrying a dark shield with a single white spot on the lower half. The iziGqoza fighting men faced them across the Mandeni valley, with their followers still secreted in the valleys running down to the Thukela beyond.

Yet the iziGqoza lost the battle even before it began. Not only had Mbuyazi's over-confidence robbed them of any real tactical options, but omens clearly suggested that they had lost the support of the spirit world. Cetshwayo had been able to secure a war-shield belonging to an iziGqoza supporter, and before his assembled army that morning he threw it on the ground and knelt upon it, thereby assuring the uSuthu supernatural ascendancy over their enemy. By contrast, as Mbuyazi and his councillors were surveying the field, in full view of their men, a gust of wind snatched an ostrich feather out of his head-dress, and cast it in the dust. Whereas Shaka had once turned a similar incident to his own advantage, Mbuyazi said nothing, and a nervous murmur ran through the ranks of his men, to whom the symbolism was only too obvious.

The uSuthu began the battle in traditional style, sending out their right horn to attempt to outflank the enemy. They moved down the Mandeni and up the sheltered Nkwaku valley on a line which would have carried then past Mbuyazi's left, had not John Dunn spotted the move. Dunn and his hunters met the uSuthu right on the banks of the Nkwaku, and opened a heavy fire on it, forcing Cetshwayo's warriors to fall back. Despite desperate attempts by their *izinduna* to rally them, the uSuthu could not stand up to Dunn's withering fire, and retreated in some confusion. Realising that this placed his whole force in danger, Cetshwayo shifted the focus of his attack to his left, sending out his left horn – the Mandlakazi and Zungu sections – to cut around Mbuyazi's right. There were no gunmen to protect the iziGqoza on this side, and under the determined uSuthu attack, Mbuyazi's right crumpled. Seeing them go, Cetshwayo launched the rest of his forces – the chest – who advanced steadily up from the Mandeni valley, drumming their spears on their shields as they did so. This was enough to intimidate the iziGqoza centre, who fell back from the crest of the ridge without standing to fight.

At first, the iziGqoza retreat was orderly enough, but as the warriors retired down the Thambo stream, they blundered into the non-combatants hidden there. The warriors became tangled up with a mass of women, children and cattle, and the sight of the uSuthu appearing over the ridge they had abandoned, and streaming down from the left, was enough to unnerve them. The iziGqoza position suddenly collapsed completely. Left unsupported, John Dunn and the hitherto victorious iziGqoza elements on the left had no choice but to retire, or face being surrounded. As the uSuthu descended into the valley and struck the iziGqoza rearguard, the killing became indiscriminate, and panic set in among Mbuyazi's followers. A terrified mass of warriors and civilians were herded towards the river, and in the rush of combat the uSuthu attacked them all. Hundreds were killed along the banks of the Thambo stream – the name post-dates the battle and means simply 'bones' – while the rest were caught among the long grass on the banks of the Thukela. Some tried to brave the waters and escape, but many more were slaughtered on the banks, or were swept away and drowned, or killed by crocodiles which still infested the surging waters. John Dunn himself only just managed to escape; Mbuyazi and those of his brothers who had joined him were all killed. Perhaps 6000 iziGqoza would survive altogether; as many as 12,000 were killed, and their bloated bodies were washed up on the beaches on either side of the Thukela for days afterwards.

The battle was an extraordinary victory for Cetshwayo. In one single blow he had completely eradicated, not only his greatest rival, but much of his support-base. A white trader, returning through Zululand to the Thukela, met the prince's triumphal return, 'a portion of the victorious army ... carrying branches of trees over Kitchwayo, walking very stately and slowly, teaching him to be king, as they said'. Another white man, a missionary, noticed the price the uSuthu had paid, however, for in the wake of the warriors, and the great herd of cattle they had captured, came the wounded, 'with gaping wounds, groaning as they went along'.

The battle was to have a curious sequel. When the victorious uSuthu had reached the river, some of them had crossed to the sandbanks near the far side, and carried off the traders' cattle which had been herded there. The warriors had offered no violence to the traders, who were, in turn, far too terrified to protest. After the battle, however, the traders complained bitterly to the Natal authorities that they had been robbed, and John Dunn – of all people – offered to visit Cetshwayo to beg for the cattle's return. This was, of course, a risky undertaking, since the part he had played in the battle had become well known, but Dunn's audacity won Cetshwayo's confidence, and the two became friends. Cetshwayo apologised for the error, rounded up the traders' cattle, and returned them; moreover, he offered Dunn a post as his white adviser. Dunn, who had never been at ease in settler society, accepted, and Cetshwayo set him up as an *induna* in the southern districts of the country, which had been depopulated by the recent fighting. Here Dunn lived a curiously cross-cultural life, marrying Zulu wives, and ruling in the manner of a traditional *inkhosi*, while at the same time maintaining a European house-hold and dressing like an English country gentleman. He remained a close personal friend of Cetshwayo until the crisis in Anglo-Zulu relations in the 1870s forced him to make a difficult choice.

After 'Ndondakusuka, Cetshwayo returned to his homestead at oNdini. Mpande was heartbroken at the death of so many of his sons, but had little choice but to accept the situation. He and Cetshwayo reached a tacit agreement whereby Mpande allowed Cetshwayo increasing control over the everyday affairs of state, but retained for himself the central duties of kingship, such as officiating at the annual umKhosi festival, and raising new *amabutho*. Mpande was by this time in any case weary of his responsibilities; he was now in his sixties, and so fat that when he travelled any distance his attendants dragged him in a two-wheeled cart. Dispirited and increasingly ineffectual, he preferred to spend his time in the *isigodlo* with his favourite wives.

Yet this, too, posed fresh challenges to Cetshwayo. After the battle, a number of Mpande's surviving sons fled to Natal, while the king carefully secured the rest – mostly children – in royal homesteads. Mpande still hoped to control Cetshwayo by hinting that he might yet nominate a fresh heir, but in 1861 he overplayed his hand, and Cetshwayo reacted with a determination which revealed his underlying ruthlessness. Mpande had come to favour one of his younger wives, Nomantshali, and gave the impression he might chose one of Nomantshali's sons as his heir. Cetshwayo was furious, and promptly assembled a group of cadets from the iNgobamakhosi regiment, placed them under a trusted *induna*, and ordered them to discreetly assassinate Nomantshali and her sons. But the affair was bungled; two of Nomantshali's sons saw what was coming, and fled to Natal in the nick of time, while the third, a lad named Mpoyiyana, took refuge with his father. Frustrated and fearful of the consequences of failure, the iNgobamakhosi confronted the king himself, dragging Mpoyiyana out of Mpande's arms, and taking him off to be killed. A day or two later they sought out Nomantshali, who gave herself up to them in despair.

Cetshwayo was furious, for the blatant disrespect for the king reflected badly on him among the nation at large, and indeed the presence of so many of Mpande's sons beyond the borders – out of his reach – continued to haunt him for years to come. It is no coincidence that during the war of 1879, at least two of them – Princes Mthonga and Sikhotha – took the opportunity afforded by the British invasion to renew their fight with Cetshwayo.

Yet in truth there were few obstacles left in Cetshwayo's path. In 1867 Mpande at last granted the uThulwana permission to marry; ironically, Cetshwayo's first wife had been one of Mbuyazi's *isigodlo* girls, who had been captured at 'Ndondakusuka. Cetshwayo's son, Dinuzulu, was born the following year.

Mpande finally died in September or October 1872, the only one of Senzangakhona's sons to die peacefully of old age, in his own hut. He had ruled for over 30 years – far longer than Shaka or Dingane before him, or

Cetshwayo after – and he had kept the kingdom together despite the consequences of two civil wars and the corrosive pressure of white economic penetration. For several months his death was kept secret, while his body, wrapped in a fresh bull's hide, was allowed to dry out in his hut, watched over by his attendants and some of his *isigodlo* girls. Then he was buried, along with at least one of his attendants, at the top of the great central enclosure of his principal homestead, kwaNodwengu.

It was nearly a year before the official period of mourning ended, and Cetshwayo prepared to assume the mantle of kingship, for which he had fought for so long. He remained, however, deeply insecure, fearing that even at this stage someone might emerge to challenge his position. Most of his rivals now lived outside Zululand, while Mbuyazi's body had never been found after 'Ndondakusuka, and there were persistent rumours that he had escaped, and was poised to return and claim his inheritance. Moreover, at least two powerful *izikhulu* in the north of the country had a reputation for independence of mind, and sufficient links with the Royal House to justify a claim. One, Hamu kaNzibe, was actually a son of Mpande, but was ruled out as his heir by a complex point of genealogy, while the other, Zibhebhu kaMaphitha, was young and ambitious, and had only recently succeeded to the chiefdom of the Mandlakazi, who were themselves a collateral branch of the Royal House.

It was partly to ward off such potential threats that Cetshwayo invited representatives of the colonial administration in Natal to attend the coronation ceremonies, which were held at the end of August 1873. He hoped that by securing their support he would intimidate any potential rivals within the country. Perhaps he did, for when the ceremonies at last took place, and the Mandlakazi and Ngenetsheni (Hamu's people) met Cetshwayo's triumphal procession through the emaKhosini valley – the resting place of the ancestral spirits – there was no confrontation. Nevertheless, when the whites insisted on crowning Cetshwayo in a farcical ceremony which followed the Zulu rites, Cetshwayo found that he had tacitly given Natal the right to interfere in internal Zulu affairs. The long-term consequences for the future of the kingdom would prove catastrophic.

Nevertheless, when Cetshwayo began the construction of a new royal homestead in late 1873, there seemed few clouds on the horizon. Internal opposition had been outmanoeuvred, and, as Cetshwayo ordered a grand parade of royal cattle from across the country, the kingdom seemed wealthier and more robust than at any time since Dingane's reign. Cetshwayo's new capital reflected this feeling of security and power. He chose as its site the Mahlabathini plain, north of the White Mfolozi river, and in the very heart of the kingdom. Mpande's kwaNodwengu was only a mile or two away – deserted now, and crumbling, as it was allowed to fall into ruin around the old king's grave – but Cetshwayo's new complex was grander even than that. Like the settlement near the coast, where he grew up, it was also called *oNdini*, though the British called it by another version of the same name, *Ulundi*. It consisted of as many as 1400 huts, arranged in huge concentric circles around a great central enclosure, which served as both a cattle-pen and parade ground. The king's quarters – the *isigodlo* – was situated at the top end, opposite the main entrance, while the huts on either side were usually full with thousands of warriors who came and went as the king required their services.

Yet for all this robust self-confidence, there were indeed clouds on the horizon. When the great royal herds were taken back to their stations around the country, it was found that some had brought bovine pleuro-pneumonia – lung-sickness, a disease introduced by cattle imported from Natal – to the great gathering, and it now spread throughout the country, decimating the herds of the king and commoners alike. Moreover, as the new king sought to establish his authority, he found that many of the great chiefs in the outlying region, who had supported him in 1856, now expected a degree of autonomy in return, and were reluctant to accept royal interference in their affairs. Mpande, faced with a steady stream of emigration out of the country and into Natal, had allowed some of the more onerous aspects of life within the *amabutho* system to slip, but Cetshwayo, a more assertive man than his father, was determined to reverse this trend, and restore the central role of royal authority. In 1875 Cetshwayo gave the iNdlondlo *ibutho* permission to marry, ordering that they should chose their brides from among a female guild called the iNgcugce, who were several years younger. The iNgcugce were indignant, complaining not only that they already had lovers their own age, but that there were not enough men in the iNdlondlo to go round. In 1876, Cetshwayo made a concession to this complaint by allowing the uDloko regiment, too, to marry. Some of the iNgcugce still defied his commands, however, and the king promptly ordered them to marry, or face the consequences. When some had not yet done so some months later, squads of men from the younger regiments were sent out to execute them. In fact, only a handful of girls were actually killed, but the occasion served as a stern reminder of the new king's authority.

Nevertheless, the incident had a sequel a few years later which highlighted the divisions that continued to exist under the surface of Zulu society. In 1878, at the annual umKhosi ceremony, the young iNgobamakhosi clashed with the senior uThulwana. The iNdlondlo were incorporated with the uThulwana, and many of the iNgobamakhosi had lost lovers to them. The two regiments clashed at the entrance to oNdini itself, and what began as a stick-fight turned rather more serious when the indignant commanders of the uThulwana – including Prince Hamu – urged their men to take up their spears. Despite

Cetshwayo's best efforts to call off the fight, it raged until nightfall. While most Zulus blamed the incident on the impudence of the iNgobamakhosi, the king was furious with Hamu, but dared not act against him. Hamu retired to the north of the country, nursing a sense of grievance which became manifest when he alone among the Royal House abandoned the king and defected to the British during the war of 1879.

Not the least of Cetshwayo's concerns over these incidents was the reaction of his colonial neighbours. For some time, the relationship between the Transvaal republic and the Zulu kingdom had been tense. While the boundaries with Natal to the south ran along clearly defined geographical features, those in the north-west of the kingdom – where it abutted the Transvaal – ran across rivers rather than beside them. This area was good, open grazing land, but it was sparsely populated. As a result, Mpande allowed several Boer groups who had moved into the area to escape the extension of British authority in Natal in the 1840s, to graze their cattle there. Over the next 20 years, the Boers had steadily encroached on Zulu territory, and some had built permanent farms. From the 1860s, Cetshwayo had added his voice to his father's protests about this process, and by the 1870s Cetshwayo was prepared to contemplate the use of force, though he refrained from doing so because the British in Natal let it be known they could not sit by and allow the Zulu to attack a neighbouring settler community.

If relations with the Transvaal were cool, however, the hostility with which Natal greeted the stories of the 'marriage of the iNgcugce' took the king by surprise. True, the stories were filtered through the medium of the missionary community in Zululand, who blamed their lack of successful evangelism squarely on Cetshwayo's administration, which they held to be hostile to Christianity, and therefore wished to undermine; but nevertheless, the colonial reaction suggested a marked shift in British attitudes.

As indeed there was. In the 1870s, Britain had embarked on a new forward policy in southern Africa. After decades of straining the patience of both the exchequer and successive Secretaries of the Colonial Office, the discovery of diamonds at Kimberley in the 1870s had suddenly offered the possibility that the region might one day be economically viable. A patchwork quilt of conflicting colonies, republics and independent chiefdoms, the British soon realised that southern Africa could not be exploited economically without some sort of united political purpose. As a result, they attempted to introduce a policy called Confederation, according to which the various disparate groups would be brought under British control to facilitate the establishment of an economic infrastructure across the region as a whole.

This, of course, begged a great many questions, not the least of which was the hostility of many of these groups to any form of British control. In April

1877, however, in a surprisingly audacious move, the British gambled that the administration of the Transvaal republic was too inefficient to oppose them, and simply marched into Pretoria, raised the Union flag, and declared it a British colony.

In due course, the Boers would make their feelings to this development all too clear on the slopes of Majuba mountain, but the immediate effect was to bring the British and Zulu kingdom into direct conflict over the question of the disputed territory. Whereas, hitherto, the British had found it expedient to support the Zulu position against rival Boer interests, they now did an abrupt *volte face*. The effect was to shatter almost 50 years of goodwill between the Zulu kingdom and the British, breaking a relationship which had been started by King Shaka and Lieutenant Farewell in 1824, and which had survived even the settlers' support for the Voortrekkers in the war of 1838.

Moreover, a new British High Commissioner in southern Africa, Sir Henry Bartle Frere, had in any case become convinced that the Zulu kingdom was a block on the road to successful implementation of the Confederation policy. It was, after all, the last major African kingdom still extant south of the Limpopo river, a beacon of strength and independence to all other beleaguered African groups in the region. The Zulus had so far resisted the effects of the developing capitalist economy; no Zulus made the long walk to hire out their services to the diggers at Kimberley. Moreover, reasoned Frere, a little judicious use of British military muscle might at a stroke remove the threat to the Transvaal posed by the disputed territory, and thereby demonstrate the advantages of British rule, while at the same time show republican elements among the Boers that the British meant business. Frere began to prepare for a direct confrontation by waging a propaganda war, presenting Cetshwayo as a tyrannical ogre, and using missionary stories of the recent killings in Zululand as evidence.

For Cetshwayo, the change in British attitudes was bewildering. He was astute enough to realise that many complaints that emanated from Natal were mere posturing, but was at a loss to define what they really wanted. The issue, however, would soon become devastatingly clear to him.

In March 1878 an independent boundary commission was established to look into the question of the disputed border. Frere confidently expected that it would support the Boer position, and was taken aback when it declared that the Zulu had never given away any lasting title to any territory to the Boers. While he was pondering his next move, however, the sons of Chief Sihayo kaXongo, who lived on the western borders of Zululand opposite Rorke's Drift, crossed the Mzinyathi river to arrest two of Sihayo's errant wives who had fled to sanctuary in Natal. They were dragged back across the river and killed. To Frere, this was a border violation of the first magnitude, and he began to construct around it the basis for a confrontation.

In November Frere's representatives sent messages to Cetshwayo, inviting his envoys to attend a meeting to discuss the findings of the boundary commission. Cetshwayo sent a number of his state officials, and the meeting took place under a spreading wild fig tree on the Natal bank of the Thukela. The *izinduna* noted with some concern that the British had turned the event into a demonstration of imperial might; a naval detachment was drawn up menacingly nearby, flanking a Gatling machine-gun. Nevertheless, the meeting began well, as Natal officials announced that the boundary commission had found in favour of the Zulu claim. While the Zulu were digesting this, however, the bomb burst. Tacked on to the award was an ultimatum, which complained that King Cetshwayo was oppressing his people in defiance of the agreements reached at his coronation, and allowing border violations to go unpunished. The British demanded that Cetshwayo not only give up those guilty of the border incidents but, to ensure his future compliance, the *amabutho* system itself. Failing that, he would find himself at war with the British Empire.

When news of the meeting reached oNdini, the king and his council were dumbstruck. Although the increasingly belligerent stance of the British authorities had been apparent for some months, the fact that they were actually prepared to go to war came as a terrible shock. Many of the king's advisers, fearing for the kingdom's future, urged him to give up Sihayo's sons, and they vented their anger on Sihayo himself, and on John Dunn, Cetshwayo's white *induna*, whom they felt had failed to warn him of the looming crisis. Yet while Cetshwayo might have given in on these points in the wider interests of the state, he was reluctant to abandon Sihayo – a personal favourite. Additionally, Sihayo's principal son, Mehlokazulu, was a popular man among the iNgobamakhosi *ibutho*, with whom he held a command, and who were indignant at the very idea of his surrender.

Moreover, neither the king nor his council could contemplate the central British demand – that he abandon the *amabutho* system. It was the very foundation of central authority within the state, the rock upon which the king's position depended; without it, power would have reverted to the regional chiefs, and the country would have been at the mercy of the voracious European economies beyond its borders. If the king opted to fight, however, there was a very real possibility of defeat at the hands of the redcoats who were now assembling at strategic points along the borders. This dilemma was, of course, exactly what Frere intended.

Uncertain how to react, effectively boxed in by Frere's political manoeuvring, the king and his council prevaricated. While he tried to reassure the British of his peaceful intentions, he at the same time summoned his *amabutho* to go through the necessary pre-battle rituals in the great *amakhanda* which lay scattered around the Mahlabathini plain. Not until the ultimatum expired, and British troops actually crossed into Zululand on 11 January 1879, did Cetshwayo decide his response.

King Cetshwayo did not take to the field in person in 1879. Nevertheless, his voice remained pre-eminent in the council which shaped the nation's response to the British invasion. It was King Cetshwayo who, more than any other individual, influenced Zulu strategy throughout the war, and it is important to understand his aims and objectives.

The king had perhaps some 29,000 warriors directly available to him, with several thousand more attached to sections like the abaQulusi and the more independent chiefdoms, whose men did not always attend the gathering of the *amabutho*. Since the Zulu intelligence system was efficient – far better, in fact, than its British counterpart – the king already knew that the British were gathering in force opposite the three traditional entry points into the kingdom: the Lower Thukela Drift in the south, Rorke's Drift along the middle border, and on the banks of the Ncome river. Yet he was aware, too, that they might also attack him from other directions. Although sand-dunes and crashing surf made much of the Zululand coast impractical to amphibious landing, there were a few places where it might be tried, and Zulu scouts had already seen British ships patrolling the length of the country offshore. Indeed, it was possible that the British might reach an accord with the Portuguese – in Zulu experience, whites had a depressing ability to put aside their differences when it came to combining to fight a black enemy – and land an army at Delagoa Bay. This raised the possibility of an invasion from the north. Moreover, inland from Portuguese territory lay the Swazi kingdom, and the British might also try to exploit Zulu–Swazi differences to mount an attack from that direction.

Indeed, Cetshwayo must have felt that he faced a worrying number of possibilities as the deadline loomed, and certainly he had too few troops to counter them all. In the event, the council agreed that the three columns mustering on the border were the most obvious threat, and that it would tackle these piecemeal. While small local forces would be used to divert two columns, the full weight of the main army – the king's youngest, most aggressive *amabutho* – would be directed against the third. The council decided to await the British movements before deciding which column that would be. In addition, chiefs living in the border districts would be detailed to keep some of their men back from the general muster to guard against any surprise moves by the British. Two senior regiments – the iNdabakawombe and uDlambedlu, whose battlefield effectiveness was in any case limited – would be kept as a reserve at oNdini, to counter any further threat that might develop from the sea, or from the north. These would hardly be sufficient to defeat a major invasion, but given his limited resources, they provided a safety-net of sorts.

In the event, Cetshwayo had guessed British intentions correctly. The British commander, Lieutenant General Lord Chelmsford, had indeed toyed with the idea of an amphibious landing, while his agents had certainly tried to persuade the Swazi to enter the war. But Chelmsford's resources were also limited – as it was, he had hoped to invade with five offensive columns, but had to reduce it to three because of a shortage of transport – and the Swazi were determined to remain firmly on the fence until they saw which way the war would go. The main British thrusts would therefore be those whose movements were already obvious to the Zulu. Within days of the start of the war, moreover, circumstances contrived to focus Zulu attention on the Centre Column.

The Centre Column crossed at Rorke's Drift on 11 January, and the following day attacked Chief Sihayo's settlements, scattering his adherents and burning his personal homestead. When the news reached oNdini, Cetshwayo immediately gave the order to prepare the assembled regiments for battle. The Centre Column had shown itself to be the most aggressive, and it was against this that the main response would be directed. Men from the *amabutho* who lived in the coastal sector would be directed to harass the British Right Flank Column, while the burden of response in the north fell to the abaQulusi. Both sectors also received nominal support from oNdini. Cetshwayo was insistent, however, that the Zulu fight an essentially defensive war. His white advisers, like John Dunn, had warned him that the British could bring limitless resources to bear from beyond the sea, and he saw little chance of resisting them indefinitely. Instead, he hoped to inflict on them a quick defeat, to make them reconsider the cost of their policies; since he felt himself the victim of unwarranted aggression, he wanted to be able to claim, in any future negotiations, that he had acted only in defence of Zulu soil. The Zulu strategy depended on one quick, spectacular victory over the British on Zulu soil; ironically, they would achieve just that, but Cetshwayo fatally underesti-mated the British capacity for revenge.

The army was placed under the command of Chief Ntshingwayo kaMahole, who had a reputation as a skilled general, and who stood high in the king's regard. He was supported by Mavumengwana kaNdlela, the son of King Dingane's great commander. While Cetshwayo outlined his strategy in detail to these two men, he was content to allow them to use their judgment when it came to tactical matters. Nevertheless, the lessons of Blood River had not been forgotten, and he warned them against attacking the British in defended positions: 'Do not put your faces into the lair of the wild beasts,' he said, 'for you are sure to get clawed.'

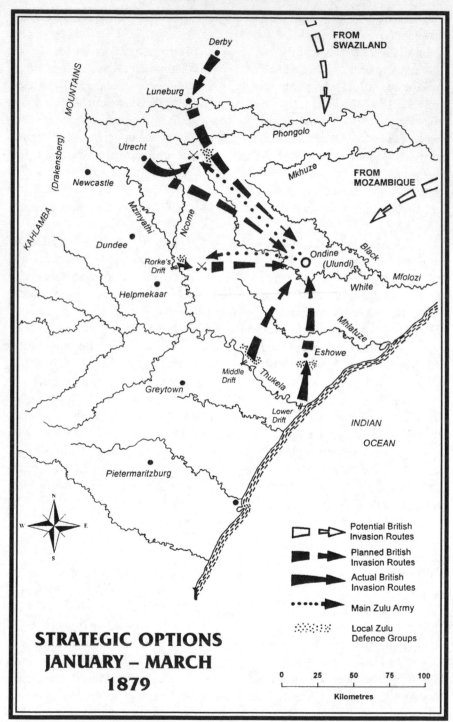

FROM
SWAZILAND

Derby

Luneburg

MOUNTAINS

Phongolo

Utrecht

(Drakensberg)

Mkhuze

FROM
MOZAMBIQUE

Newcastle

Ncome

Mzinyathi

Black

KAHLAMBA

Dundee

Ondine
(Ulundi)

Mfolozi

Rorke's
Drift

White

Helpmekaar

Mhlatuze

Eshowe

Middle
Drift

Thukela

Greytown

Lower
Drift

INDIAN

OCEAN

Pietermaritzburg

N

W   E

S

Potential British
Invasion Routes

Planned British
Invasion Routes

Actual British
Invasion Routes

Main Zulu Army

Local Zulu
Defence Groups

**STRATEGIC OPTIONS
JANUARY – MARCH
1879**

0   25   50   75   100

Kilometres

On 17 January the ceremonial preparation of the army was complete, and the king addressed the assembled warriors. He told them to march slowly, so as not to tire themselves, to eat up the enemy, but not to cross the border.

When the army marched away from the Mahlabathini plain that evening, it marched beyond the king's immediate control, although Cetshwayo was kept informed of its progress by runners, who brought him news, probably several times a day, of its movements. Yet the further the army marched, the older the news was when it reached him, so that by the time he first heard, on 22 January, that the army was attacking the British camp beneath Isandlwana hill, the battle was probably already over.

As soon as the news arrived, however, Cetshwayo retired to the hut which held the *inkatha ye sizwe ya'kwaZulu* – the sacred coil of the nation which Shaka had created, and which represented the combined spiritual power of the nation. Cetshwayo, who, as king, was the medium though which all communication with the powerful ancestral spirits of the Royal House was channelled, squatted over the *inkatha*, and by joining himself with it, focused all the great spiritual resources of the nation behind the army and its crucial enterprise. The king remained secluded there as more runners arrived, bringing the latest story of the battle. Yet when it seemed that the Zulu were on the point of victory, Cetshwayo left the *inkatha* for a few minutes, breaking the psychic bridge to the after-life. The royal women scolded him, warning him that to leave the *inkatha* before the battle was won was highly dangerous, and he returned to it immediately. When the army limped home a few days later, 'carrying the fury of war on their backs', and the huge price they had paid for their victory became obvious, many within the closed inner circle of the king's household saw this as the result of his lack of concentration.

Indeed, it was difficult to tell in the aftermath of the day's toll whether it had been a victory or defeat. According to Zulu spiritual belief, 22 January 1879 was *olumnyama usuku*, a 'dark day', to be followed by the night of the new moon. This was a time of ill-omen, when dark spiritual forces were thought to be lurking close to the everyday world, and the Zulu had intended to avoid battle that day. Curiously, however, circumstances combined to force them into battle on all three fronts that very day, for as well as the attack on Isandl-wana, and its sequel at Rorke's Drift, the coastal contingents had blundered into Col. Pearson's column at Nyezane river, while in the north the abaQulusi had been driven from one of their strongholds, Zungwini mountain. And indeed, perhaps the omens had been correct, for the total losses on all three fronts amounted to more than 2000 men – a figure which at least equalled later, more decisive engagements, such as Khambula.

Moreover, the day's fighting exhausted both sides. The great army took several days to return to parade before the king at oNdini, weighed down as it was by so many wounded and dying men. Indeed, hundreds of warriors were so exhausted by the experience that they simply returned home, without reporting to the king, as custom dictated. For weeks, the whole country seemed to be in mourning, stunned by the sheer magnitude of the fighting.

For the British, meanwhile, whatever glory they heaped upon the heroic garrison at Rorke's Drift, there was no escaping the fact that they had been defeated. The Centre Column had been shattered, and the survivors retired quickly on Rorke's Drift. While the Right Flank column reached its first objective safely – the deserted mission station at Eshowe – the collapse of the Centre Column left it unsupported, and it could go no further. Unwilling to retreat, it simply dug in. Panic swept across Natal in daily expectation of a Zulu counter-attack, and indeed Lord Chelmsford had left the colony perilously undefended, with few garrisons of any consequence. He could do little but try to hold his ground, and appeal for reinforcements from overseas.

In fact, however, it was neither possible nor within his plan for King Cetshwayo to attack Natal. His army had dispersed to the warriors' own homes to rest and recuperate, and after such a costly battle it would be weeks before the king could reassemble them. Only on the coast – where the defeat of the local elements had not been so severe – was he able to maintain sufficient troops in the field to prevent Pearson from withdrawing to Natal, while in the north the abaQulusi, supported by the retainers of the Swazi renegade, Prince Mbilini, continued to skirmish with the Left Flank Column.

Cetshwayo's praises hailed him as the 'Thunder that crashed above Isandlwana hill', but any hope the Zulu had of winning the war slipped away in those grim weeks after Isandlwana. Every day that passed allowed Chelmsford time to rebuild his forces, and intensified British resolve to avenge the disaster. Perhaps a determined raid into Natal, attacking civilian targets and overrunning a border town, might have raised the international profile of the war, and forced the home government to reconsider Frere's objectives, but more probably it would have merely provoked the British still further. The grim truth – which only dawned on Cetshwayo in the last months of the war – was that once they had embarked on a policy of confrontation, the British were sure to pursue it until they had secured a comprehensive Zulu defeat.

By the middle of March it was clear that the war was about to enter a new phase. British troops were arriving daily along the border, and in particular were concentrating at the Lower Drift, assembling to march to the relief of Eshowe. As a precaution, Cetshwayo ordered the *amabutho* to reassemble. At the same time, however, he made diplomatic overtures to the British, sending messengers to ask what terms they would accept to end the hostilities. But the British saw in the king's actions a certain duplicity, and, sensing that the war was turning in their favour, they rejected his attempts at negotiation.

The war erupted with equal ferocity at the end of the month. The king, pressed by Mbilini and the Qulusi *izinduna* to lend some support against Colonel Wood's column, agreed to send the main army to defend the northern sector, while – as he had in January – he sent a smaller force to oppose the British concentrations on the Thukela. Once again, Cetshwayo entrusted Ntshingwayo with command of the main army, but this time he was more specific in his tactical instructions. The army was to avoid British laagers at all costs, and to feint towards the border, hoping to draw the enemy into the open.

Yet his words were not heeded. On 28 March the main army arrived in the vicinity of the Hlobane mountain, to find the abaQulusi hotly engaged with Wood's mounted men. The British were already in difficulties, and as the main army drew close, they retired off the hill in something akin to panic. Buoyed up by this success, the main army ignored the king's advice, and went on to attack Wood's camp at Khambula the following day. The young *amabutho* rushed forward recklessly, calling out 'We are the boys from Isandlwana!', only to be mown down by devastating volley fire. When they began to tire, the British sent their mounted men to chase them from the field. The army was exhausted and broken. Worse, within a few days this disaster was followed by another at the other end of the country, as the coastal section attempted to stop Lord Chelmsford's Eshowe Relief Column at Gingindlovu. Here, too, the Zulu were scattered. Within days Eshowe had been relieved, and Chelmsford had retired to the border to regroup.

When news of these disasters reached Cetshwayo, he was devastated. He was furious that the army had disregarded his instructions, attacking the British in secure positions, and in particular he blamed Mnyamana Buthelezi, his most senior adviser, who had accompanied the army to Khambula as his direct representative, but who had not prevented the catastrophe. The sheer numbers killed in less than a week's fighting were appalling, with at least 3000 dead. Once again the army dispersed to recover, and for the first time the king noticed a reluctance to respond to his order to re-assemble.

Cetshwayo now believed that it was, in any case, impossible to win the war by military means. Throughout April he made a concerted effort to open negotiations with the British, but the latter were now heavily reinforced and preparing a second invasion, and had nothing to gain by talking. They would not rest until Isandlwana had been avenged.

The British began their invasion at the end of May, this time in two main thrusts, one advancing up the coast, and the other from the north-west, across the Ncome river. While the coastal districts had little fight left in them, many Zulu in the central areas remained behind to defend their homesteads and cattle, and here the British advance was accomplished in the face of constant skirmishing.

Nevertheless, the kingdom's capacity to resist was limited. By the middle of June the *amabutho* had once again assembled at oNdini. While many warriors had come to respect the awesome firepower of the British, they did not yet feel beaten, and they were determined not to let the British destroy the kingdom without one last fight. Cetshwayo chided them, pointing out that their continued truculence would only lead to greater loss of life. But the king himself had run out of alternative strategies.

By the end of June, the British had advanced to the southern bank of the White Mfolozi river, just a few miles short of oNdini itself. As they descended the great ridges which overlook the valley, their mounted patrols had ravaged the emaKhosini, destroying the royal homesteads which had existed there since before the time of Shaka's father. Unknown to them, as they fired the huts indiscriminately, they also destroyed the great *inkatha* of the nation, the sacred grass coil which bound the kingdom together; it was a dreadful omen which foreshadowed the collapse of everything Shaka had built up.

Lord Chelmsford paused at the Mfolozi, allowing himself a few days to make final preparations for the last battle which both sides knew must come. Cetshwayo was filled with foreboding, and he sent a herd of his pure white royal cattle to the British as a peace offering; but the uKhandempemvu regiment, guarding the river, refused to allow the king to humiliate himself, and turned it back.

The final battle of the war took place on 4 July. Leaving his baggage under guard at the river, Chelmsford crossed the White Mfolozi and drew up his forces in a hollow rectangle on the Mahlabathini plain. For almost 45 minutes the Zulu army attacked him there, charging in some places to within just ten paces of his line before being mown down. But the Zulu could not penetrate the terrible zone of rifle, artillery and Gatling fire, and few displayed the determination they once had at Isandlwana and Khambula. When they began to retire, Chelmsford ordered his cavalry in pursuit, and the Zulu were ruthlessly chased from the field. When the fighting was over, the British systematically set fire to the great *amakhanda* which surrounded the plain, including oNdini itself.

The king could not bring himself to watch the breaking of his army. He had left oNdini before the battle began, and retired to a homestead a few miles away. He heard the rumble of gunfire, and knew from the faces of the first messengers to arrive that the battle was lost. Accompanied by his servants and hand-maidens, he made his way over the next few days to the homestead of Mnyamana Buthelezi. From here, he tried to open negotiations with the British, and sent out instructions tentatively ordering his younger *amabutho* to reassemble. But even they now realised the British had defeated them, and they would not come. As the British began to accept the surrenders of his regional chiefs and *izinduna*, the king knew that his power was broken, and he had only to think of his personal safety. He moved further north, into the sparsely populated Ngome forest, but the British would not let him rest, and on 28 August he was captured by a patrol of British dragoons.

The king was taken down to the coast, where he learned that the British had suppressed the last traces of resistance in Zululand, and were already disposing of his country. Zululand was to be divided among thirteen regional chiefs, some of whom – like John Dunn and Zibhebhu kaMaphitha – were members of the former elite, but all of whom the British now felt they could trust. Cetshwayo's fate, too, was decided; he was placed upon a surf-boat, transferred to a steamer offshore, and taken to Cape Town, and exile. The dignity with which he received the news impressed his captors, and more than one British officer was touched by the image of the king in his last days in Zululand, leaning on his long staff, staring in silence at the distant green hills of the land of his ancestors.

The British had prepared quarters in the old Dutch Castle at Cape Town for his confinement. The king was accompanied by four of his *isigodlo* girls, and two *izinduna*, and the British proved courteous gaolers. Nevertheless, once Cetshwayo had recovered from the shock of his capture, he refused to pass into obscurity, as the British hoped he would. Instead, he began an eloquent campaign for his reinstatement. Supported in Natal by the family of the great liberal humanitarian, Bishop Colenso, who had always spoken out against the injustice of the Zulu War, Cetshwayo petitioned the British government, offering to return to Zululand to rule in their name. He argued that he alone had the power to ensure stability, a position which seemed increasingly convincing as the post-war settlement slid steadily towards anarchy. The impact of Isandlwana had ensured the king a certain notoriety, and encouraged a steady stream of visitors from among the fashionable travellers who passed through Cape Town. Most were deeply impressed by his intelligence and manner, and began to question the policies which had brought about the war.

Cetshwayo asked the Colonial Office for permission to visit London to argue his case, and in 1882 this was finally granted. The king's visit to London is not the least remarkable aspect of his extraordinary life story. He arrived on 5 August, to find that news of his coming had already attracted considerable press interest. A large crowd had gathered at the docks to see the famous and terrible ogre, who had been presented to them in the illustrated papers at the time of the war as a scowling savage. Instead they saw a tall, dignified man, impeccably dressed in European clothes. His appearance and behaviour underlined a growing sense of popular unease about the war, which, combined with a natural sympathy for a romantic and tragic figure; and delight at the king's evident acceptance of British authority produced a wave of public sympathy. Over the next fortnight, Cetshwayo found himself lionised by fashionable society, and cheered through the streets whenever he ventured outside his lodgings. Queen Victoria agreed to meet him; she presented him with a silver drinking mug as a memento, and instructed her portrait-painter to paint his likeness.

Undoubtedly, the public reaction added weight to Cetshwayo's cause, but his success in his principal objective – restoration – was limited. The Colonial Office finally agreed to allow him to return to Zululand, but under strict supervision. He was not to be allowed to revive the *amabutho* system, while in order to guarantee the security of elements within the kingdom who were opposed to his return, such as John Dunn and Zibhebhu – both of whom had attacked his supporters and raided royal cattle during his absence – large areas of the country were set aside. To serve as a buffer between the new kingdom and colonial Natal, a large slice of the south of the country was to be administered directly by the British, under the name of the Reserved Territory. In effect, the king was to be surrounded by his enemies, and denied any proper means of defending his authority.

Moreover, his return was opposed by the colonial administration in Natal, who had backed his rivals during his absence, and who considered the Royal House to be anathema to settler interests. Thus when the king landed on the shore of Zululand on 10 January 1883, he found that his supporters had not been informed of his arrival, and only a handful of Zulu were present to greet him. As he began the journey inland, word of his return spread, and hundreds of Zulu who had remained loyal to him throughout his exile gathered to meet him. Zibhebhu merely rode into his camp to welcome his colonial escort, ignoring the king himself, a pointed snub which did not bode well for the future.

Cetshwayo planned to re-establish himself at oNdini. There was little left of his old homestead apart from a dark circle of bush growing up through the ashes, and the bones of many of his followers still lay on the plain where they had fallen. Nevertheless, the king still regarded the Mahlabathini plain as the heart of his kingdom, and he instructed the young men who visited him to pay their respects to begin construction of a new homestead, a mile or two from the ruins of the old one. The new oNdini – the third to bear that name – was smaller than the old, no more than a thousand huts, but it was nonetheless an impressive complex, a tribute to the prestige the king still held within the country.

Yet the fortunes of the new oNdini would prove no better than the old. Even before the young men had completed it, it was destined to be destroyed in a catastrophe no less overwhelming than the tragedy of 1879.

To the king's supporters – who called themselves by the name which had been associated with him from his youth, *uSuthu* – Cetshwayo's arrival, not unnaturally, offered the prospect of a return to the glorious days before the war. Indeed, the king himself called upon many of his chiefs and *izinduna* to visit him, to assess the degree of support he still enjoyed, and to re-establish his authority. Although the *amabutho* had not assembled since 1879, and there were no longer royal homesteads to house them and royal cattle to sustain them, many nonetheless still acknowledged their allegiance both to the king and the institutions, and gathered at oNdini to answer his summons. Many royalists had suffered harassment and losses over the previous few years, as the chiefs set up by the British had sought to intimidate them into submission. In particular, the uSuthu nurtured a bitter hatred for Zibhebhu kaMaphitha, the Mandlakazi chief who had fought bravely for the king in 1879, but who accepted a position in the new post-war order, and had been resolutely opposed to the Royal House ever since.

Encouraged by the king's return, several of his brothers, led by Prince Ndabuko, assembled a force of uSuthu warriors at the homestead of Chief Mnyamana of the Buthelezi, in northern Zululand. Mnyamana's territory abutted the Mandlakazi district, and from here at the end of March 1883 Ndabuko launched an attack against Zibhebhu. It was a disaster; Zibhebhu lay in wait in the broken ground of the Msebe valley, and on 30 March he ambushed the uSuthu force and utterly routed it.

News of the battle caused consternation at oNdini. Whereas Cetshwayo may have known of Ndabuko's plans, he had not sanctioned the attack, nor had he directed it. Nevertheless, the country was suddenly on the verge of a full-scale civil war, and while the uSuthu looked to the king for leadership, the British continued to regard him with suspicion, and to oppose any attempts by his party to raise an army. It was an impossible situation, and faced with the possibility of a Mandlakazi counter-attack, Cetshwayo abandoned any pretence of abiding by the British restrictions, and prepared for war. By the middle of July he had assembled several thousand warriors at oNdini, and many of the *izikhulu*, chiefs and *izinduna* who still supported him had gathered there to discuss the crisis.

It did not save them. At dawn on the morning of 21 July, about 3000 Mandlakazi appeared over the hills to the north-west of oNdini, led by Zibhebhu himself. They had made a daring march through the Black Mfolozi valley, covering the distance from the Mandlakazi territory in a single night. They were not spotted until the first women from oNdini rose to go about their chores. By the time the inhabitants of the royal homestead mustered to meet the challenge, Zibhebhu was already sweeping down on them. While the young men of the *amabutho* streamed out of the gate in some confusion, the senior men and *izinduna* rushed to the king. Some were close to panic, and urged him to flee while there was still time, but the king replied indignantly, 'Am I to run away from my dog?' Indeed, Cetshwayo seems to have kept his head, for he hastily gave orders appointing commanders to the various *amabutho*, and instructing them on their dispositions.

Yet it was too late. Taken by surprise, and with many of their *izinduna* still in conference inside the homestead, the uSuthu regiments moved forward hesitantly. The Mandlakazi were now only a mile or two away, and advancing with great determination. As they came within range, the uSuthu opened fire, but this seemed to have little effect on the Mandlakazi, whose relentless advance caused the uSuthu to panic. The youngest regiments, on the uSuthu right, collapsed before the Mandlakazi reached them, making the position of the centre and left untenable. The whole uSuthu line fell back towards oNdini, and Zibhebhu's men charged right in among them. Elements of the uThulwana regiment tried to stand in oNdini itself, but were overwhelmed and wiped out. For the most part, the uSuthu army simply broke and fled. The Mandlakazi chased after them, killing them as they ran. Many of the younger warriors were quick enough to escape the pursuit, but the senior men, including a number of the great *izinduna* who had served not only Cetshwayo but Mpande before him, were overtaken and killed. The slaughter was so great that many historians agree that the defeat at oNdini in 1883 was far more damaging than the war of 1879, and marked the true end of the old Zulu kingdom.

During the fighting, some of the huts at the entrance to oNdini caught fire, and the conflagration soon spread to the rest of the complex. For the second time, oNdini went up in flames at the hands of Cetshwayo's enemies. As it burned, the Mandlakazi looted the huts, carrying away many of Cetshwayo's personal possessions; among them was the three-handled cup he had been presented with by Queen Victoria. Somewhere on the line of retreat its new owner dropped it, and it lay hidden until it washed out of the side of a donga in the 1930s.

Cetshwayo himself had lingered at oNdini until the rout became obvious. Helped by his attendants, he mounted a white horse and tried to ride to safety, but he was too heavy, and the animal stumbled under his weight. Instead, he made off on foot towards the Ntukwini stream, which flows into the White Mfolozi. Here he paused to rest among a clump of trees, while his attendants made off in a different direction, to deceive the Mandlakazi. Nevertheless, he was spotted crouching in the grass by a group of young Mandlakazi warriors. Thinking he was the king's brother, Ziwedu, they called upon him to stand up, then threw three spears at him. One missed, but the other two struck the king in the right thigh. Indignantly, Cetshwayo called out to one of the warriors, whom he recognised, 'Do you stab me, Halijana, son of Somfula? I am your king!' The king's person was widely held to be sacrosanct, even in the heat of battle, and the young Mandlakazi were appalled by what they had done. They approached Cetshwayo, addressing him with the royal salute, and apologising profusely. A passing Mandlakazi *induna* scolded them, and directed them to help the king with his wounds. The spears were pulled out, and the wounds washed with water, blown through a straw. The young warriors then pointed out the best escape route, and allowed Cetshwayo to go on his way.

The king slipped into the valley of the White Mfolozi, then made his way across country to the territory of Chief Sigananda kaSokufa, of the amaCube people. The amaCube lived in the wild, broken country near the Nkandla forest, and their territory was regarded as a secure refuge. And indeed, Sigananda took Cetshwayo in, and sheltered him in his personal stronghold – an inaccessible cave behind a waterfall where the Mome stream tumbled into its spectacular gorge.

Cetshwayo lived among the amaCube for more than two months. From here he sent messages, trying to rally his supporters, and appeal to the British to intervene on his behalf. But his supporters were in hiding across the country, while the British refused to move, blaming Cetshwayo's alleged belligerence for his own position. At last, on 15 October, the king admitted the inevitable, and surrendered himself to the British Resident at Eshowe, in the Reserve.

The British had little succour to offer him. Convinced that the Zulu Royal House was behind all the disturbances in Zululand, they gave him nothing but sanctuary while the Mandlakazi ravaged his former territory. The king was settled in a homestead on the outskirts of Eshowe, and here he entertained his brothers and the mournful stream of supporters who came to visit him. The uSuthu cause seemed to lie in ruins; with no hope of a military resurgence, there appeared to be no political options available to them.

Then, quite suddenly, on 8 February 1884, Cetshwayo kaMpande, the last independent king of the Zulu, collapsed and died. A military doctor was summoned to examine the body; the king's attendants would not allow a post-mortem, and the doctor officially entered the cause of death as fatty degeneration of the heart. Privately, he suspected that Cetshwayo might have been poisoned, and indeed, the king's death was suspicious. He had been seen strolling about that morning, apparently in his usual health; early in the afternoon he had eaten a meal, and had been seized by a sudden convulsion, and died very soon afterwards. Certainly, many Zulu still believe to this day that he was poisoned at the orders of Zibhebhu.

The king's brothers took charge of the funeral rites, which were carried out as far as possible in the traditional manner. The body was wrapped in a bull's hide, then left in a sealed hut until it desiccated. His supporters had hoped to take the body to the traditional burial place of the kings, the emaKhosini valley, but the country was too unsettled, and the British in any case forbade it, fearing that it would only provoke further fighting with Zibhebhu. Instead, the body was placed in a large coffin, and loaded on to an ox-wagon, to be taken instead back to the territory of Sigananda's amaCube. It was buried in a remote spot, deep in the Nkandla forest, and the wagon placed upon the grave, and allowed to fall into disrepair, so that it would never be used for a lesser purpose again.

Cetshwayo's sad death was, perhaps, in keeping with the more tragic aspects of his life. As a young man, he had been ruthless in his pursuit of his birthright, but he had been regarded by most Zulus as a strong and just ruler. Certainly, the war with the British had been forced upon him, and he had reacted to the calamity with courage and dignity. He had proved a skilled politician, a competent battlefield commander, and a perceptive strategic thinker. Moreover, he had not flinched on the several occasions when his own life was in danger, and had shown remarkable resilience during his misfortunes. Yet in the end these qualities were not sufficient, for the odds were too heavily stacked against him. The attack upon the Zulu kingdom had not just been waged with cannon- and rifle-fire, for it was part of a broader, more subtle, and ultimately far more destructive assault upon African society by the forces of European industrial capitalism. While the leaders of the old Zulu order, Cetshwayo among them, dimly perceived the danger, and understood that a way of life itself was under threat, yet they had little beyond their lives, and the lives of their supporters, to offer against it, and in the end it was a hopeless and unequal struggle.

With the death of King Cetshwayo, the Zulu kingdom passed into a new era, and the civil war entered a fresh, and equally bloody, phase.

4

NTSHINGWAYO kaMAHOLE
'There is no going back home!'

Such was the bitterness engendered by the divisive settlement imposed by the British in 1879 that it is said that, in the aftermath of his devastating attack on oNdini in July 1883, Zibhebhu kaMaphitha showed little remorse for the lives of the many great chiefs and *izinduna* whom his warriors had run down as they fled across the grassy Mahlabathini plain, and stabbed to death. These were men who, like himself, were *izikhulu* – the great ones of the nation – who had once enjoyed all of the considerable trappings of power and prestige which the Zulu kingdom could afford, and who, just four short years before, had fought alongside Zibhebhu in the common cause of resisting the white invader. Now they were turned against one another in the most ruthless of civil wars and, in the full flush of his greatest victory, Zibhebhu offered them no mercy.

One death he did regret, however. Lying somewhere close to oNdini was the body of one of the elderly uSuthu commanders. W. A. Walton, a correspondent of the London *Pictorial World*, sketched him there, sprawled across his war-shield, his body scored with stab-wounds, and still clutching a knobkerry in his right hand. Walton noted on his sketch that he was 'Chingwio, [who] led at Rorke's Drift'. This was the sort of misinformation which characterised many British observations regarding the Zulu commanders in 1879, but Walton did at least record for history the poignant fate of King Cetshwayo's most senior general, his commander-in-chief, Ntshingwayo kaMahole. It had been Ntshingwayo who had led the king's main army throughout the war, and who had commanded personally during the two most decisive battles, Isandlwana and Khambula. Ntshingwayo's sad end personifies the post-war tragedy of the Zulu kingdom; yet death in battle in the service of the king was perhaps not inappropriate for a man regarded as one of the great warriors of his day.

Ntshingwayo was among a handful of individuals who shared in the decision-making process of the nation at the highest levels. In a simple but expressive Zulu phrase, he was *pakathi*; one of those 'on the inside', a confidant and councillor to no less than two of the great kings. Ntshingwayo was born about 1820, the head of a section of the Khoza people, whose traditional lands lay on the upper reaches of the White Mfolozi. The Khoza had been brought into the Zulu kingdom by Shaka himself, yet the association of Zulu and Khoza chiefly lines stretched back beyond that time. Ntshingwayo's father, Mahole, was said to have been in the same age-group as Senzangakhona, Shaka's father, and might even have been present on the famous occasion when Senzangakhona first encountered Nandi of the Langeni, who was to be Shaka's mother. In later life, Mahole became an attendant to Senzangakhona, establishing a precedent which lasted across a generation.

In 1879, when his skills were put to the test, Ntshingwayo was widely regarded as a man of great military skill and experience. Unfortunately, there is little information about his early career. As a young man of 19 or 20, however, he probably took part in King Dingane's campaigns against the Voortrekkers, and he may well have held regimental commands during Mpande's several expeditions into Swaziland. Certainly, he rose to prominence as an *induna* under Mpande, and by the time of Mpande's death was counted by some to be second only in influence to the king's great councillor, Masiphula kaMamba. Under Mpande, Ntshingwayo was attached to the emLambongwenya royal homestead, where Cetshwayo was born, and it may be that the friendship between the two first began there. When Prince Mbuyazi's followers, the iziGqoza, lingered too long on the banks of the Thukela in their flight from Cetshwayo, it was Ntshingwayo whom Mpande trusted with a secret message, urging Mbuyazi to hurry across the border; Ntshingwayo was intercepted and turned back by Cetshwayo's warriors, but the fact that he remained on good terms with Cetshwayo suggests something of the respect in which the latter held him. He clearly remained highly regarded by the king, too, for when Mpande was involved with the Transvaal Boers in a dispute over land ownership on the north-western borders, it was Ntshingwayo whom he instructed to establish a royal homestead in the region, as a mark of his authority. In the last years of Mpande's reign, Ntshingwayo played a prominent part at many of the great national ceremonies, directing events with Masiphula on the king's behalf. Ntshingwayo was known for his commanding presence, strong voice, and for his ability to declaim the praises of the Royal House.

Despite these close associations with Mpande, Ntshingwayo survived the transition to Cetshwayo's reign smoothly enough, unlike Masiphula. Cetshwayo had never forgiven his father's chief *induna* for openly supporting Mbuyazi in the civil war of 1856, and Masiphula's fall was swift and final. In August 1873 he presided over the ceremonies which installed Cetshwayo as king, but publicly declared his intention shortly afterwards to retire as senior *induna*. It was not enough to save him, however, for his influence was far too great for Cetshwayo to tolerate comfortably; a few days later, after sipping from a gourd reserved for his own use in the new king's hut, he was suddenly taken ill, and died that night. Cetshwayo had already let it be known that he favoured Mnyamana kaNgqengelele of the Buthelezi as his senior councillor, but Ntshingwayo seems to have remained secure in his position as second councillor, and enjoyed much the same relationship with Mnyamana as he had with Masiphula. Indeed, Mnyamana and Ntshingwayo were of a similar age, and became close personal friends and political allies.

By the time of the war with the British, Ntshingwayo was nearly 70, a short man with a powerful physique and strong limbs, whose paunch and grey hairs belied his commanding presence. Cetshwayo had moved him from emLam-bongwenya, and instead made him head of the kwaGqikazi *ikhanda*, not far from oNdini. In the difficult months leading up to the outbreak of war, Ntshingwayo had followed Mnyamana's lead, urging caution, and counselling the king to accept British demands rather than risk the destruction of the kingdom for the sake of Sihayo's 'rash boys'. Nevertheless, when it became clear that the British could not be so easily deflected, Ntshingwayo was among the innermost circle who, together with Cetshwayo, planned the country's military response to invasion.

When the great army was assembled and doctored for war in the third week of January, it was entirely in keeping with his status that Ntshingwayo should be placed in command of that portion which was to bear the brunt of the fighting. To assist him, Cetshwayo appointed Mavumengwana kaNdlela as his co-commander. Mavumengwana was a much younger man – he was in his forties – but was a close friend of the king's, and had been enrolled with him in the same regiment, the uThulwana, among whom he commanded a wing. Mavumengwana's reputation in military matters was also impressive, and he, too, was part of the inner circle who surrounded the king; his father, Ndlela kaSompisi, had been Dingane's general, while his brother, Godide, was appointed to the command of the troops defending the coastal sector.

The great *impi* marched out from the Mahlabathini plain on the evening of 17 January. It was one of the largest forces ever assembled by the Zulu kingdom, and the most important *amabutho* were present in force. By and large, these were young, unmarried warriors, and many of them – the uVe, iNgobamakhosi, uKhandempemvu and uMbonambi regiments – had been too young to fight at 'Ndondakusuka, and had yet to see serious military action. They were full of pride in their military heritage, confident that they could defeat the white men, and as they marched through the emaKhosini valley on their way to the front, they sang the great war-songs of Shaka and Dingane's day, and called upon the nation's ancestral spirits to support them in their endeavours. To the women, children and old men watching them with pride, it seemed that nothing on earth could ever stop them.

The army's target was the British Centre Column, which had crossed into Zululand at Rorke's Drift. The king had warned the *amabutho* not to tire themselves, so they moved westwards at a leisurely pace, with Ntshingwayo and Mavumengwana setting an example by walking at the head of their men, rather than riding horses, as some *izinduna* did. As the great *impi* climbed out of the valley of the White Mfolozi and its tributaries, and on to the high land which separated it from the enemy, it split into two columns – a traditional tactic to prevent the entire army being surprised. Ntshingwayo led the left column, and Mavumengwana the right. On 20 January it camped on the eastern slopes of Siphezi mountain; on the other side, just fifteen miles away across undulating country, Lord Chelmsford's column was encamped at Isandlwana.

Isandlwana was such a calamity for the British army that it is often tempting to consider the battle purely as a British defeat. By concentrating on British movements, however, on the capabilities or otherwise of the British commanders, of their dispositions, errors of judgment, lame excuses, and red-herrings such as the supposed ammunition failure, it is easy to overlook the fact that Isandlwana was also a Zulu victory. Indeed, although the long-term political consequences were disastrous, and the battle itself costly, Isandlwana remains probably the greatest victory achieved by the Zulu army in the 60-year history of the old kingdom. It is instructive to consider how and why that victory came about, and the extent to which Ntshingwayo kaMahole was personally responsible for it.

One undoubted reason for the Zulu success was that Lord Chelmsford split his forces on the eve of battle. Historians are divided as to whether this was a deliberate Zulu ploy, but on balance it seems not. On 21 January there was a disagreement in the Zulu camp at Siphezi. The king's army had been joined by the followers of a local chief, Matshana kaMondise, who had hitherto remained in their home districts to harass British patrols. Since the main army was operating in Matshana's territory, he expected to be allowed considerable influence in decisions regarding its deployment. The Zulu commanders disagreed, however, pointing out that they had been personally selected to their posts by the king, and Matshana left in a huff, taking his followers back to the hills which constituted his stronghold, just a few miles to the south-west of Siphezi. On the evening of the 21st, a British reconnaissance from the camp at Isandlwana blundered into some of Matshana's men, and mistakenly assumed they had discovered the main *impi*. When the news reached Chelmsford in the small hours of the morning of the 22nd, he immediately decided to take half his force out of camp to meet the Zulu challenge. This decision was much criticised with hindsight, and indeed Chelmsford might have reacted in any number of other ways; to suppose that he had been deliberately misled by a careful Zulu plan to decoy him away from Isandlwana credits the Zulu commanders with a better understanding of British practice than they at that time possessed.

Moreover, there is a good deal of evidence to suggest that the Zulu did not want to fight on the 22nd, when the battle actually took place. Indeed, Cetshwayo had hoped, right up until the last minute, that his commanders might have been able to avoid an armed confrontation, and open negotiations with the British instead; while this was never really an option, the Zulu commanders do not seem to have abandoned the possibility until the very morning of the 22nd. To have embarked on a decoy plan several days in advance would have committed them to military action before they were actually ready to do so. The 22nd was also *olumnyama usuku* – a 'dark day', the time of the new moon, when dark spiritual forces were abroad. The Zulu had probably hoped to attack the camp at dawn on the 23rd, a more propitious time, and any diversionary tactics would surely have been timed for then.

Like many great military master-strokes, the Zulu victory was a combination of skill, courage and good luck; and this first crucial element in their success must still be regarded as fortuitous.

On the 21st, the army moved from Siphezi, not towards Matshana's stronghold in the south-west, but into the Ngwebeni valley, to the north-west. This took them to a position only five miles from the camp at Isandlwana, separated from it by the high ground of Mabaso and the iNyoni escarpment.

The fact that they accomplished this move undetected by British scouts was arguably their greatest achievement of the campaign. Luck no doubt played its part here, too, but military competence was the far greater factor, and for this Ntshingwayo, as senior commander, must take the credit. The area between Siphezi and the Ngwebeni is comparatively open, and any movement across it must have been acutely vulnerable to determined British scouting. In fact, however, the army set off on the evening of the 21st, moving by companies, rather than regiments, so as to be less conspicuous, and making best use of natural folds in the ground. Furthermore, scouts under Zibhebhu kaMaphitha were thrown far out to keep away any British patrols, and indeed skirmished with a British party from Isandlwana, but drove them off before the British came within sight of the main army.

The *impi* spent the night in the Ngwebeni valley, lighting no cooking fires so as to reduce the risk of detection, and living instead on cold mealies roasted a day or two before. Early on the morning of the 22nd, Ntshingwayo held a council of war with his senior commanders and regimental *izinduna*. While the possibility of opening negotiations with the British may still have been discussed, they must, too, have talked through contingency plans in case the camp was to be attacked. Certainly, the Zulu had far more intelligence available to them than the British. While the British knew nothing of the Zulu movements, and had only the roughest maps to work from, Zulu scouts had kept Chelmsford's column under constant surveillance. Moreover, Isandlwana lay within the territory of Chief Sihayo, and both Sihayo and his son Mehlokazulu were present with the *impi*, so that Ntshingwayo and Mavumengwana had access to information from men who knew the terrain intimately. Thus, although the battle, when it happened, was provoked by a spontaneous encounter, the Zulu were able to recover themselves far more quickly than the British, which can only have been possible if the regimental *izinduna* were fully aware of both the situation and Ntshingwayo's general operational intentions.

The Zulu had hoped to lie quietly throughout the day of the 22nd, but at about noon a party of horsemen from the camp, pursuing Zulu foragers across the iNyoni heights, stumbled across their bivouac. The uKhandempemvu *ibutho*, which was lying closest to the British incursion, immediately rose up to attack them, drawing the other regiments after it on either side. There was no time to form them into a circle to receive the last ritual preparations and orders, and the younger regiments spilled out of the Ngwebeni valley in some confusion. The best Ntshingwayo and Mavumengwana could do was hold back those *amabutho* who were camped furthest from the encounter. These were middle-aged men from the regiments associated with the oNdini homestead itself, who had perhaps lagged behind on the march, and arrived last at the camping ground; Ntshingwayo formed them up and addressed them in the manner of all great commanders on the eve of battle, reminding them of their tradition and duty with typical Zulu imagery. After calling out the praises of Senzangakhona and Shaka, he held up his great war-shield, proclaiming, 'This is the love charm of our people. You are always asking why this person is loved so much. It is caused by the love charm of our people. There is no going back home!' The oNdini regiments were then deployed as the reserve; although they took no part in the attack on the camp, they later went on to attack the British outpost at Rorke's Drift.

In the crucial first few minutes of the Zulu deployment, Ntshingwayo's influence can have been limited only to the reserve. By the time the *impi* had crossed the three or four miles of undulating upland which separated it from the camp, however, the *amabutho* had shaken off their initial confusion, and taken up the traditional 'chest and horns' attack formation, a remarkable testimony to the initiative and skill displayed by the regimental commanders. While the right horn swung, unnoticed by the British, into the valley behind Isandlwana, the left horn raced out to cross the open ground in front of the mountain, and outflank the British on the other side. The chest, coming up more slowly from behind, advanced across the iNyoni heights directly towards the camp.

While the Zulu had managed to recover well from the initial shock of the encounter, the British utterly failed to make a true assessment of the threat to the camp. The British commander, Lieutenant Colonel Pulleine, pushed his firing line well out from the camp and in extended order. From here his men could command the hollows at the foot of the iNyoni ridge, but were far too extended to withstand an assault in depth. Once the full extent of the Zulu attack became evident, Pulleine was dependent on his firepower to break up the Zulu centre, with little hope of repositioning his men. And for a while it did; as they descended the heights, the regiments in the chest – the uKhandempemvu and uMbonambi – came under such heavy fire that the attack stalled, and the warriors went to ground, lying out in a line of dongas and broken ground which afforded them some cover only 300 yards from the British position.

It was probably at about this time that Ntshingwayo re-established personal control of the battle. He, Mavumengwana and their staff must have followed in the wake of the chest, for they appeared after the fighting had begun, and stationed themselves on top of a patch of exposed cliff on the escarpment. It was usual for senior commanders to take up positions which had a good view of the action, and this spot is no exception; the entire camp was stretched out before them, while directly below them lay the dongas where the chest had gone to ground. More unusual was the fact that this position was very conspicuous to both sides, and well within range of British artillery, for Zulu generals were expected not to place themselves at risk; Ntshingwayo, however, consistently preferred to ignore such dangers in favour of encouraging his men with his presence.

From the iNyoni rocks Ntshingwayo could see that whereas the two horns appeared to be advancing rapidly to secure their objectives of encircling the camp, the chest – which was suffering most from British fire – was in danger of being driven back. Realising that the battle would turn on this point, he sent one of his *izinduna*, Mkhosana kaMvundlana, chief of the Biyela, and a commander of the uKhandempemvu, to urge the uKhandempemvu to renew the assault. Mkhosana is justly remembered among the Zulu as the man who strode fearlessly about among the prostrate warriors, calling out Cetshwayo's praise-name, and spurring them on to attack. Shamed by this tart reminder of their duty, the uKhandempemvu rose up; crouching low and holding their shields in front of their faces, they charged forward. Mkhosana himself fell dead, shot through the head, but the movement was enough to encourage the uMbonambi and iNgobamakhosi on the left to follow suit.

The British position, which had always been over-extended, promptly collapsed. The companies in the firing line retired to take up a position closer to the tents, but the Zulu charged in among them before they could do so. The British were driven through the camp, and tried to make a stand on a saddle of land below the southern peak of Isandlwana, only to find that the right horn was already in place to attack them from behind. The British stands were steadily broken up by pressure from the chest and left horn, and driven down into the valley behind the mountain, where the right horn finished them off.

Isandlwana remains an extraordinary example of a classic Zulu victory. While the two horns did not quite meet in time to seal the line of retreat entirely, only about 300 African auxiliaries and 50 white troops escaped. Over 1300 British troops and their allies from the Natal chiefdoms were killed. Both senior British officers were killed, and the Zulu captured a huge quantity of stores and ammunition. Although that portion of the column which had marched out with Lord Chelmsford was to survive, the Centre Column effectively ceased to exist as an operational force, and Chelmsford himself retired to Natal.

Despite the spontaneous nature of the attack, Ntshingwayo must be considered the main architect of Zulu victory. Working within a traditional framework which his men instinctively understood, he had made the best possible use of his numbers and of the terrain, and had fully exploited the British weaknesses. Nevertheless, the cost had been appalling, for his attack had inevitably exposed the chest to the full effects of concentrated modern firepower. Over 1000 Zulu lay dead around Isandlwana, and perhaps as many again were wounded, many of them suffering terrible injuries from the heavy-calibre British bullets. Once the Zulu had finished off the last resistance, and had thoroughly looted the camp, they retired to the Ngwebeni valley, carrying their wounded with them. There were so many of them that the army remained at its old bivouac for three days, until the worst of the injured had recovered sufficiently to travel, or had died. Among the wounded were two of Ntshingwayo's own sons, who are thought to have died later from their injuries.

Indeed, the army was so exhausted that many warriors made directly to their homes, rather than report to the king, as was customary. While Ntshingwayo returned to oNdini to report on the battle, the rest of the *amabutho* straggled behind him, looking more like a beaten army than a victorious one. There was general concern about the extent of the losses, and British border patrols reported widespread wailing among civilian homesteads opposite during the following weeks. On the whole, however, the Zulu preferred to believe that the casualties had been a result of their failure to follow last-minute protective rituals, rather than an inevitable consequence of British firepower, so that when the second phase of fighting began in March, the army took to the field with its confidence undiminished. Indeed, the men of the young *amabutho* were to go into battle at Khambula chanting, 'We are the boys from Isandlwana!'

Nevertheless, when the king sent the army to attack the northern column, he was more specific in his instructions, telling his commanders to avoid attacking heavily defended positions. Once again, Ntshingwayo was placed in overall command, although Mavumengwana had returned to his homestead near the coast, and, together with Prince Dabulamanzi, was directing the investment of the British garrison at Eshowe. This time, however, the *impi* would be accompanied by Mnyamana Buthelezi. Since Mnyamana was Cetshwayo's most senior councillor, he outranked Ntshingwayo; this was not a criticism of Ntshingwayo's role at Isandlwana, but rather an indication of the importance of the coming round of fighting. Cetshwayo was only too aware that another Zulu victory might persuade the British to reconsider their position, while a Zulu defeat would undo any advantages he had gained at Isandlwana. While Mnyamana was in overall command of the king's strategy, Ntshingwayo retained control of the army in the field.

As it had during the Isandlwana campaign, the army divided into two columns when it drew near to the British positions. On 28 March the right wing, consisting of the uKhandempemvu, iNgobamakhosi and uVe *amabutho*, crested the iNyathi heights, south of Hlobane mountain, to find that the British were attacking the abaQulusi section on the mountain itself. While the right wing advanced rapidly, catching some of the British troops as they withdrew from Hlobane, and turning retreat into a rout, the left wing hung back. Advancing on a line to the west of Hlobane, it took no part in the fighting, and it is unlikely, therefore, that either Mnyamana or Ntshingwayo played any great part in the events of Hlobane. Nevertheless, the success of the right wing at Hlobane undoubtedly boosted their confidence and heightened their aggressive spirit, which was to have dramatic consequences in the ensuing battle.

At first light the following morning, the reunited army was assembled and formed into a circle. There was ample time, now, for the *izinyanga*, the specialist war-doctors, to spatter the warriors with the last of their protective medicines, and for the commanders to address them. It was Mnyamana who spoke, and while he succeeded in stirring their anger against the white man, he unsettled them, too, as he stressed the dire consequences for the nation of defeat. Then the army formed up in five columns and moved forward towards the British positions on Khambula hill.

It was probably Ntshingwayo who made the final dispositions as the army advanced, although once again his command was compromised by the impetuosity of his younger regiments. While it seemed briefly that the army would follow the king's instructions, and bypass the British garrison in an attempt to lure them away from their fortifications, as they drew near the camp the regiments suddenly shifted direction to surround it. Whatever the intentions of their leaders, it seems that the young *amabutho* had no patience for complex strategies, and felt it was their duty to attack the British wherever they appeared. As had happened at Isandlwana, Ntshingwayo once again found himself attempting to control a battle which had begun without his instructions. In that respect, he was following in the footsteps of Ndlela kaSompisi, who had faced exactly the same problems at Blood River 40 years before.

The British position consisted of a chain of fortified laagers and an earthwork fort, lying on top of a narrow ridge. While the ground to the north of the camp was an open slope, that to the south fell away more steeply into the valley of one of the streams which formed part of the headwaters of the White Mfolozi. The Zulu approached the position from the south-east, with the right horn circling round to the north, and the left horn following the line of the valley. But the bottom of the valley was marshy and in the wet conditions of late summer 1879, going was heavy. The right horn was in position first, halting a mile away from the camp, apparently waiting for the rest of the army to come into position. Suddenly, it advanced rapidly, then halted once more, much closer to the British position. The Zulu later explained that the iNgoba-makhosi thought the rest of the army was about to attack, and it wanted to be among the first to 'stab' the enemy; from their position on top of the ridge, however, the British commanders could see that this was far from the case, and that the rest of the Zulu army was still moving into position.

This gave the British a golden opportunity to provoke the Zulu right into launching an unsupported attack, and a small force of mounted troops was sent out from the main laager to fire into the right horn at close range. The indignant iNgobamakhosi and uVe promptly rose up and charged forward. The horsemen fell back before them, and as they came within range of the British positions the Zulu were suddenly exposed to the full fury of their fire. Some elements managed to press forward to reach the British laager, but for the most part the attack melted under a storm of shot and shell. Unable to sustain their exposed position, the Zulu right retired to the shelter of some rocks a few hundred yards away.

It is probably true to say that the Zulu lost the battle with that initial repulse. While the left and centre were now advancing to the attack, the British had ruined their co-ordination and, moreover, the British could now shift their artillery to meet each new attack in turn. Once again, Ntshingwayo seems to have arrived after the battle had begun, and again he took up a position on an exposed knoll, well within British range. This time, however, despite his obvious presence, he was unable to regain control of the battle.

With the right horn temporarily spent, the focus of the battle shifted to the southern slopes, where the left horn was able to advance to within a few hundred yards of the British position under cover of the dead ground afforded by the valley. From here it was able to charge right up to one of the outlying

British posts, driving a company of British troops out of a small cattle laager. Any attempt to get closer was met by the same impenetrable zone of fire, however, and the British commander, Colonel Wood, ordered a sortie to disperse the warriors sheltering in the valley. Although the chest subsequently mounted a bold attack along the ridge itself, which left dead slumped against the British ramparts, and the right horn recovered to make a second assault, it proved impossible for Ntshingwayo to concentrate his men properly. Instead, the army battered itself to destruction in a series of increasingly point-less attacks, and once it showed signs of exhaustion, the British made a fero-cious counter attack which drove it from the field.

The assaults on the camp at Khambula had been no less costly than at Isan-dlwana, but it was during the retreat that the Zulu army really suffered. At first, the Zulu fell back in good order, but the British shelled them as they retired, then followed up with a stiff cavalry pursuit. Many of the warriors were so tired that they could not lift their shields to defend themselves, and hundreds were slaughtered. When darkness forced the British to desist, the Zulu army was close to collapse. Over 750 bodies were buried by the British close to their positions, and many more lay out on the line of retreat. By the time the number of mortally wounded were taken into account, the total Zulu casual-ties might not have been far short of the figure of 2000 dead claimed by the British.

Why had the battle gone so disastrously wrong? Certainly, the ill-discipline of the younger *amabutho* had brought on the battle prematurely, but whereas at Isandlwana the lack of British preparedness had allowed Ntshingwayo to regain the initiative, the open ground at Khambula – coupled with the fact that the British were forewarned of the attack by the action at Hlobane the previous day – meant that Ntshingwayo was given no such opportunity a second time. Certainly, the Zulu attack was no less daring than it had been at Isandlwana, and their assaults had exploited whatever weaknesses the British had presented, but the grim truth was that a concentrated British formation, particularly when secured behind fortifications, was largely unassailable as far as the Zulu were concerned. As Rorke's Drift had proved earlier in the war, if the Zulu could be kept beyond the reach of their stabbing spears, they could be shot down almost with impunity. Ntshingwayo's one chance had been to assault the British position on all sides simultaneously, and hope that the British had insufficient guns to man the perimeter; and he had been robbed of that chance in the first few minutes of the battle.

With the defeat at Khambula, the king accepted that there was little hope of bringing the war to a successful conclusion by military means. While he tried with renewed desperation to open negotiations with the British, it soon became clear that they were not interested in peace until they had defeated the Zulu in the field. While the capacity of the Zulu army to resist had been weakened, the young *amabutho* were still prepared to mount one last challenge to the British invasion. The battle which took place on the Mahlabathini plain, opposite oNdini, on 4 July was, therefore, a necessary gesture for both sides, although the outcome was largely a foregone conclusion.

It is difficult to determine the role of any of the principal Zulu commanders in the final battle. The king had apparently held his last formal council on 2 July, and almost certainly Mnyamana, Ntshingwayo, Zibhebhu and a number of the king's brothers were present. The strategy they had devised was to lure the British on to rising ground in the centre of the plain, then attack from all sides. Curiously, Lord Chelmsford had selected exactly the same spot as his chosen ground, so the battle took place where both sides had intended. But Chelmsford's judgment proved more sound than that of the Zulu commanders, and the Zulu were once again unable to penetrate the British fire. With Chelmsford's force arrayed in a large square, there was little opportunity for even the most talented *induna* to display tactical flair, and Ntshingwayo's part in the battle is unknown.

When the battle was over, and the British had looted the king's homestead, and set fire to the great *amakhanda* on the surrounding hills, the Zulu scattered. Cetshwayo retired to Mnyamana's homestead, between the White and Black Mfolozi, while his *izinduna* and warriors dispersed to their homes. Even while the war was still in progress, the British had tried to prise the king's followers from their loyalty to him, offering the important chiefs easy terms if only they would surrender. After Ulundi, they added to the carrot the threat of the big stick, parading through Zululand to overawe those still inclined to resist. Whereas in the south of the country, already occupied in large numbers by British troops, the chiefs were quick to submit, those elsewhere were reluctant to do so while the king remained free.

On 14 August Mnyamana, Ntshingwayo and more than 150 other chiefs came into the camp of Lord Chelmsford's successor, Sir Garnet Wolseley, at oNdini. They drove before them 617 head of cattle, which they had collected at the king's request. Their objective was to negotiate for the king's life. As Ntshingwayo later put it, 'We had been sent by the king; we had not run away to the Whites. We had gone simply to ask for his head, that he might live and not perish.'

Yet the war was clearly over, and even the most loyal of the king's supporters was thinking of what might lie ahead. When, on 28 August, the king was at last captured, the chiefs had little option but to accept whatever settlement the British might propose.

Wolseley's solution was to break the country up into thirteen independent chiefdoms. This was purposely divisive, since he intended to prevent the kingdom ever uniting to pose a further threat to white interests, but even he did not realise how truly divisive it would become. Although some of the appointed chiefs were men who had defected to the British during the war, like Hamu or John Dunn, others were men of established rank. Wolseley hoped the latter would be more acceptable to the majority of ordinary Zulus, while at the same time being grateful to the British for a degree of independence that they had not enjoyed under the Royal House.

For that reason, he was particularly keen that Mnyamana should be given a chieftainship. If the king's former minister accepted a post under the British, it would have been a sure sign that the old order had been overthrown. Mnyamana, however, proved unwilling. While on the one hand he was reluctant to break faith with Cetshwayo, he was also concerned for his own future, and felt that by accepting a chieftainship he might rule out future influence with other members of the Royal House. Moreover, many of his followers were placed under Hamu, and he complained that he did not wish to be separated from them. Wolseley took the refusal in his stride, and simply offered Mnyamana's proposed territory to Ntshingwayo instead. The latter, too, had reservations, but the realisation that Mnyamana's refusal had left him politically isolated probably helped to overcome his qualms. Ntshingwayo's territory included the area of his own Khoza people, and lay between the upper reaches of the two Mfolozi rivers, stretching from Hlobane mountain in the north to Nlazatshe in the south.

The next few years were difficult for the appointed chiefs. All had accepted their positions on the understanding that Cetshwayo would never return to Zululand. Some, like Dunn and Zibhebhu, seized the opportunity this gave them and wholeheartedly embraced the new order. Others, Ntshingwayo among them, found themselves caught uneasily between their new position and a lingering respect for the old order. Many senior members of the Royal House were still living in Zululand, dispossessed by Wolseley's settlement, and they naturally applied pressure on those chiefs who were most sympathetic to their cause. Therefore, when the first messengers approached Bishop Colenso in Natal, in early 1880, to petition for the restoration of the king, they listed among their patrons not only the Princes Ndabuko, Shingana, Ziwedu and Sitheku – all of whom had been deliberately excluded from the settlement – but Ntshingwayo and Mnyamana as well. Nevertheless, as the campaign for the restoration grew, the position of the appointed chiefs who had supported it became increasingly uncomfortable. Not only did they risk the disapproval of the British, but by exercising their authority they inevitably aroused the resentment of the royalist party. When Ntshingwayo confiscated some cattle which had once been the property of either Cetshwayo or Mnyamana – accounts differ – he found himself accused by the royalists of betraying them. By the time the king's return had been approved, he had clearly lost patience with this situation, and declared he would have nothing to do with the 'House of Chaka', but would rather move with his people into the area of the British Reserve.

Nevertheless, he did not leave, and when Cetshwayo landed at Port Durnford in January 1883, it was to assume responsibility for a portion of Zululand which included Ntshingwayo's territory. A rapprochement seems to have been in the air, for Ntshingwayo was among the many important survivors of the old order who made their way to oNdini to *konza* – to proclaim their allegiance to – the king. Even then he was not entirely forgiven by ordinary royalists, who were still smarting from their sufferings under the British settlement, and who apparently insulted and abused him.

Significantly, Ntshingwayo was not involved in the disastrous Msebe expedition at the end of March, though it would undoubtedly have benefited from his military experience. He did, however, answer the king's summons in July when a fresh clash seemed to be imminent. As such, he found himself among those who awoke at dawn on 21 July to find the Mandlakazi army already bearing down on them.

Little is known of Ntshingwayo's part in his last battle. Cetshwayo appointed him to the command of the uDloko *ibutho* – themselves veterans of Rorke's Drift – which formed part of the uSuthu centre, but in the confusion it seems probable that he, like many of the other uSuthu leaders, only caught up with their men as the fighting began. The Mandlakazi advance was so determined that the uSuthu collapsed before it, and only the centre made any sort of stand. While the young, fit warriors were able to flee before Zibhebhu's advance, the more senior men, middle-aged and big-bellied, were too slow. Some, like Vumandaba kaNtati, turned on their pursuers and went down fighting, while others threw aside their weapons and tried to run, but were overtaken and stabbed just the same.

Ntshingwayo, by now in his mid-seventies, was among them. No details of his death have survived, but he clearly died with his weapons in his hands, and it is tempting to imagine him fighting to the last.

For the man who commanded the great army at Isandlwana and Khambula to die at the hands of fellow Zulu was a tragic indictment of the divisions unleashed within the kingdom by the British conquest.

5

PRINCE DABULAMANZI kaMPANDE

'His enemies talk about him ...'

On 12 July 1879, a week after Ulundi, the last great battle of the Anglo-Zulu War, Prince Dabulamanzi kaMpande rode in to surrender to British troops. Dabulamanzi's personal territory was in the south-eastern coastal strip, and this area had effectively been occupied by Lord Chelmsford's First Division in such numbers that resistance had seemed futile, even before the news became widespread of the destruction of the great cluster of *amakhanda* in the heart of the country which constituted King Cetshwayo's capital. Dabulamanzi's surrender was greeted with delight by the British, who took it as a sure sign that the war was all but over, since the prince had achieved an enviable reputation as the most daring, dangerous and irreconcilable of the Zulu commanders. As one officer wrote:

> Of all the chiefs who have come over to us, the most important is Dabulamanzi, a half-brother of the King's. He was a general in the army of Cetewayo [sic], and famous for his dauntless courage and great ability. It was he who led the charge on the British troops at Isandhlwana [sic], he also fought conspicuously at Kambula [sic], and signalised himself in the attack on the British square at Ulundi.

In Zulu culture, a great man is addressed by the praise-name *Ndabazitha*, which literally translated means 'his enemies talk about him', and by that criterion Prince Dabulamanzi was indeed a great man. Yet the respect accorded him by the British was not entirely shared by his own countrymen, who had a more realistic view of both his record and his capabilities. 'Dabulamanzi is not a good general,' commented Mehlokazulu kaSihayo, an officer in the iNgobamakhosi *ibutho*, 'he is too hasty.' And indeed, the prince's reputation among his enemies was undoubtedly inflated, almost beyond the realms of feasibility. The British had gone into the war knowing little of the personalities who constituted the Zulu military elite, and because Dabulamanzi was one of the first names to be seized upon by the British and colonial press, as one observer commented wryly, he was by them 'forthwith constituted commander-in-chief of the Zulu army, and its leader in every battle, quite irrespective of such trivialities as time and place'. Certainly, the officer who sang his praises so highly was almost entirely wrong, for Dabulamanzi took only a peripheral role at Isandlwana, and he was present neither at Khambula nor Ulundi; in fact, a few days after Khambula, he was commanding a division in another action, Gingindlovu, across the other side of the country. Nor was his record as a commander particularly successful, for although he fought several times in 1879, and played a prominent part in the bitterly destructive internecine fighting of the post-war years, his career as a general is best summed up as one of gallant and heroic failure. That he achieved such an extraordinary standing among his enemies was due to one fact alone; he had been the commander of the greatest and most gallant Zulu failure of the war, the attack on Rorke's Drift.

Dabulamanzi had been born to one of Mpande's wives, Sanguza, shortly after Mpande 'broke the rope', and crossed into Natal in October 1839. His name itself commemorated the incident, being derived from *ukudabula*, meaning to tear aside, or pass through, and *amanzi*, the water. Dabulamanzi was of the same house as his elder brother, Prince Cetshwayo, and the closest to him in age; this was a position of some prominence within the royal family, and Dabulamanzi's fortunes would prove to be inextricably linked with those of Cetshwayo.

His introduction to military life was to underline this point. Like all Zulu men, Prince Dabulamanzi was enrolled in an age-set regiment – *ibutho* – once he reached the appropriate age. Indeed, his royal status may have led to him being drafted into a regiment at a rather younger age than was typical. Many of Mpande's senior sons, including both Cetshwayo and Mbuyazi, were enrolled in the uThulwana, which was raised about 1850. At the age of ten or eleven, Dabulamanzi was too young to be included in the call-up, though he may well have carried sleeping mats and food for his elder brothers. Instead, he was enrolled in the next regiment, the uDloko, which was raised about 1850; even so, he was young by usual standards, and can have been no more than sixteen, when most of his companions were probably a year or two older. Nothing is known of Dabulamanzi's introduction to military life, though it would have differed little from that of any other Zulu of his age and class. The uDloko were present at Cetshwayo's great victory over his rivals at 'Ndondakusuka in 1856, and Dabulamanzi probably saw his first taste of action there. An early glimpse of his personality emerges from the ceremonies which marked Cetshwayo's first marriage, in 1867, suggesting that Dabulamanzi already possessed self-confidence, a trait which was indulged by his brother. Cetshwayo was, apparently, notoriously stingy, a serious fault in any chief, who was expected to demonstrate his benevolence by regular distribution of largesse, including food. No one dared criticise the crown prince in this regard, until Dabulamanzi took advantage of the ribaldry which accompanied aspects of the wedding ceremony to compose a song, which was sung by girls of the groom's party. It included the lines:

Babbler, who promises much,
    but gives nothing.
In vain do we incite him
    to accept us. Will we ever find
that he will feed us?

Cetshwayo was considerably put out, but the customs of the wedding demanded that he maintain his good humour throughout. Nonetheless, it says much for Dabulamanzi's character that he felt able to make so public and witty a criticism of his elder brother's behaviour. Dabulamanzi was emerging as an assertive – even aggressive – individual, confident of his own opinions, and of his relationship with his brother. Cetshwayo, it seems, was particularly fond of him, for although etiquette dictated that he ate his meals accompanied only by those of his household who were of the same age-group, he nonetheless occasionally sent food from his own meat-platter to Dabulamanzi's hut, a gesture that conveyed on Dabulamanzi a greater status than his role as a junior brother implied. This was not lost on some of the more senior members of Cetshwayo's household, and may in the end have had tragic repercussions.

Dabulamanzi grew up in southern Zululand. This area was the part of Zululand most exposed to white influence. The Lower Drift on the Thukela, not far from the river mouth, was one of the great entry points into the Zulu kingdom, and from the 1840s had been used by a steady trickle of white traders and hunters, making their way to see the king in search of permits to operate within his territories. After the battle of 'Ndondakusuka, when the white adventurer John Dunn had visited Cetshwayo to make his peace with him, the king had offered Dunn a position as an intermediary with the white world, and had established him as a chief over part of the southern districts. Since most of the white traffic was channelled through Dunn, Dabulamanzi had far greater access to the white world than many members of the Royal House. Indeed, Dunn and Dabulamanzi became friends, and frequently hunted together, and it was probably Dunn who taught Dabulamanzi to ride and shoot. Dabulamanzi's skill and courage as a hunter were widely known throughout Zululand, and is recalled in an anecdote about a snake which lived near a path to the kwaGqikazi royal homestead. This snake had killed several people, and defied many attempts to catch it, until at last Dabulamanzi led a group of hunters to destroy it:

Dabulamanzi went off to hunt the snake with his dogs. They picked up its scent ... Then the dogs raced one another for it, for there was the snake up in an acacia tree. It was coiled up, and lying quite still, watching the dogs and every now and then spitting at them. It began to descend, while the dogs scratched at the tree. Dabulamanzi came close up to it by climbing another tree. It was descending, and had almost reached the ground, when, 'Ka-a!', he shot it, blowing its head off. When other hunters came up it was lying in a heap on the ground ...

Contact with Dunn allowed Dabulamanzi access to European-made trade goods, and he developed a fondness for European clothes, and for gin. Nevertheless, the prince's astute and sometime autocratic manner won him few friends among the white traders who occasionally visited him, if only because he was not overawed by them, and could not easily be cheated. The British traveller, Bertram Mitford, who visited him in 1880, left a description of the prince's physical appearance, which also reflected the prevailing opinion in settler society about his character:

Dabulamanzi is a fine-looking man of about thirty-five [sic], stoutly built and large-limbed like most of his royal brethren. He is light in colour even for a Zulu, and has a high, intellectual forehead, clear eyes, and handsome, regular features, with jet-black beard and moustache. But although a handsome face, it is not altogether a prepossessing one, for it wears a settled expression of insincerity and cunning which would cause you to have little doubt as to the deservedness of public opinion about him if only you had heard it, and if you had not, readiness of belief when you should come to do so. That opinion I have heard expressed by those who knew the man, in two words, 'a blackguard'. With missionary and trader alike he is in disrepute, and many are the tales of sharp practice, if not downright rascality, which were told me about him ...

Of course, any African who refused to accept the dealings of white men at face value was likely to find himself judged in such terms!

Following the death of Mpande in 1872, Cetshwayo at last secured his birthright, and moved to the Mahlabathini plain, in central Zululand, to build himself a new oNdini. The men of influence who had supported him – his brothers, the *izikhulu* and many district chiefs – naturally then came into their own. The uDloko regiment, together with a number of others, was allowed to marry, and Dabulamanzi established two homesteads in the south of the country: eZulwini, *the heavens*, on the slopes of the eNtumeni hill inland, not far from the mission station at Eshowe, and eZiko, *the fire*, in the hot coastal lowlands. Although he held no great office in his brother's administration, he was the principal officer in charge of the eSiqwakeni royal homestead, which was sited not far from his own eZulwini residence.

Yet Cetshwayo was not long allowed to enjoy his reign. By 1877 relations with the British colony of Natal, on his southern boundary, had deteriorated to such an extent that war seemed a possibility. Despite his reputation, Dabulamanzi was among those who urged the king to placate the British, and to give into their demands rather than risk the security of the kingdom.

By December 1878, however, it had become obvious that the British would not be placated. On the 11th, British representatives met the king's envoys at the Lower Thukela and demanded that the king disband the *amabutho*. This was unthinkable, and the king reluctantly summoned his army and prepared for war. Like many others in the so-called 'peace party', Prince Dabulamanzi wholeheartedly committed himself to the war once it had become inevitable.

The Zulu army collected at the great concentration of *amakhanda* around oNdini in the third week of January. By that time, British troops had already entered Zululand at three points along the border, and the British Centre Column, under the direct command of the British commander-in-chief, Lord Chelmsford himself, had destroyed homesteads belonging to Chief Sihayo kaXongo, opposite Rorke's Drift. The king and his senior generals decided to deploy holding forces to harry the two flanking columns, while concentrating their main response on the centre column.

The main Zulu army, in excess of 20,000 men, left the Mahlabathini plain on the afternoon of the 17th. Many notables within Zululand held specific commands, while a number of the *abantwana* – the princes of the royal house – were also in attendance. Among them was Prince Dabulamanzi. Although he held no particular position, he was present with his regiment, the uDloko. His relationship to the king, and his autocratic manner, gave him a natural authority.

The army moved slowly westwards to meet the invader. On 20 January it camped behind Siphezi mountain, about fifteen miles from Lord Chelmsford's advanced base at Isandlwana. On the 21st, while Chelmsford's reconnaissance searched for it to the south-east, it moved north-west, slipping through the undulating country in columns, and taking up a position in the sheltered Ngwebeni valley. Here it spent the night of the 21st/22nd, just five miles or so from the British camp. The uDloko, which had been marching with a number of other regiments associated with the king's oNdini homestead – the uThulwana, the iNdlondlo, and the iNdluyengwe – had remained in the rear of the column, and arrived at the bivouac last. These were some of the most senior men in the army, all married men in their forties; they were probably less fit than the young regiments in the vanguard, and may simply have lagged behind. In any case, dawn on the 22nd found them encamped at the far end of the valley, furthest away from the British position.

The Zulu force did not intend to attack on 22 January but at about noon, parties of British troops from Isandlwana crested the Mabaso heights and almost blundered into the uKhandempemvu *ibutho* camped below them. In the heat of the moment the uKhandempemvu rushed forward to attack, drawing the young regiments nearby with them. There was no time even to perform the last-minute preparatory rituals which were necessary to secure victory for the regiments in the coming fight. The battle began spontaneously, with no direction from the senior commanders; the best Ntshingwayo and Mavumengwana could do was intercept the oNdini regiments, at the far end of the valley, and prevent them from joining the rush. The oNdini regiments, including the uDloko, were hastily formed into an *umkhumbi*, a circle, to receive final instructions from the commanders, and to be spattered with protective medicines carried by the *izinyanga* – doctors – who specialised in military matters. When the ceremonies were complete, the regiments were deployed to form the loins – the reserve in the traditional attack formation – and sent to cut off the line of the British retreat.

In many ways, the battle of Isandlwana proved to be the ultimate Zulu battlepiece. Despite the fact that the *amabutho* had emerged from the Ngwebeni valley in some confusion, they had completed their deployment in attack formation by the time they had covered the iNyoni heights, and spilled over to within sight of the British camp. The attack may have been launched without last-minute preparations, but the Zulu intelligence was so good that the *amabutho* had achieved their aim of encirclement almost before the British had become aware of them. By contrast, the British commanders had made their initial dispositions without any clear idea of the threat they were under, and were never able to regain the initiative. Their line was over-extended and insupportable; the horns surrounded it on either side, and it collapsed under pressure from the chest. Only a gallant fighting retreat by several companies of the 24th Regiment, which helped prevent the various elements in the Zulu deployment drawing together until the very end of the battle, allowed some of the survivors to escape.

The part played by the reserve during the battle is often underestimated, if only because it saw little fighting. This is not to say, however, that it was not of the greatest importance. Swinging wide of the right horn, the reserve entered the valley of the Manzimnyama stream, behind Isandlwana. As such, it placed a significant body of troops between the camp and its line of retreat, forcing the British infantry to abandon the road as a means of escape, and retire instead into the broken ground along the banks of the stream, where the last of their concentrations were overwhelmed. With this objective secured, the reserve then moved off across country towards Rorke's Drift, detaching one *ibutho* – the iNdluyengwe, the youngest among them – to harry

Right: Although clearly romanticised, this is the only portrait of King Shaka sketched by one who met him.

Below: White traders, armed with firearms, look on as Shaka's warriors clash with the Ndwandwe.

Above: The dying Shaka curses his assassins in this colourful Victorian version of the scene.

Below: King Dingane listens as two of his *izinduna* energetically argue the merits of one of his *amabutho*.

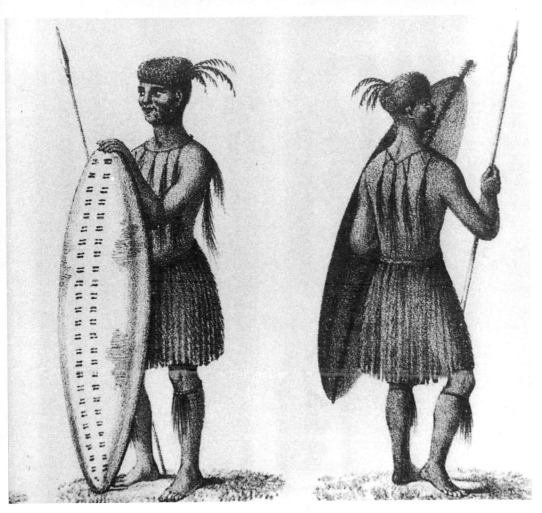

Above: Warriors of King Dingane's army. They are wearing war dress – a simplified version of the more lavish ceremonial costume.

Below: The battle of Blood River; taking shelter in the donga close to the laager, the Zulu are trapped by the merciless fire of Pretorius's sortie. (Voortrekker-monumentmuseum)

Above left: King Cetshwayo kaMpande. Cetshwayo commanded the uSuthu at the battle of 'Ndondakusuka in 1856, and played a prominent part in shaping the Zulu strategy in 1879.

Above: King Cetshwayo in London, 1882. Expecting to see the scowling savage portrayed in British newspapers at the time of the Anglo-Zulu War, the British public were surprised and delighted by the king's dignified bearing.

Left: An unusual image from the 1879 war, depicting Cetshwayo in heroic mode, ordering his army to the attack at Ulundi (oNdini). In fact, the king did not witness the final defeat of his army. (Rai England Collection)

Above: This impressive Zulu elder is believed to be Ntshingwayo kaMahole, the senior Zulu general in 1879, who commanded at Isandlwana and Khambula.

Right: A small British stand is swamped by overwhelming Zulu numbers in this contemporary interpretation of Isandlwana. Such imagery was typical of Victorian representations of the battle, which implicitly excused the British defeat suggesting that the Zulu victory was due to odds alone, rather than superior generalship.

Above: The height of the battle of Khambula. Major Hackett's sortie disperses the Zulu 'left horn' in the dead ground to the south of the British camp.

Below: Prince Dabulamanzi and his attendants, c. 1873. As this photo suggests, the prince moved easily in the world of white traders, and was both a good shot and a competent horseman.

Right: The desperate struggle for the barricades at Rorke's Drift.

This engraving of the scene at Rorke's Drift on the morning of 23 January suggests something of the terrible price paid during the attack by the senior men of the uThulwana *ibutho*.

Right: The Zulu army emerges from the Nyezane valley to attack Lord Chelmsford's square at Gingindlovu. Prince Dabulamanzi commanded the right wing and was wounded during the battle. (Killie Campbell Collections)

Right: The last shots of the Eshowe campaign; Lord Chelmsford's foray to destroy Dabulamanzi's homestead, 4 April 1879.

Right: Prince Dabulamanzi, sketched on the day of his surrender to the British forces, July 1879.

Dabulamanzi.
C. in. Chief Zulu army.

Above: 'The hyena of the Phongolo'; Prince Mbilini waMswati, right, with his *induna* Mbambo. (SB Bourquin)

Above: Mbilini's devastating attack on the stranded convoy of the 80th Regiment at Ntombe Drift, 12 March 1879.

Below: The death of Captain Campbell of Colonel Wood's staff at Hlobane mountain, 28 March 1879. Some sources suggest Mbilini himself was among the Zulu party who shot him. (Rai England Collection)

Above: A historic photograph of Mehlokazulu kaSihayo, guarded by British Irregulars and black Border Police, at the end of the 1879 war. Mehlokazulu's raid into Natal in 1878 had been used by the British as a pretext for the invasion; Mehlokazulu himself fought throughout the war as a junior officer of the iNgobamakhosi. (Christie's Images)

Below: Mehlokazulu's homestead in flames, 1906 Rebellion.
(Local History Museum, Durban)

Left: Zibhebhu kaMaphitha, one of the most dynamic Zulu commanders in 1879, and the scourge of the Royal House in the civil wars of the 1880s. Photograph c. 1873. (Natal Archives)

Below: A Zulu force under Zibhebhu's command ambushes British irregulars at Ulundi, 3 July 1879. (Rai England Collection)

Above: King Dinuzulu; the young warrior, photographed wearing an *iziqu* 'bravery bead' necklace at the time of his surrender after the rebellion of 1888.

Above: Prince Ndabuko kaMpande, Cetshwayo's full brother, and a fervent royalist supporter in the troubles of the 1880s.

Below: Into exile: King Dinuzulu and his uncles leave Eshowe gaol under guard by the Zululand Police, 1889.

Right: Bambatha kaMancinza (right), and an attendant. Bambatha's rejection of colonial authority provided the focus for a doomed nostalgic attempt to restore the old Zulu kingdom in 1906.

Left: King Dinuzulu at the time of the Bambatha rebellion, 1906.

Below: The start of Bambatha's rebellion; the attack on the police convoy at Mpanza, 5 April 1906. (Rai England Collections)

Above: Zulu Police (Nongqayi) with guns taken from the rebel dead after the battle of Mome Gorge. The action at Mome effectively crushed the 1906 rebellion in Zululand. (Killie Campbell Collections)

Below: The end of it all; the severed head, supposedly belonging to Bambatha, removed from his body for purposes of identification after the battle of Mome Gorge. (Killie Campbell Collections)

the British survivors as they reached the Mzinyathi river. The Mzinyathi was the border with Natal, and in theory offered the survivors some hope of escape; in fact, the river was in spate, and the iNdluyengwe struck the survivors just as they reached it. Dozens of men who had made the difficult and terrifying journey thus far were killed on the banks or swept away in the river. The toll was particularly heavy among the column's white troops, who were less used to moving in the harsh, hot, boulder-strewn landscape than their African auxiliaries; out of 1700 troops in the camp when the battle began, only about 300 escaped, and less than 60 of those where whites.

The reserve was directed in the pursuit not by Prince Dabulamanzi, but by Zibhebhu kaMaphitha. Zibhebhu was probably the most dynamic and talented Zulu commander to serve in 1879, and during the advance to Isandlwana he had commanded the scouting parties which had skilfully kept British patrols at a safe distance, enabling the army to move without being discovered. He was, however, the senior officer of the uDloko *ibutho*, and seems to have taken command of the reserve throughout the battle, perhaps because a number of more senior officers, attached to the uThulwana, had left their regiment to direct the attack on the camp. At some point during the pursuit, however, Zibhebhu was wounded in the hand, and retired from the fight. Since the king had specifically ordered the *amabutho* not to cross into Natal, he probably concluded that the battle was, in any case, all but over.

In fact, the reserve regiments decided not to halt at the river, but to cross into Natal. With Zibhebhu gone, Prince Dabulamanzi was the most senior man present. In a move that most of his contemporaries judged to be rash, he led the reserve on to attack the British post at Rorke's Drift. Sadly, although many white traders and travellers discussed the war with Dabulamanzi in the years immediately following, none were to record the prince's version of events in any detail, nor has it survived through Zulu sources. The king's prohibition on crossing the river was well known – he wanted to be able to claim that he had merely acted in defence of Zulu soil in any subsequent peace negotiations – and the only justification which Dabulamanzi offered was that he 'wanted to wash the spears of his boys'. This was undoubtedly a rationalisation of the feeling of the moment, that the reserve had missed out on most of the glory of the afternoon's activity, and were reluctant to return home without seeing action or without their share of the loot. It is a comment which reveals a distinct lack of tactical purpose and objective, and certainly the wild stories current in Natal shortly after the fight – that Dabulamanzi had intended to invade the colony itself – were unfounded. The reserve had already covered many miles of rough country, and some elements had engaged in a running fight with the British survivors. They had not eaten since mid-morning, and had no food with them, nor were they in sufficient strength to attempt a prolonged assault on the British garrisons which – they must surely have guessed – lay along its lines of communication. That there was a British outpost at Rorke's Drift was, however, common knowledge, and since the site had been a popular source of trade goods since it had been established in the 1840s, the possibility that it contained rich pickings must also have been widely known. In short, Dabulamanzi's incursion into British territory was little more than a raiding expedition, an opportunist attempt to take advantage of the sudden British collapse.

This is borne out by the behaviour of the *amabutho* themselves. The iNdluyengwe moved upstream from Sothondose's Drift, where they had struck the survivors, and crossed by way of a narrow gorge, where huge slabs of rock allowed them a comparatively safe passage. They were in no particular hurry, and British lookouts at Rorke's Drift saw them emerge on to the ridge above the Mzinyathi valley and pause to take snuff. The senior regiments – the married men of the uThulwana, iNdlondlo and uDloko – kept to the more open country above Sothondose's Drift, manoeuvring to cut off any survivors who had escaped the cordon, until they struck the river near its confluence with the Batshe stream. Here the Mzinyathi was wider and shallower, and the senior regiments formed a human chain to help one another across. Once on the Natal bank, they, too, paused to regroup.

The advance of the reserve had been only too clear to the British lookouts on the top of Shiyane hill, which overlooked the post at Rorke's Drift, but for a long time the British had mistaken the Zulus for their own Native Contingent. They did not realise their error until the Zulu were so close that the British could see through their field-glasses that they were led, not by white officers, but by their own *izinduna*. By the time the lookouts raced down from the hill, the news of Isandlwana had been spread among the garrison by survivors, streaming past. The senior British officers, Lieutenants Chard and Bromhead, decided against a retreat, despite the fact that the most reliable element under their command was a single company of the 24th Regiment. The post was, however, full of stores which had been stockpiled pending the arrival of a convoy from the camp at Isandlwana, and Chard and Bromhead ordered their men to improvise a hasty barricade from sacks of mealies and heavy wooden crates of army biscuit.

The apparent lack of urgency among the Zulu allowed them crucial time to complete the task. The British post was on the far side of the Shiyane hill, out of sight to the Zulus who had recently emerged on the south bank of the Mzinyathi downstream. After the iNdluyengwe had finished resting, several companies peeled off to scour the countryside inland, raiding the African homesteads, and a single European farm which had been abandoned along the border. A small party of scouts moved up towards Rorke's Drift, gingerly passing between Shiyane and kwaSingqindi hill, to the left, until they had the post in sight. By that time the iNdluyengwe had drawn up into line, and begun to follow them. The senior regiments, who had crossed a little later, also deployed to follow the same line of advance, led by two chiefs on horseback, one of whom was undoubtedly Dabulamanzi. At full strength, these regiments numbered over 4500 men, but they had already lost a number of companies who had been drawn into the fight at Isandlwana, while a number of casualties, and the absence of the groups sent to raid the foothills, probably reduced them to an effective strength of about 3500 men.

As the iNdluyengwe drew near to Shiyane, they were suddenly fired upon by a group of the Natal Native Horse, who had escaped from Isandlwana, and had volunteered to try to slow the Zulu advance. In fact, however, the Native Horse were in no position to mount a serious challenge, and as the iNdluyengwe broke into a rapid advance, the horsemen fled. This was to have a serious effect on the British garrison, where a company of auxiliaries of the NNC saw them break, and promptly ran after them. In the last few minutes before the attack, the British garrison was reduced to less than 150 men.

The iNdluyengwe passed around the south-western edge of Shiyane, and ran straight at the post, which came into sight on their right front. Their attack showed no great tactical sophistication; probably, after the events at Isandlwana, they did not expect any serious resistance. Even by this time, however, the British position, which consisted of two long, low, thatched buildings, had been surrounded by a barricade, and was at its most secure facing Shiyane. The British garrison opened a heavy fire at about 450 yards' range, and despite pushing forward to within 50 yards of the post, the iNdluyengwe attack stalled. While a number of warriors threw themselves down in the grass, to open a close-range fire-fight with the garrison, the rest veered off to their left, on a course which took them past the end of the nearest building, and allowed them to swing round on the other side. This was in fact the front of James Rorke's old trading post, and a cultivated garden, an orchard and a patch of bush allowed the iNdluyengwe to take some shelter. From here they launched the first of a series of attacks on the building in front of them – Rorke's old house, which the British had turned into a makeshift hospital. Despite the fact that this was the weakest point of the British defence – the barricade was flimsy and incomplete – this first attack was driven back at the point of the bayonet.

It had no sooner been repulsed, however, than the uThulwana, iNdlondlo and uDloko regiments swung round from behind Shiyane in support. Whether or not Dabulamanzi had any specific plan in mind, it was immediately obvious that the iNdluyengwe were already engaged, thereby severely limiting his options. He could hardly pass the post by and abandon them, even if his men had let him, nor could he take time to plan a co-ordinated assault. Rather than attack the back of the post – directly in front of them, where some of the iNdluyengwe were still pinned down under British fire – the senior men took a more westerly course, streaming past the end of the hospital building, and swinging round to join those iNdluyengwe who were already attacking the front. As they came within range, a careful shot by one of the garrison struck and killed Dabulamanzi's mounted companion. Nothing daunted, the senior men poured into the bush at the front of the post, and began to feed elements forward to join the attacks already under way by the iNdluyengwe.

From the start, therefore, the Zulu attack at Rorke's Drift had developed in a piecemeal fashion. Once the majority of the warriors were committed, the *izinduna*, Dabulamanzi included, could do little more than try to exploit short-term advantages. Although the Zulu had the advantage of overwhelming numerical superiority, the very nature of the British position, and the tiny frontage they occupied, meant that it was impossible to bring those numbers effectively to bear. Even once the Zulu had extended to surround the bush on all sides, most of the warriors spent much of the battle lying out in the grass or bush, exchanging fire, and waiting for an opportunity to reach the front. Furthermore, the British had made the most of the natural features around the post to render their barricades almost impregnable. A natural terrace of rock, a ledge in places four feet high, ran along the front of the position, and Chard had built part of his barricade on top of it. This gave the defenders an enormous advantage, since the attacking Zulus were faced with a barrier over six feet high, and the soldiers, firing down into them from above, were able to shoot them almost with impunity.

Nevertheless, there is clear evidence that Dabulamanzi tried to control the fight as best he could. The repeated assaults on the front of the hospital building finally drove the defenders to retire, and allowed the Zulu to occupy the veranda and batter at the doors themselves. While these assaults were progressing, dozens of Zulu bearing firearms occupied a line of broken strata which ran around the shoulder of Shiyane hill, and from the cover of shallow caves and fallen boulders opened a heavy fire on the back of the post. Indeed, according to local legend, Dabulamanzi himself took up a position below this ledge, a spot which certainly would have given him a commanding view of the battlefield. From the ledge, the Zulu marksmen could look right down into the British position, and the backs of the men defending the opposite – front – barricade were particularly exposed to their fire. The range was between 300 and 400 yards, however, and most of the weapons carried by the Zulus were antiquated flintlock or percussion models, which were no longer effective at such a range. Nevertheless, while the chances of accurate firing were virtually nil, a proportion of the Zulu shot was bound to strike down into the British position purely by chance, and indeed Chard's men began to take casualties. By early evening, Chard was increasingly worried that the front barricade was at risk from both Zulu fire from behind, and from the continual assaults along the front. He had prepared a contingency plan in case he could not hold the entire perimeter, and at about 6.30 he gave the order to abandon the yard between the buildings, and retire to a smaller perimeter in front of the storehouse.

This move can only have encouraged the Zulu. It was now drawing towards dusk, and the Zulu traditionally did not fight after nightfall. However, the sight of the redcoats scurrying back to their new line seems to have spurred them on to greater efforts. The hospital building had effectively been abandoned outside the new perimeter, though there were still both soldiers and sick men inside it. As the Zulu rushed forward to occupy the barricades abandoned by the British, nothing could prevent them from forcing a way into the hospital, and a terrible fight raged in the claustrophobic interior as the British retired from room to room. To drive them out all the quicker, the Zulu set fire to the thatched roof, which after a slow start took hold, and lit up the battlefield in the gathering gloom. Remarkably, most of the soldiers inside the hospital managed to escape, running the gauntlet to join Chard's men in front of the storehouse.

The capture of the hospital was complete shortly after nightfall. Chard's men now occupied the storehouse, a few square yards of ground in front of it, and a stone cattle kraal which abutted the store on one side. Nevertheless, driven into a corner with no alternative but to fight, they stubbornly resisted fresh Zulu attacks to their front. By this time the hospital was blazing so fiercely that it lit up the approaches to the barricades, and as the Zulu assaults burst out of the darkness, the soldiers poured such a volume of fire into them at close range that the bodies tumbled over one another into heaps. In the lulls between the attacks, the British garrison could hear the Zulu commanders calling to their men, no doubt regrouping and preparing for fresh assaults, while the warriors responded with war-songs, and by drumming their spears on their shields. As the night progressed, the Zulu shifted the focus of their attack to the cattle-kraal at the far end of the storehouse, and successfully drove the defenders out of it, until they held only the wall closest to the store. Nevertheless, hampered by the kraal itself, the Zulu could not bring enough men to bear to force a way through this final line. By this time, Chard's men had converted a heap of mealie-bags, lying in front of the storehouse in the centre of their position, into an improvised redoubt, and from the top a handful of men could bring an extra line of fire to bear, over the heads of those manning the perimeter. It was enough to break up each fresh Zulu attack as it reached the barricades, and drive the warriors back into the shadows.

The Zulu attacks continued without respite until about midnight, but thereafter the gaps between them became longer, and the attacks themselves less determined. The last rush took place at about 2 a.m., but a fierce fire-fight continued for at least an hour after, and the last shots spluttered on until shortly before dawn.

Probably it was about midnight when Dabulamanzi gave up any hope of carrying the post, and the first of his men began to withdraw. For men approaching middle life, they had expended a prodigious amount of energy. They had crossed at least fifteen miles of difficult country, and forded the flooded Mzinyathi, even before the attack had begun. They had not eaten since the morning before, and yet they had sustained a ferocious attack for more than seven hours. They had destroyed the hospital building, but had proved quite unable to dislodge the British garrison from its final bastion, and it was probably this lack of hope of success which discouraged them most. Throughout the early morning, while it was still dark, most of the warriors abandoned their positions, leaving only a rearguard to mask their withdrawal. It is not clear when Dabulamanzi himself left the field, but he may well have been with the main body, which crossed at Rorke's Drift, and reached the Manzimnyama stream, near Isandlwana, at daybreak. Here, in one of the most curious incidents of the war, the Zulu encountered the remnants of Lord Chelmsford's force, who had returned to spend a dreadful night on the stricken field at Isandlwana, marching in the opposite direction. Both sides were so exhausted that they were reluctant to renew the fight, and the Zulu passed across the front of Chelmsford's column without hindrance, only a few hundred yards away. The last Zulu elements were still lingering on the hills nearby when Chelmsford's column finally arrived at the post.

The extraordinary price paid by the Zulu for their courage and persistence was only too obvious to the British. Great heaps of bodies were piled up close to the barricades, or sprawled in a thick carpet across the front of the hospital, where the fighting had been heaviest. Chard reported that over 350 bodies were collected around the post and buried, but later admitted that the Zulu losses were much higher. Bodies turned up for weeks afterwards, concealed among boulders on Shiyane hill, or lying in long grass on the line of retreat. A pile of bloodied shields found by Chelmsford's men at the drift suggested that the Zulu had carried many of their wounded at least that far, but it would have been impossible to get them all over the river, and many were probably drowned as their colleagues tried to drag them across. Some Zulu sources at the time put the figure as high as 600 dead, with hundreds more wounded – an extraordinary proportion of casualties which may have reached as much as 25 per cent of the attacking force. Some of the wounded who survived had been hit several times while lying out in the terrible zone of fire close to the

British barricades, and even those who escaped unscathed were so exhausted that they could only drag their shields behind them in the grass.

The battle of Rorke's Drift was undoubtedly a comprehensive Zulu defeat, although its strategic significance was in fact limited. Against the background of the destruction of the British column at Isandlwana, the failure of Dabulamanzi's men to loot a few tons of stores was largely inconsequential. Blame for the defeat might squarely be laid at Dabulamanzi's feet, on the grounds that he had exceeded his orders, and attacked a strongly fortified position. Yet time and again, the lesson of the battles of 1879 was that the sheer volume of British firepower made them almost invulnerable, so long as they were in a tight defensive formation. Dabulamanzi was simply the first commander of his generation to learn the lesson that against the combination of concentrated rifle-fire and a stout barricade – beyond the reach of the Zulu stabbing spears – the *amabutho* had no effective answer. At Rorke's Drift, too, the desperate plight of the British garrison added a particular intensity to their resistance. As one Zulu veteran told the traveller Mitford simply, 'The soldiers were behind a *schaans* (breastwork), and ... they were in a corner.' Although the evidence suggests that once the battle had begun, the Zulus were handled competently enough, it was not enough to overcome this fatal weakness.

When news of the attack became known throughout the nation, most Zulu regarded it as a rather pointless side-show. According to one vivid account, the battered and exhausted uThulwana were greeted with derision: 'You went to dig little bits with your assegais out of the house of Jim, which had never done you any harm!' In the manner of unsuccessful commanders the world over, Dabulamanzi hedged his report to the king, trying hard to find something positive to draw out of the sorry incident. According to Cetshwayo's own account, 'Dabulamanzi reported that he had successfully stormed and taken "the house". He attacked, and then retired, but admitted he had suffered heavily.' Most Zulu, both astonished by their success at Isandlwana, yet appalled by the casualties, were not impressed by such claims. 'You!' they taunted the survivors. 'You're no men! You're just women, seeing that you ran away for no reason at all, like the wind!'

Contrary to lurid reports which began to circulate in the Natal press soon after the battle, Cetshwayo made no efforts to punish Dabulamanzi to whom he had, after all, always been close. Nevertheless, the shame of the defeat made life at the royal homestead uncomfortable, and Dabulamanzi soon retired to his own homesteads near the coast. Clearly, Rorke's Drift had not permanently discredited him, however, for he was soon involved in a new aspect of the war.

The Zulu success at Isandlwana effectively paralysed both sides for a matter of weeks. Although the Zulu realised they had won a great victory, the cost had been terrible, and the nation needed to mourn its losses. The survivors, too – particularly those who had killed an enemy, or been wounded themselves – were considered polluted by the act, and had to undergo purification rituals before they could rejoin their regiments. Even had the king and his council wanted to – and they did not – there was no possibility of following up the success with further action immediately.

Indeed, the strategic implications of the Zulu victory were by no means clear. True, the British Centre Column had been completely repulsed, the survivors abandoning Zululand and scurrying into laager at Rorke's Drift. The flanking columns, too, were on the defensive, and both had dug themselves into heavily fortified positions. Nevertheless, there was no sign that the British intended to abandon the invasion, and indeed, the Right Flank Column had easily brushed aside the efforts of those Zulu who lived in the coastal sector to halt its progress. On the same day as Isandlwana, the British commander on the coast, Colonel Pearson, had defeated a force of 6000 Zulu on the Nyezane river. The following day he had occupied the deserted mission station at Eshowe, not far from Dabulamanzi's territory at eNtumeni. Although the collapse of the Centre Column prevented Pearson from advancing further, he had decided to hold his ground, and had turned the mission into an impressive fort.

The king was incensed that Pearson had apparently settled in Zululand, acting as if the country were already conquered; but if nothing else, Rorke's Drift had highlighted the folly of attacking entrenched positions. Unable to recall the army immediately, the king and his council decided on a strategy of containment. Local elements in the north would harass the British Left Flank Column, while a similar holding force would invest Eshowe. In the hope – vain, as it turned out – that the British might be more amenable to negotiation after Isandlwana, Cetshwayo also attempted a new diplomatic offensive, sending messengers to his contacts in Natal, asking how hostilities could be brought to a close.

Dabulamanzi was given command of the forces around Eshowe, together with Mavumengwana kaNdlela, one of the successful commanders at Isandlwana, who also lived locally. The British position was secure but uncomfortable, with over 1700 men cooped up in a narrow earthwork which had been thrown up around the mission. During the day, the British were forced to drive their transport oxen away from the fort in search of grazing, and as their rations dwindled, they were also increasingly dependent on foraging for food. The king's orders to Dabulamanzi and Mavumengwana were quite specific; they should not attack the post itself, but should watch the British movements, harassing their patrols where they could. Only if the British were provoked into making a sortie away from their fort were they to be challenged; similarly, any relief column was to be attacked in the open, before it could join up with Pearson's command. The Zulu commanders had perhaps as many as 5000 men at their disposal, drawn largely from local elements who had not fought at Isandlwana, and who were housed at some of the royal homesteads nearby, including the original oNdini.

The result was a low-intensity war of minor raids and skirmishes which raged throughout February and March. Some 500 Zulu were placed in temporary shelters close to the British fort, ready to provide the first line of attack, while groups of 40 or 50 warriors watched the British daily from nearby hilltops. Attempts were made to ambush British vedettes, while working parties who ventured out of the earthwork were subjected to shouted taunts and sniper-fire. Occasionally, the British made forays to raid the gardens of nearby deserted homesteads, only to find that the Zulu mustered with remarkable speed and attempted to intercept their retreat. Such skirmishes were seldom conclusive, however, and the siege of Eshowe became a waiting game at which the British were distinctly disadvantaged. In the cramped and uncomfortable conditions inside the fort, where there was no room to pitch tents, the men slept on the ground each night, often in the pouring rain. Dysentery inevitably made its appearance, and a steady trickle of men were buried on a grassy slope below the fort. Isolation and boredom told on the men's nerves. The Zulu were soon preventing messengers from slipping through to the border, and it was weeks before signalling equipment could be improvised to open up some form of limited communication with the border.

In an attempt to revive his men's flagging spirits, Pearson decided to mount an attack on eSiqwakeni, the nearby royal homestead of which Dabulamanzi was an *induna*. Indeed, one of Dabulamanzi's personal homesteads was said to be close to eSiqwakeni, and Pearson hoped to show the Zulu that he was still a force to be reckoned with by attacking the prince himself. Accordingly, he mustered a mixed force of about 500 men, with one 7-pdr gun, and marched out at about 2 a.m. on the morning of 1 March. ESiqwakeni lay about seven miles away, west of Eshowe, but Pearson's scouts had planned the route carefully, and the raiding party covered the ground in silence before daybreak. The head of the British column had actually deployed on a ridge overlooking the homestead when the sun rose next morning, but Pearson squandered the advantage of surprise by delaying until the gun – which had lagged behind – could be brought up. A solitary Zulu, emerging from a small family *umuzi* nearby to answer the call of nature, suddenly spotted the redcoats silhouetted against the dawn sky, and raced off towards the inhabitants of the *ikhanda*. Although Pearson sent some mounted men to intercept him, he outran them and raised the alarm. Almost immediately, hundreds of Zulu spilled out of the huts of eSiqwakeni and retired on to a hill beyond, about 1500 yards away, driving their cattle with them. Pearson sent men down to set fire to the *ikhanda*, while the gun lobbed a shell into the crowd of warriors; but once the Zulu had recovered from their surprise, they began to descend from the hill to threaten the column's flanks. Pearson decided not to push his luck and continue to Dabulamanzi's personal homestead, but instead ordered a withdrawal. Immediately, the Zulus advanced to harass the rearguard, making excellent use of bush and natural features to work within a few hundred yards of the troops, and open a heavy fire. Indeed, as the rearguard moved off, the Zulu raced ahead of them, keeping to the flanks, but occupying patches of bush or rocky knolls past which the British then had to retire. From these positions they kept up a heavy fire, which would undoubtedly have caused serious casualties had it been more accurate, as a Lieutenant Lloyd observed:

> It was really a pleasure to watch the manner in which these Zulus skirmished. No crowding, no delay, as soon as they were driven from one cover they would hasten rapidly to the next awkward bit of country through which our column would have to pass. Luckily for us their shooting was inferior or we should have suffered severely.

The Zulu were directed by a conspicuous chief on a black horse, who was probably Dabulamanzi himself. Certainly, after his surrender, the prince told British officers that in his opinion the Zulu had had the better of the encounter; and although Pearson's men had achieved the limited objective of destroying eSiqwakeni, it is difficult not to feel that he was right. By the time the Zulu called off their pursuit two miles from Eshowe, and the British reached the safety of the fort, Pearson showed every sign of having been chased from the field.

Effective though the strategy of containment at Eshowe was, however, the Zulu were unable to exploit their advantage to the extent of forcing the British to withdraw. Moreover, as March drew on, it became evident that the war was about to enter a new phase. British reinforcements had been flooding into Durban, and it was clear to Zulu scouting parties that they were concentrating along the border. In particular, military activity at the Lower Thukela suggested that Lord Chelmsford might be about to mount an expedition to relieve Eshowe, while there was an increase in diversionary raids from Colonel Wood's column, still secure in the north of the country.

In the third week of March, the king summoned his councillors to discuss the situation, and both Dabulamanzi and Mavumengwana left the Eshowe front to attend. The king's peace overtures had been repeatedly rebuffed, and the *ibandla* concluded that there was little choice but to summon the army yet again. Since Wood's column had been much more aggressive than Pearson's beleaguered garrison, the main army would be despatched to the north, to attack Khambula. A smaller force was to be assembled near Eshowe, however, ready to attack the relief column before it could effect a junction with the garrison at Eshowe. Dabulamanzi and Mavumengwana returned to the coast to assist in the preparations.

The Zulu assessment of the British intentions was largely correct, and on 29 March Chelmsford set out from the Thukela with a force of 5500 troops, some 3000 of whom were white troops of the 3rd, 57th, 60th, 91st and 99th Regiments and the Naval Brigade, and the rest auxiliaries of the NNC. The weather was bad – alternately hot and wet – and Chelmsford's advance was cautious. This allowed the Zulu ample time to concentrate their forces at the various *amakhanda* around Eshowe. They mustered nearly 10,000 men, of whom about 3000 were auxiliaries from the tributary 'Tsonga chiefdoms around St Lucia bay, while the rest were drawn from members of the king's *amabutho* whose family homes were close by. Since Dabulamanzi had never been an appointed general, it is unlikely that he would have been seriously considered as senior commander, especially given his record at Rorke's Drift. In fact, the king appointed one of his close friends, Somopho kaZikhale, to overall command, assisted by Phalane kaMdinwa and Sigcwelecwele kaMhlekehleke, the senior officer of the iNgobamakhosi and a veteran of Isandlwana. All of these men lived locally and knew the country well. Dabulamanzi continued to command those troops who had been stationed around Eshowe to watch the garrison.

The Zulu forces assembled in the hills below Eshowe, above the Nyezane river, on the evening of 1 April. By that time, Lord Chelmsford's column had camped in a laagered position on the other side of the river, on a rise close to the ruins of the kwaGingindlovu homestead. Some of the Zulu commanders were keen to attack immediately, but Dabulamanzi, with uncharacteristic restraint, pointed out that some of the warriors who had only just arrived were tired and hungry, and urged them to wait until morning. Since first light – 'the horns of the morning' – was a favourite time of attack, the general agreed. Accordingly, shortly before sun-up on 2 April, when a dense mist hid their movements in the Nyezane valley, the *amabutho* manoeuvred into position to attack Lord Chelmsford's camp.

The British had expected the Zulu to oppose their advance near the Nyezane. Indeed, Lord Chelmsford had persuaded John Dunn, the 'white chief of the Zulus', to abandon his allegiance to Cetshwayo and defect to the British, and Dunn had personally scouted the Nyezane the night before, and pronounced it full of Zulu campfires. Nevertheless, it was still an awesome sight when the early morning sun burnt off the mist, and several long columns of warriors were seen to be already advancing up from the river. They swung round in a wide arc, the chest aiming for the front of Chelmsford's square, the left horn for Chelmsford's right face, while the right horn appeared on the crest of a low hill a mile from Chelmsford's left face.

The battle of Gingindlovu has assumed the character of an easy British victory, a walkover, but it most certainly did not appear so at the time. The Zulu chest was first to mount its attack, running forward in open lines, screened by skirmishers, and making good use of cover. The 60th Rifles, on the front face of the laager, opened volley fire at about 400 yards, and they were soon joined by the boom of the guns and the chatter of the Gatlings. Nevertheless, the Zulus pushed forward to within 50 yards of the front face with a determination that made the 60th – fresh out from England – waver. The Zulu could not sustain a full assault from such a position, and instead took what cover they could and mounted a series of desperate rushes. Several of these were directed against the front right corner, and one came close enough for a warrior to touch the Gatling gun positioned there before being shot down. Nevertheless, the fire was so heavy that many Zulu veered off to their right, manoeuvring instead to attack Chelmsford's left face.

As the first attack of the chest and left stalled, the right horn advanced rapidly. This was commanded by Dabulamanzi in person, and the prince could clearly be seen urging his men on from horseback. The Zulu could not believe that the British had sufficient troops to man the square on all sides, and when from some way off they saw the sun glinting on what they thought were spears, they jumped to the conclusion that the rear face was only held by the NNC. For this reason the attack on this front was particularly determined, since the Zulu were convinced that a fierce assault would cause the NNC to panic. Despite the fact that the rear face was in fact held by the 91st Highlanders, who met the attack with controlled volleys, the Zulus were so persistent that Chelmsford ordered two companies of the 60th from the front face – where the attacks had slackened – to the rear. A veritable firestorm broke up the Zulu assault, leaving the nearest Zulu corpse just 31 yards from the line. Dabulamanzi himself was hit in the fleshy part of the thigh while encouraging the attack. The right horn faltered, then veered further to its right, curling to tackle Chelmsford's right face. It was no more successful there, however, and for a while the warriors went to ground all around the square, opening a heavy but largely ineffectual fire on the defenders. At last Chelmsford judged the moment right to send out his mounted men – a mixture of Natal Volunteers and Mounted Infantry – and they charged into the stubborn knots of warriors still clinging to knots of cover near the square. Gradually, the Zulu began to retire on all sides, the mounted men taking heart from their withdrawal, and attempting to turn what started as an orderly retreat into a rout. Once the bulk of the Zulu were away from the laager, Chelmsford ordered the NNC out to clear the ground and finish off the wounded. Many injured Zulu were carried down to the Nyezane by their comrades, only to be abandoned on the banks of the river itself, and slaughtered by their pursuers.

The battle had lasted less than an hour and a half, and the British casualties had been inconsequential – five dead and 35 wounded, four of them mortally. There were at least 500 Zulu lying out around the laager, and many more on the line of retreat. Probably a thousand had been killed altogether – perhaps as many as 1200. Once across the Nyezane, the regiments made some attempt to regroup, but there was no doubt that they had been heavily defeated. They retired to some of the royal homesteads nearby, but then dispersed to their homes to recover. Dabulamanzi himself – whose wound was not serious – returned to his eZulwini homestead at the foot of eNtumeni hill.

The battle of Gingindlovu was a major Zulu reverse. They had caught Chelmsford's column in the open, as they had hoped, only to find that the British had built a fort out of their own bodies. Against such a concentrated position, and in the face of such a terrible fire, they had proved no more capable of charging home than they had at Rorke's Drift. This realisation must have come as a particular blow to Dabulamanzi, whose attack had been the most courageous of the day. Moreover, all their efforts had been for nothing, for they had not checked the British in the slightest. The following day a flying column from the Gingindlovu camp relieved Eshowe.

Ironically, Lord Chelmsford had already decided against holding Eshowe. The position was too advanced, and he was planning a new thrust along the lines of the old Centre Column. Once the euphoria of relief had passed, the garrison was faced with the dreary task of breaking up its camp, and abandoning a position it had held for 72 days.

Lest the Zulu considered this to be a retreat, Lord Chelmsford was determined to make one last gesture of defiance before he went. Dabulamanzi's name was already well known among the British for his role at Rorke's Drift, and for the part he had played in conducting the siege. On the morning of 4 April, as the rest of the force prepared to leave, Chelmsford led a foray to attack the eZulwini homestead. Despite a forced march, however, the British failed to catch the Zulu by surprise, and by the time they reached the homestead, the Zulu had abandoned it and taken up a position on a hill about 1300 yards away. The British moved forward and set fire to the homestead, and as the huts caught there was a splutter of shots from within, as the fire consumed loaded guns stored there. The Zulu on the hilltop defiantly sang a war-song, and opened fire at extreme range. Most of the shots were hopelessly inaccurate, but Lord Chelmsford and his staff attracted the attention of one particularly good marksman:

Then came a puff of smoke, and a bullet whished over our heads, then
came others, and lower and lower until we heard them hit the ground
among us, and then we were ordered to separate and not give such a
big bull's eye to them. As I led my horse away by his bridle, a bullet
came right between my hand and my horse's head and went into the
ground about fifteen feet further on ...

John Dunn, who had accompanied the expedition, studied the Zulu group
and declared that the rifleman was Dabulamanzi himself. He had taught the
prince to shoot in the happy days before the war, and now the two old friends
pitched their skills against each other. Chelmsford's staff, watching through
their field-glasses, declared Dunn the winner, since they saw the Zulu duck
several times as the shots went over their heads. The range was too great to
do any real damage, however, and after a few minutes the British retired,
leaving eZulwini in ruins behind them.

Within a few days, Chelmsford had withdrawn to the Thukela, leaving only
a few advanced outposts on the Zulu side of the border. Yet it was clear even
to the Zulu that this was no sort of victory. On 29 March, the day Chelmsford's
column had started for Eshowe, the main Zulu army had attacked Wood's
camp at Khambula, in the north of the country. After several hours of heavy
fighting, the Zulu had been heavily defeated, and driven from the field with
terrible casualties. This, coupled with Gingindlovu a few days later, on the
other side of the country, had seriously damaged both the king's major
concentrations of troops. For the following weeks, while the warriors recovered, there would be nothing to stop any British advance, and furthermore it
was becoming obvious to the king and his council that the Zulu were losing
the war of attrition, for while Zulu losses could not be replaced, fresh British
reinforcements were continuing to arrive at Durban.

Throughout April Lord Chelmsford planned his fresh offensive. In place of
the three columns of the first invasion, he now intended to make one major
thrust, with another column in support. A new column, the 2nd Division, was
to cross into Zululand north of Rorke's Drift, effect a junction with Wood's
column, and then march on oNdini. The remnants of Pearson's column, reinforced with new arrivals from home, would be formed into a new coastal
column, to be commanded by General H. H. Crealock, and styled the 1st Division. Chelmsford intended to command the 2nd Division himself, while the
role of the 1st Division was to offer support by tying down the coastal districts.

In fact, the advance of the new British coastal column would prove
ponderous, hampered as it was by lack of adequate transport. Not that this in
any way helped the Zulu, who were completely unable to resist. Throughout
May the 1st Division assembled on the Zulu bank of the Thukela, and finally

began to creep forward in early June. By that time, too, Chelmsford's 2nd Division had begun its advance, and the king called up his warriors for the third time. After the losses of the earlier fighting, it was clear that the army had only limited capacity to resist, and the king kept it close by him at oNdini, ready to make one last gesture of defiance in the heartland itself.

This decision meant that most of the coastal district was denuded of its fighting men. Many of the chiefs, including Dabulamanzi, remained at home, hoping to save their crops and herds from the invaders; but even though the 1st Division raided and destroyed both royal *amakhanda* and ordinary homesteads alike, there was little fighting. The Zulu on the coast had been completely disheartened by their inability to prevent the British achieving any of their aims there. Indeed, the British made a serious effort to open communications with the chiefs, hoping to prise them from their allegiance to the king with promises of lenient treatment if they submitted, and thinly veiled threats of what might happen if they did not. They paid particular attention to Dabulamanzi, whose surrender would have been a propaganda coup, but although the prince was prepared to negotiate, he was not among the first to surrender. On 5 June Somopho and Phalane, two of the commanders at Gingindlovu, asked for terms, and on 5 July most of the remaining important chiefs in the area submitted.

This was a reflection of the widespread belief that the war was already lost. And, indeed, unknown at that time to the coastal chiefs, Chelmsford had reached oNdini just the day before, and in the last set-piece battle of the war, had scattered the *amabutho* and razed the great cluster of *amakhanda* which served as the capital, including oNdini itself. Cetshwayo himself had guessed the outcome, and rather than witness the slaughter of his young men, had fled into the hills.

Once news of the battle became known, most of the remaining chiefs surrendered. Only a few areas, away from the main British concentrations, continued to resist. Dabulamanzi finally rode into the 1st Division camp on 12 July, accompanied by several attendants. The fabled leader at Rorke's Drift – and rumoured commander at almost every engagement of the war – caused quite a stir among his enemies, who were surprised to find him smartly dressed in European style, wearing a pea-jacket and a braided forage cap.

True to their word, the British allowed most of the chiefs who had surrendered in good time to return to their own territories. There was to be no lenient treatment, however, for Cetshwayo, who was hunted down by British patrols, and finally captured in the wild country north of the Black Mfolozi on 28 August. He was taken down to the coast and put on a ship, destined for exile in Cape Town. The British had already done their best to dispose of his kingdom. Chelmsford's successor, Lord Wolseley, whose brief was to prevent the Zulu ever again providing a threat to their neighbours, had divided the country up among thirteen client chiefs.

The post-war settlement was not kind to Dabulamanzi, nor to any member of the Royal House who had remained loyal to Cetshwayo. As part of a deliberate plan to create a buffer along the borders, John Dunn had not only been confirmed as chief of his old districts, but had his territory extended along the length of the Thukela. Dabulamanzi now found himself living under an erstwhile friend, with whom he had come to trade shots, and who, in any case, was despised by the royal family for betraying the king's trust. Most of the new rulers of Zululand were deeply suspicious of the surviving members of the royal family, and Dunn was no different in this regard. Like Zibhebhu and Hamu to the north, Dunn kept a watchful eye on the royalists in his territory, and enthusiastically confiscated cattle which had formerly been part of the royal herds.

This sudden reversal of fortune was hard for the royalists to bear. Conditions were particularly difficult in the north, where Prince Ndabuko quarrelled with Zibhebhu – who had been placed over him – about the fate of members of the royal household given into Zibhebhu's care. Zibhebhu retaliated by attacking royalist supporters and raiding their cattle. As early as May 1880 a deputation of leading royalists – who were again beginning to call themselves by the name of Cetshwayo's faction in 1856, the uSuthu – walked all the way to Pietermaritzburg to appeal to the Natal authorities to intervene. Their appeals fell on deaf ears, and a series of stormy meetings with the British resident in Zululand made it clear that official British opinion was firmly opposed to them. Against an ominous background of sporadic violence, a second deputation walked to Pietermaritzburg in May 1882. Significantly, this included Dabulamanzi and a number of other chiefs from Dunn's area, who had grown resentful of an increased burden of taxation which, as Dunn made no effort to conceal, went into his own coffers.

Although the second uSuthu deputation was no more successful than the first, the deteriorating situation in Zululand was beginning to worry the British authorities. Although the peaceful settlement of Zululand was never part of Wolseley's remit – which had been solely to prevent the country posing a threat to its white neighbours – the spiral of raid and counter-raid was threatening to get out of hand, with obvious dangers to the border regions. Moreover, sympathy for Cetshwayo, in exile in Cape Town, had grown as the British public had come to regard the war as unjust. Cetshwayo lobbied tirelessly to be allowed to return to Zululand, to reassert his authority, and end the violence. In August 1882, the king was allowed to visit London, to argue his case. The Colonial Office was prepared to consider allowing him to return, provided he did not revive the *amabutho* system.

Provision had to be made for those among the new chiefs who would not accept his authority, however, while Natal officials were still deeply suspicious of the king's influence. A compromise was reached which would effectively condemn Zululand to a fully fledged civil war. The southern part of the kingdom – Dunn's district – would be placed under British administration, and known as the Reserve Territory. In the north, meanwhile, Zibhebhu was confirmed as an independent ruler. Cetshwayo was effectively to be confined to a strip of central Zululand, hemmed in both north and south by his enemies. It was a recipe for disaster.

The king landed at Port Durnford, a windswept stretch of beach in the Reserve Territory, in January 1883. There were no crowds of supporters to meet him, for the British had kept the landing secret; just Sir Theophilus Shepstone, the great colonial manipulator, and a squadron of dragoons. The king journeyed inland to the Mthonjaneni heights, where the uSuthu were at last allowed to greet him, and then descended to oNdini, where the official installation took place. Many of his leading supporters took the opportunity to make speeches publicly attacking the colonial policies in a damning indictment of British ineptitude and duplicity. Among them was Dabulamanzi, forthright as ever, who made a stinging attack on Shepstone's personal role, 'You are killing him [Cetshwayo] still as you did before,' he declared, 'when you first made him king, and then killed him.'

Such outbursts were an effective expression of the frustration felt by the king and his supporters. Once the British party had departed, the king selected the site for a new homestead, not far from the ruins of the old oNdini. Although it was built along traditional lines, however, it was already an anachronism, for the infrastructure which supported it, the *amabutho* system and the vast herds of royal cattle, were already gone. Nevertheless, the uSuthu took encouragement from Cetshwayo's return, and began to prepare their vengeance on their persecutors. In March, northern uSuthu under Prince Ndabuko and Mnyamana Buthelezi assembled an army on Zibhebhu's borders, and marched on his principal homestead. But Zibhebhu was far too astute for them, and led them into an ambush in the Msebe valley in which they were spectacularly routed. USuthu supporters across the north of the country fled to the hills, leaving the triumphant Mandlakazi to destroy their homes and crops and loot their cattle. With the country in uproar, Cetshwayo abandoned his pledge to the British not to arm, and summoned his supporters from across the country. Many of those living in the Reserve or Zibhebhu's territory made the journey to oNdini to attend him, and among them was Dabulamanzi. In mid-June, Dabulamanzi led a force of 3000 uSuthu north to attack Zibhebhu, in an attempt to relieve the pressure on the king's supporters, but when his force reached the Black Mfolozi, it ran into a numerically smaller Mandlakazi force sent to oppose it. So low was the morale among the uSuthu that Dabulamanzi's men refused to fight, and returned to oNdini. For the second time in his career, Dabulamanzi found himself sternly rebuked by his brother, the king.

The uSuthu plan was to mount a major expedition from oNdini, but with characteristic panache, Zibhebhu struck first. Assembling his own forces on his southern borders, he made a daring march through the Mfolozi valley, and appeared on the hills at oNdini at dawn on 21 July 1883, taking the uSuthu completely by surprise. Even as the Mandlakazi deployed to attack, the uSuthu stumbled out of their huts in confusion. The king refused to flee, however, and rapidly appointed officers to command his forces. Chief Sekethwayo was appointed to overall command, with three of the king's half-brothers, Ziwedu, Sitheku and Dabulamanzi, as his lieutenants. The uSuthu gingerly advanced to meet Zibhebhu, but the Mandlakazi fell on them with such determination that they collapsed before the onslaught and fled. In the heat of the battle, the Mandlakazi pursuit was ruthless, and dozens of important *izinduna* of the old order were killed. The oNdini homestead was set ablaze, and Cetshwayo himself was wounded as he escaped. During the rout Dabulamanzi's young son, Mzingeli, trod on an acacia thorn which pierced his foot, and his father helped him away, commandeering a horse from a passing *induna*. Both escaped the slaughter.

For the uSuthu, the defeat was apocalyptic. Not only were many of their leaders killed, but their army was scattered, and there was little to stop the Mandlakazi rampaging at will across the king's former territory. Cetshwayo himself, with a handful of loyal attendants, managed to slip into the Reserve Territory, and eventually surrendered to the British Resident in Eshowe. Here, in a doleful homestead on the outskirts of the fledgling European town, he received his defeated supporters, including his brothers Ndabuko, Ziwedu and Dabulamanzi. Before the king could address his situation, however, on 8 February 1884, he collapsed and died.

According to his brothers, one of the king's last acts was to appoint his fifteen-year-old son Dinuzulu as his heir, and nominate Dabulamanzi as his guardian. 'Dabulamanzi,' he is said to have cried, 'there is my child. Look after him for me. Bring him up well, for I have no other sons. Dinuzulu is my only son. There is your task Dabulamanzi, to look after my child.'

Certainly, the king's brothers had every cause to support Dinuzulu's claim, as the uSuthu clearly needed a new leader. The choice of Dabulamanzi as guardian was unusual, since Ndabuko was the senior brother, but probably reflects the king's affection for his younger brother. The task was, perhaps, a poisoned chalice, since years later one of Dabulamanzi's sons expressed the belief that Ndabuko had been offended by the choice, and had plotted to have

Dabulamanzi killed. For a few months Dinuzulu lived under Dabulamanzi's protection in the Nkandla forest, but events were in any case gathering momentum. Acting in Dinuzulu's name, the uSuthu sent a deputation to appeal to the Transvaal Boers to intervene on their behalf. In April 1884 Dinuzulu slipped out of the Reserve, and into the Transvaal, where an alliance was being hammered out which would at last destroy Zibhebhu's ascendancy.

Dabulamanzi was left in the Nkandla, to look after royalist interests in the Reserve. In many ways this was an obvious task for him, since he knew the area well, and his own homesteads were not far away. Here he assembled a force of some 2000 warriors. The British Resident, Melmoth Osborn, clearly saw this as a threat to his authority, and raised 3000 levies from among the chiefs nearby in Eshowe who had accepted his authority. At the head of these, and under personal escort from the Zululand Territorial Carbineers – a unit of Zulu troops raised under white officers – he marched out to Nkandla to demand that the uSuthu refugees there submitted to him. When they proved reluctant to do so, he confiscated some of their herds, and light skirmishing broke out. With typical audacity, Dabulamanzi immediately led his warriors to attack Osborn. It was the first time royalist forces had directly challenged the British administration since 1879, and it would prove to be Dabulamanzi's last fight. Typically, it was characterised by rash gallantry on his part. At about 3 a.m. on 10 May, on a clear, moonlit night, Osborn's scouts rushed into his camp with news that a hostile *impi* was approaching. The garrison just had time to deploy – the levies screened by the more disciplined carbineers – when the Zulu came up and attacked. They were met with such a heavy fire that, even in the dark, it was impossible for them to charge home. They contented themselves with recapturing confiscated cattle, and retired. Nevertheless, Osborn's levies had proved so unreliable that it was obvious he could not defend himself in the event of a further attack, and he retired immediately to Eshowe.

Meanwhile, the struggle between the uSuthu and Mandlakazi reached its dramatic climax in the north. A large royalist army, assembled by the great uSuthu leaders and accompanied by Dinuzulu himself, had taken to the field, supported by a Boer commando. On 5 June it encountered Zibhebhu's forces along the foothills of the Tshaneni mountain, the Mandlakazi were scattered, and the jubilant uSuthu had their revenge.

Yet the price paid by the uSuthu would be severe. The Boers promptly presented claims for farms as reward for those who took part in the expedition, and these amounted to almost five-sixths of the country outside the Reserve. The uSuthu protested bitterly, and at last the British shouldered some of the burden of responsibility which had rightly been theirs since 1879, and intervened. They agreed to recognise Boer claims provided those claims were reasonable, and a prolonged wrangle ensued. In particular, the uSuthu bitterly resisted losing their right to the country around the emaKhosini valley, where the ancestors of the Royal House were buried.

It was this wrangle which finally cost Prince Dabulamanzi his life. The prince had been a typically forthright supporter of Dinuzulu's position, and on 21 September 1886 Dabulamanzi and his son Mzingeli were arrested by a Boer *Veldkornet* on trumped-up charges of cattle-theft. The following morning they were taken to Vryheid – capital of the new Boer territory, under the guard of two Boers, Wilhelm Joubert and Paul van der Berg. When the party was passing the Nondweni river, and not far from the border of the British Reserve, the two Zulus suddenly put their horses to a gallop, and crossed the river. When they reached a nearby homestead they dismounted, and asked if they were now in British territory. On being told that they were, Dabulamanzi commented, 'The Boers can't do us any harm.' Within a few minutes, however, the two Boers rode up, and demanded that Dabulamanzi come out of the homestead, threatening to fire into the huts if he refused. 'I am in the Reserve and you have no right to touch me,' replied the prince, 'nor take me to Vryheid; I have stolen no man's cattle, nor done any harm; if you take me anywhere, take me to the [British representative].' The Boers agreed, but no sooner had Dabulamanzi emerged from the huts than van der Berg seized him and tried to tie him up. According to Mzingeli:

> [van der Berg] and my father then struggled together, my father seizing hold of [van der Berg's] bandolier. After a bit they separated, my father having possession of the bandolier, and [van der Berg] of my father's knobkerrie. I was prevented from assisting my father by the other Boer who threatened to shoot me. [van der Berg] said, 'Give me back my bandolier.' My father replied, 'Return to me my knobkerrie.' My father threw the bandolier to [van der Berg] who then seized the gun from Wilhelm and said he would shoot my father if he wouldn't go to Vryheid. My father replied, 'You won't shoot me on Government ground.' [van der Berg] said he would, and after some more words he shot my father, who was standing within two or three yards of him, through the body, the bullet entering his stomach below the left side and coming out above his right hip. My father ran away and as he was doing so [van der Berg] shot at him again twice, the first shot struck him above the left hip, the second shot passed through the right elbow and left wrist. [van der Berg] then fired two shots at me as I was riding away on which the horse bucked me off and I sprained my knee. My father, after receiving the second shot, fell close to me; he had only run about 200 yards. After this I saw the Boers seize our horses and ride

away, and presently the people from a nearby kraal came up and carried us to their huts.

Dabulamanzi lingered throughout the night, but died at dawn the next morning. His last words were, 'I don't know why they killed me on Government ground.' His body was later loaded on to a wagon, much as Cetshwayo's had before him, and taken down to the coast, to be buried on the site of his eZulwini homestead, at the foot of eNtumeni hill.

The circumstances of Dabulamanzi's death amounted to little more than cold-blooded murder, arousing suspicions that he had been deliberately assassinated. Whether his death was due to his opposition to the Boer land claims, or whether – as his family believed – his assassins had been in the pay of his jealous brothers, has never been firmly established. In any event, it was a tragic and squalid end to a man who had achieved an extraordinary reputation among the whites. That his achievements as a general did not always live up to his name cannot diminish his standing as a steadfast and courageous warrior in the royalist cause.

6

PRINCE MBILINI waMSWATI
'The hyena of the Pongolo'

In October 1879 the citizens of Exeter, in Devon, threw a banquet for one its sons, recently returned home as a conquering hero from the Anglo-Zulu War. Colonel Redvers Buller had earned himself a dashing reputation, which had been recognised by the award of the Victoria Cross, for gallantry at the battle of Hlobane mountain. Buller took the opportunity to make a strong and impassioned speech which painted a graphic picture of Zulu cruelty. Buller had served on the Transvaal–Zulu border, the most remote theatre of operations of the war, and a district which had been unsettled even before hostilities broke out. In particular, Buller recalled a ride through the border country on the eve of war, when he saw 'dozens of burnt-down and deserted farms', and dwelt on the horrors of 'the slaughter of men, women and children in Swaziland by the Zulu band of Umbelini's followers'.

It was a speech destined to reassure the ruling classes in Britain that their role in Zululand had been fully justified, although it is interesting to note that among the press, even at that time, there were some who remained unconvinced. That Buller chose to cite the name of 'Umbelini' – Mbilini waMswati – in such a context was quite deliberate, and his words reflected the mixture of fear, revulsion and grudging respect which characterised their reaction to the man who was arguably the most relentless and implacable Zulu leader in the war. The very qualities which made Mbilini's name a byword for vicious cunning among the British were those that served to make him a consistently effective commander. Another officer who campaigned against him, Captain Tommasson, perfectly summed up British ambivalence when he described Mbilini as 'a savage chief of freebooters', but admitted that 'he was certainly one of the most dashing of all the Zulu generals', and 'was the very man to carry out those guerrilla tactics that the Zulus ought to have relied upon for success'.

That Mbilini achieved such distinction was all the more remarkable because he was not a member of the closely knit circle of men from the Royal House or great ones of the nation who traditionally made up the Zulu military elite. Indeed, Mbilini was not even a Zulu; he was a prince of the Swazi royal house, who had fled Swaziland, and given his allegiance to King Cetshwayo.

Mbilini was born about 1843, the eldest son of King Mswati of Swaziland by his first wife, laMakhasiso. From an early age, he was brought up to be a warrior. In the 1850s, when still a boy, he accompanied Swazi punitive expeditions along the Lebombo mountains, and at the age of twelve he was reputed to have had the fresh and bloody pelt of a particularly vicious dog drawn over his head, so that he might draw strength from its spirit. The effect of this on an adolescent mind, in a culture which accepted implicitly the power of the supernatural, should not be doubted, and perhaps explains another brutal – but probably apocryphal – anecdote from his youth, that Mbilini once killed a prisoner, bound hand and foot, with repeated spear thrusts.

Certainly, Mbilini's reputation for ruthlessness was already established by the time his father died in 1865. Mbilini was the eldest of Mswati's sons, and the only one approaching adulthood; furthermore, he had been among his father's favourites. Nevertheless, he was technically barred from the succession because his mother's status, as first wife, was inferior to that of other members of the king's household. The succession was discussed by senior members of the Royal House, but opposition to Mbilini was considerable, because of his ambitious nature, and instead one of his brothers, a minor named Ludvonga, was chosen to succeed. Mbilini was bitter at the decision, and tried to muster support among the Swazi army; when that failed he asked the Transvaal Boers to help. The Boers were usually willing to intervene in the domestic disputes of neighbouring African groups – at a price – but on this occasion Mbilini's following was so small that it was clearly not worth the risk, and the best the Transvaal authorities were prepared to do was offer Mbilini sanctuary. No longer safe in Swaziland, Mbilini accepted, but established himself on the slopes of the Tafelberg, a natural fortress, pitted with caves, which overlooked the confluence of the Ntombe and Phongolo rivers.

His choice of site was typically calculating, for the Phongolo river basin was a remote frontier zone, over which no less than three administrations claimed authority. Here Swazi- and Zulu-speaking peoples lived close together, and the Swazi kingdom had long-standing claims to the district. The area had been severely dislocated, however, by King Shaka Zulu in the 1820s, and a Zulu *ikhanda* – ebaQulusini – built there. Moreover, following King Mpande's expeditions against the Swazi in the 1860s, the Zulu kings claimed the area as their own, as far as the Umkhondo (Assegai) river further north. This claim was disputed by the Transvaal republic, who maintained that their authority extended across the Umkhondo to the headwaters of the Phongolo. Their claim was based on the fact that King Mpande had allowed Boer farmers to graze cattle and cut wood in the area from 1848. A Boer settlement, Utrecht, had grown up to the west, and Boer farmers had begun to push their boundaries ever further into areas claimed by the Zulu. This action had angered the Zulu, who took a strong line opposing Boer incursions, especially after

Cetshwayo became king in 1873. The resultant tensions would bear a bitter fruit once the British annexed the Transvaal in 1877.

Not that the area, in any case, was thickly populated. White settlement consisted of scattered farms and a small hamlet at Luneburg, on the Ntombe, in the very heart of the disputed territory. This had been built by God-fearing German immigrants in 1869, and they had been sensible enough to ask permission of both the Transvaal government and King Mpande. Most of the land settled by Boer farmers lay between Luneburg and the Transvaal town of Utrecht, 35 miles to the south-west, while only a few adventurous souls had moved into the more contentious territory further east. Black population around Luneburg was also patchy, and by far the largest African group – the abaQulusi – were concentrated 30–40 miles further south, east of the head-waters of the White Mfolozi. The abaQulusi were descendents of the people attached by King Shaka to the ebaQulusini homestead, who had settled in the area, and by the 1870s had come to number several thousands. They considered themselves a section of the Zulu Royal House, and were ruled over by *izinduna* appointed by the king, rather than by hereditary chiefs; but their territory, remote from the centres of royal authority, gave them considerable autonomy.

Such a patchwork quilt of peoples, aims and objectives, spread over an area of strikingly beautiful but rugged and inaccessible country, allowed Mbilini free rein to improve his fortunes. He was astute enough to seek the protection of King Cetshwayo, to whom he tendered his allegiance, but his ambitions were almost always self-serving. Indeed, Mbilini's relationship with the king was crucial to his subsequent career, yet it remains difficult to disentangle. For Mbilini, the king's support offered him considerable protection whenever he antagonised his neighbours – which was often – and for that reason he was generally careful not to anger his patron. In 1868 a missionary had encountered him staying at the then Prince Cetshwayo's oNdini homestead, at that time on the coast, and described Mbilini as an outcast, a refugee with few cattle or followers – a position which royal patronage could only improve. Nevertheless, Mbilini's own aims were often at odds with Cetshwayo's, and he acted as independently as he dared, sometimes flagrantly disregarding the king's policies, and courting disaster as a result. For Cetshwayo, in turn, Mbilini's allegiance gave him an excuse to intervene in Swazi politics, and there is considerable evidence that, once the crisis with the British deepened, Cetshwayo considered the possibility of shifting some of the centres of Zulu authority into Swazi territory, and used Mbilini as a means of testing the strength of the border region. Even when Mbilini's actions embarrassed the king, he was reluctant to act against him, for fear of giving the impression that he had abandoned a man under his protection.

Mbilini's initial following was small, and probably drawn from a mixture of disaffected Zulu and Swazi who saw a chance to enrich themselves in his service. Throughout the 1870s, Mbilini launched a number of raids, aimed mainly at local Swazi groups, some of them living on Transvaal territory. His intention was to make his presence felt and to increase his cattle and followers; on each occasion his attacks were quick and ruthless, and he had retired to his mountain stronghold before the victims could mobilise to oppose him. The Boers complained to Cetshwayo, who gave them permission to retaliate but – significantly – did nothing himself. In 1877 the Boers did just that, and a commando besieged one of Mbilini's homesteads for several days, only to find at the end of it that Mbilini had slipped away. Indeed, when things became too tough on the border, Mbilini found it expedient to abandon his homes there, and pay his respects to Cetshwayo in person, so much so that one member of the king's household commented that Mbilini seemed to be permanently in residence at oNdini for the best part of three years in the 1870s.

Once the Boers had departed following the clash in 1877, Mbilini returned to the Phongolo, and built a new homestead on the southern slope of the Hlobane mountain. Hlobane was one of the great strongholds of the abaQu-lusi, and Mbilini's presence there was an indication of the successful relation-ship he had forged with them. He gave his new homestead the name iNdlabeyitubula, a wry reference to his recent difficulties; it means *they* – the Boers – *gave my home a shove*. Far from discouraging him, however, the recent Boer successes made him all the more determined to make good the cattle he had lost, and in October 1878 he raided a number of Swazi home-steads across southern Swaziland. A Swazi *impi* attempted to cut of his retreat, but abandoned its pursuit on the Phongolo river.

This raid was, in the words of a Zulu who knew Mbilini, 'like setting fire to dry grass which can no longer be extinguished'. The British had now assumed control of the Transvaal, and were sensitive to events in the disputed border; it was on this occasion that Redvers Buller visited the area to see for himself the carnage caused by Mbilini's depredations. Coming on top of Zulu attempts to stake their claim to the Luneburg district – King Cetshwayo had directed the abaQulusi to build a small royal homestead within three miles of the settle-ment – it convinced the British that the settlers on the frontier were in danger. The nearest British garrison had been established at Utrecht, south-west of Luneburg, in the Transvaal, and the British commander, Colonel Wood, promptly despatched two companies of the 90th Regiment to protect Luneburg. Given King Cetshwayo's contention that Luneburg was in Zulu territory, this merely served to heighten Zulu suspicion that the British were intent on a confrontation.

Indeed, by the end of 1878 Anglo-Zulu relations were approaching crisis point. When Bartle Frere's ultimatum was presented to the Zulu envoys at the Lower Drift, it included, alongside the demands that the *amabutho* system be abolished, the insistence that Mbilini be surrendered to British justice. Even as the king and his council debated how best to meet the British challenge, however, rather than surrender Mbilini Cetshwayo ordered him to move closer into Zululand.

The Zulu could find no effective way to appease the British, and the Anglo-Zulu War began on 11 January 1879. Even before that date, Wood had moved forward from Utrecht and established a base at Thinta's kop, inside Zulu territory. It was clear to both sides that the war threatened to fall particularly heavily on the northern border region, and the settlers, the Zulu and the Swazi had all taken steps to prepare themselves. The whites living on the more exposed farms had abandoned their properties and fled to the safety of the Luneburg garrison, leaving – in some cases – their farms to be ransacked by the Zulu. In their turn, the Zulu had begun stockpiling grain and preparing their strongholds in the caves along the Ntombe and Phongolo rivers, while the Swazi had abandoned their border settlements in case the war spilled over and affected them.

When the fighting began in earnest, it was Mbilini who emerged as the most resourceful commander in the region. He was still a young man – in his mid-thirties – and slight of build, with a dark complexion. He was unmarried, but some indication of his self-assurance can be found in the fact that he had adopted the *isicoco*, the gummed headring which characterised the married man's estate, because he considered himself the head of his own household. In his manner he appeared quiet and pleasant, but this disguised a subtle and aggressive mind; it is no coincidence that he was said to be an expert at the game of Sokhexe, in which players tried to outmanoeuvre one another amidst a maze traced in dust on the ground. According to one who knew him, his charm concealed a natural ruthlessness which had been tempered by years of insecurity and violence; his true nature was in fact that of 'a hyena'. Unlike the more conventional Zulu commanders, who were given control of the king's *amabutho* – many of whom had not seen action for at least twenty years – Mbilini had a wealth of recent experience to draw upon, which combined aspects of both the Swazi and Zulu military outlook, and knew instinctively how to use them to best effect in the local terrain. Moreover, Mbilini rode a horse and was a good shot, and he lacked the lingering sense of awe with which many of his contemporaries viewed the white world; indeed, his experience had given him a sound practical appreciation of both the strengths and weaknesses of his opponents. By inclination and training, he was, in fact, ideally suited to the role of a dynamic guerrilla leader, a role he embraced wholeheartedly once the fighting began.

Not that his British opponent in the northern theatre, Colonel Wood, was ill-equipped for the challenge either. Wood was a slight, rather vain man, who was prone to illness and had suffered, during a highly adventurous career, a variety of bizarre accidents, which included being trampled by a giraffe. Self-assured and restless, he was highly experienced in colonial warfare, was unafraid to take chances – sometimes to the point of recklessness – and was popular with his men. The Zulu had given him the name *Lukani*, after a hard-wood they used to make knobkerries, and this was both a pun on his name and a tribute to his military capabilities. Wood depended heavily on his commander of cavalry, Colonel Redvers Buller, a growling bulldog of a man, then in his prime, and no less tough and aggressive than his chief. It was to Buller's command in particular – which consisted of a number of small irregular mounted units, recruited in southern Africa from hard-bitten adventurers who could ride and shoot – that much of the burden of the coming campaign would fall.

Wood soon realised that the semi-independent status of the local Zulu commanders cut both ways. No sooner had the ultimatum expired than he began to put pressure on chiefdoms lying to the south and east, relentlessly raiding them for cattle, while at the same time offering them easy terms for surrender. As he had hoped, a number of chiefs soon came to recognise that while oNdini was a long way away, and the king preoccupied, the British were only too close to hand, and after only token resistance several surrendered. This news caused some consternation at oNdini, and the king sent messengers to order Mbilini and the abaQulusi to stand firm. They needed no further bidding, and their combined forces soon became the centre of resistance to the British invasion.

Mbilini had moved south from the Ntombe valley to his homestead below the Hlobane mountain when the ultimatum expired. Together, his followers and the abaQulusi numbered several thousand men, and in their discipline and determination they offered a far more formidable foe than the dispirited waverers Wood had so far faced. Furthermore, the abaQulusi district included a range of three interconnected mountains, which had served as strongholds for generations, and which provided a secure base from which to operate. The nearest of these, Zungwini, lay about 30 miles north-east of Wood's camp at Fort Thinta; beyond Zungwini, further east, lay Hlobane, and finally Ityenka. Of the three, Hlobane was the most formidable, an irregularly shaped flat-topped plateau, which rose over a thousand feet from the undulating plain, and whose summit was surrounded by an almost impenetrable wall of cliffs, 200 feet high. The abaQulusi did not live on these mountains – the peaks were exposed to summer thunderstorms of terrifying ferocity – but in times of stress drove their herds up steep, rocky paths which cut through the cliffs here and there, sealing the paths behind them with loose walls of stones.

On 20 January, Buller led a patrol to probe the Zungwini range. He was almost surprised by a force of abaQulusi who rushed out to surround him so smartly that he was forced to retreat. The lesson was not lost on Wood, who determined to drive the Zulu away from their strongholds. On 22 January he led a mixed force of cavalry and infantry which caught the Zulu by surprise, driving them off Zungwini after a skirmish. During the incident there was a partial eclipse of the sun, and the Zulu saw ominous signs in Wood's audacity. Mbilini's *itonya* – the mysterious spiritual force which assured him of success in battle – was associated with the sun, and it seemed to some of his followers that his power was deserting him. Sure enough, when Wood returned to the area two days later, he once again caught the Zulu unawares, dispersing about 3000 warriors who had hastily gathered to oppose him. Although Mbilini was not in command, he had nonetheless been present with his men, and shared the blow to Zulu prestige.

In fact, however, it was the British fortunes which were about to be eclipsed. Right in the middle of the skirmish of the 24th, Wood received a message telling him that the British Centre Column, under the direct command of Lord Chelmsford, had been heavily defeated two days previously at Isandlwana. Wood immediately ordered his forces to break off the engagement, and to retire to Fort Thinta. Despite his successes locally, his position was precarious; he was now unsupported, and might expect to be attacked by the main Zulu army at any point. Moreover, the abaQulusi and Mbilini could reasonably be expected to be encouraged by the Zulu victory, while the Transvaal border appeared suddenly exposed and vulnerable. The settlement at Luneburg seemed particularly at risk, while even Utrecht itself was not out of range of Zulu attack. Wood decided to abandon his camp at Fort Thinta, and move to a new position which placed him closer to Luneburg, and lay squarely between the Zungwini range and Utrecht. He chose a narrow grassy ridge known as Khambula hill. To show that he was not daunted by the wider strategic reverse, however, he despatched Buller's men on 1 February to mount a daring raid on the ebaQulusini *ikhanda* itself, on the far side of Hlobane. The move was so unexpected that Buller's men achieved their objective – setting fire to the homestead and carrying off the cattle – almost without opposition.

Wood's constant pressure on the Zungwini strongholds made effective resistance difficult, but the vulnerability of Luneburg was not lost on Mbilini. Rather than continue the costly skirmishing around Hlobane, Mbilini slipped north, returning to the Ntombe valley with his own followers and several hundred abaQulusi. Here, Manyanyoba had been engaged in constant skirmishing with the Luneburg garrison, which, the Zulu realised, was too small to effectively police the district. Moreover, it was too far away for immediate help to be sent from the main garrison at Khambula. Accordingly, Mbilini, Manyanyoba and a Qulusi *induna*, Tola kaDilikana, made a careful plan to take advantage of the garrison's weaknesses. Their target was not the British military, but the hundreds of Christian Africans – *amaKholwa* – who had attached themselves to the Luneburg settlement, and who had been given smallholdings along the Ntombe valley. These were people who had adopted much of the European lifestyle, had opted to side with the whites, and were particularly despised by the Zulu as a result. The raid took place on the night of 10/11 February, and clearly demonstrated the Swazi influence of Mbilini's upbringing. Swazi armies often moved at night, secretly, then lay in wait close to their targets before launching their attack at daybreak. On this occasion, the combined Zulu force slipped into the valley at night, separating into four parties which then surrounded the unsuspecting amaKholwa, and fell on them before dawn. Mbilini had issued strict instructions that the warriors carry only spears, so that the Luneburg garrison would not be warned by the sound of gunfire. The onslaught was ferocious, for all it was silent; the Zulu killed 41 amaKholwa men, women and children, burned their homes, and carried off their cattle and sheep. A few mounted men from Luneburg, aided by the irate amaKholwa, tried to cut them off as they retired, killing a few stragglers as they crossed the Ntombe and recovering some of the livestock, but the attack had been an undoubted success. The Zulu retired to the caves which marked the lower slopes of the Ntombe valley, while Mbilini himself slipped away to Hlobane. As he had guessed, the attack immediately provoked British reprisals. Buller's men rode out from Khambula over the next few days to burn deserted homesteads and to try – unsuccessfully – to force the Zulu from their caves, while British garrisons further north, in the Transvaal, launched forays against local Zulu cattle outposts.

The stern British response masked the fact that fighting in the northern theatre had reached a stalemate, a war of raid and counter-raid in which neither side appeared able to gain the upper hand. The Zulu, well aware that they could not match British firepower in open battle, continued to avoid direct confrontation, and concentrated instead on easy targets. While the British, in turn, could mount effective punitive expeditions in the short-term, they lacked the resources to drive the Zulu out of their strongholds, or to maintain effective control of the countryside. No sooner did the British withdraw than the Zulus re-emerged to harass small British patrols on the road around Luneburg.

Indeed, Mbilini was soon to prove – in spectacular fashion – that even large parties could be at risk. From the first week in February, the garrison of Luneburg had been replaced by five companies of the 80th Regiment, under the command of Major Charles Tucker. When Lord Chelmsford had deployed his forces at the beginning of the war, the 80th had been attached to a defensive column, under the command of Colonel Hugh Rowlands, which was posted to the north of Wood, further along the Transvaal border. Although the garrison at Luneburg fell under Wood's jurisdiction, the 80th continued to draw their supplies, not from Utrecht, but from Lydenburg in the Transvaal, many miles away. This meant that they were fed by regular convoys which travelled the long and exposed road that bypassed the hamlet of Derby, crossing the Ntombe stream near the Reverend Myer's deserted mission station, just four miles from Luneburg.

One such convoy, consisting of eighteen ammunition and supply wagons, set out at the end of February. Since the first part of the journey was through a safe district of the Transvaal, it was not accompanied by a military escort. Instead, Major Tucker sent out a company of the 80th from Luneburg to join it at Derby, once it neared the Zulu border, to bring it in. The journey was plagued by misfortune from the start. The weather was so bad that the road distintegrated, and the drivers found it impossible to keep the convoy together. By 5 March the convoy was only eight miles from Luneburg, but progress was dreadfully slow. Tucker, worried that the track through the Ntombe valley was the most dangerous part of the journey, sent orders for the escort to march in by nightfall, but the commander misunderstood him, and the 80th promptly arrived at Luneburg, having abandoned the wagons on the road. On the 7th, Tucker sent out Captain David Moriarty with a company-sized detachment of the 80th to bring the wagons in.

Moriarty found the convoy in dire straits. The leading wagons had reached the north bank of the Ntombe, but the stream had become so swollen by the constant rain that it was impossible to get them across. Normally a shallow stream only a few yards across, the Ntombe had risen eight feet to burst its banks, and was a sluggish brown barrier nearly 40 yards wide. Moriarty's men were able to cross using rafting materials they had brought with them, and after securing the party on the bank, Moriarty set off further down the road to find the rest of the wagons. They were spread over several miles of road and, ominously, the drivers reported that during the absence of any escort, small parties of Zulus had harassed them and carried off some of their cattle. It took another day for Moriarty to bring in the stragglers. By that time, the water level had dropped sufficiently for the drivers to get two wagons across, but had then risen again. Moriarty now found his charges spread over both sides of the river, utterly unable to proceed, and overlooked just three miles away by Mbilini's Tafelberg stronghold.

Moriarty made the best of his position. He arranged the sixteen wagons on the north bank into an inverted V, with the base resting on the river. The wagons were not close together, however, while Moriarty's own tent was pitched at the point of the V – outside the protected area. Even now, his troubles did not end. The river continued to rise until it reached half-way up the wheels of the nearest wagons and flooded part of the enclosed area; then it dropped again, leaving an unguarded gap between the wagons and the banks. The laager was a sea of mud and Moriarty's men were exhausted and miserable, having been living in wet clothes since they had left Luneburg. A fatal mixture of despondency and complacency seems to have hung over the camp.

On the 11th, Major Tucker rode out from Luneburg to see for himself the reasons for the delay. He pointed out to Moriarty that the laager was not secure, and urged him to cross the river forthwith. Moriarty replied that he was doing his best, and with that Tucker returned to Luneburg. Later that day, a party of friendly Africans were allowed into the laager to sell mealies; one of the civilian wagon-drivers claimed to recognise Mbilini among them, and reported the fact to one of the 80th's NCOs, Sergeant Booth, but if the information was passed on to Moriarty, he ignored it. When dusk fell that evening, the British position was as divided as ever; Moriarty, with sixteen wagons and 71 men, was on the north bank, while two wagons, guarded by Lieutenant H. H. Harward, Sergeant Booth and 34 men, were on the other.

As Tucker had feared, the stranded convoy proved far too tempting a target for the Zulu. Manyanyoba Khubeka, still living in his retreat in the Ntombe valley, upstream from the drift, had soon become aware of the convoy's vulnerability, and had sent an urgent message to Mbilini, urging him to combine in an attack upon it. It took a day or two for the Zulu to assemble their forces; Mbilini himself had been living at his homestead on the slopes of Hlobane mountain, miles away to the south. From here he assembled a force which consisted of his own followers, abaQulusi, and members of the king's regiments – which were then dispersed at their family homesteads – who lived locally. From Hlobane he moved north to the Tafelberg, to effect a rendezvous with Manyanyoba. Although some British sources insisted that the combined Zulu force numbered as many as 9000 men, it was probably no more than 800 strong, though this in itself was an unusually large *impi* given the conditions that prevailed in the northern sector. If it is true that Mbilini himself scouted out the British position – and it is typical of his audacity – he must scarcely have been able to believe his luck. The British position was divided, the men demoralised, and the laager inadequate. Late on the night of the 11th, the Zulu force moved quietly down from the Tafelberg under cover of darkness.

At one point, it seemed that bad luck might betray them. Sometime in the early hours of the 12th, the British sentries heard a single shot – probably a nervous finger on a sensitive trigger – and called on the camp to stand to. On

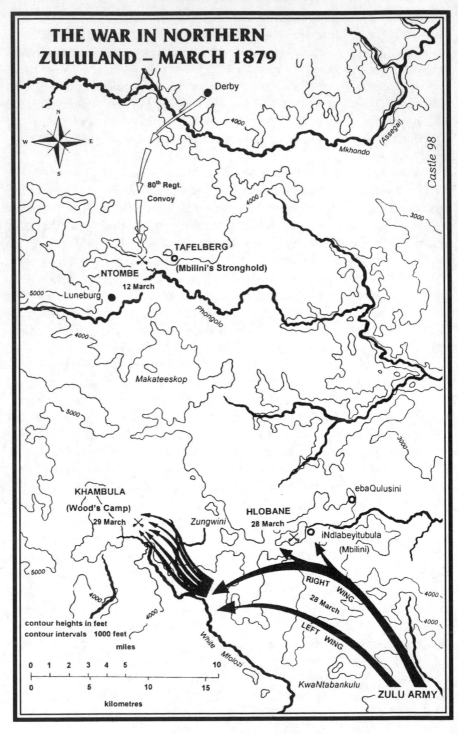

THE WAR IN NORTHERN
ZULULAND – MARCH 1879

Derby

4000

Mkhondo

(Assegai)

Castle 98

3000

N
W E
S

80th Regt.
Convoy

4000

TAFELBERG

×
NTOMBE
(Mbilini's Stronghold)
12 March

5000
Luneburg

Phongolo

4000

Makateeskop

5000

KHAMBULA
(Wood's Camp)
29 March ×

Zungwini

HLOBANE
28 March
×

ebaQulusini

iNdlabeyitubula
(Mbilini)

5000

RIGHT WING
28 March

LEFT WING

4000

4000

contour heights in feet
contour intervals 1000 feet
miles

White Mfolozi

KwaNtabankulu

ZULU ARMY

4000

0	1	2	3	4	5		10

0	5	10	15

kilometres

the south bank, Harward's men turned out of their tents, but the order was countermanded by Moriarty, who seemed dismissive of any danger, and ordered the men back to bed. Harward wisely told his men to sleep with their equipment on, but on the north bank Moriarty's lax attitude encouraged many men to strip off their wet uniforms and huddle naked under their blankets.

The storm broke shortly before dawn. A dense mist hung in the valley, and as it began to lift with the first grey light of day, a sentry on the north bank suddenly spotted a large body of Zulus, who had advanced to within 70 yards of the face of the wagons without being seen. The sentry fired a warning shot, and was immediately met with a ragged volley and a shout of 'uSuthu!' The warriors fired once, then tossed their guns into the long grass and rushed in with their spears. A frantic shout of 'Guards out!' was too late to save most of the men on the north bank, who stumbled out of their tents, half asleep and in various states of undress, as the Zulus were among them. In one of the wagons, two civilian conductors heard the sound of the war-cry, and rolled out from under the canvas; one landed inside the laager, and managed to escape, but the other emerged outside, right in front of the warriors, and was killed. Moriarty himself emerged from his tent at the apex of the laager to find it already surrounded. He blazed away with his pistol, until hit by a thrown spear, which caused him to stagger. As he called out, 'Fire away, boys! I'm done!', he was struck by a shot which killed him.

The position on the north bank was overrun with very little resistance; those soldiers who did attempt to fight were easily surrounded and killed, while the survivors threw themselves into the river to escape. Many were caught and killed on the banks, or shot or killed with thrown spears midstream, while some were swept away and drowned. On the south bank, however, the terrifying sound of the attack at least gave Harward's party a few moments' grace, and Sergeant Booth rallied a number of men, directing their fire at a large party of Zulu who were preparing to cross the river. Once the Zulu reached the south bank, however, Harward's position proved no more defensible than Moriarty's, and Harward himself abandoned his command, riding off to Luneburg. When later called to account for his action, he claimed that he was the only man with a horse, and had gone to raise the alarm. Many of his men, demoralised by the speed of the Zulu attack and the slaughter on the opposite bank, followed his example, and fled towards Luneburg. Sergeant Booth and Lance Corporal Burgess managed to keep a handful of men together, however, and made an orderly retreat, stopping to fire volleys to drive away the pursuing Zulus or to cover the retreat of the survivors. Many of those who tried to get away in ones and twos were, however, overtaken and killed. The Zulu finally abandoned their pursuit less than two miles from Luneburg itself.

The whole battle was probably over within fifteen or twenty minutes, and it had been a dramatic Zulu success. Mbilini had scattered the garrison, and captured the camp and convoy. His warriors proceeded to strip it of everything of value, driving off the oxen, taking the rifles, ammunition and supplies, and thoroughly ransacking what remained. British casualties amounted to 79 dead, including Moriarty, a surgeon attached to the 80th, two white wagon conductors, and a number of black drivers. Mbilini's losses were small for so great a result, a tribute to the careful way the Zulu commanders had planned and executed the attack; the British later found about 30 Zulu bodies along the banks of the river. Although the Zulu carried away most of their wounded – some of whom undoubtedly died later – their total losses were probably still less than those of the British.

The Zulu, moreover, were allowed to loot the camp undisturbed. Harward reached Luneburg and woke Major Tucker, but by the time Tucker had assembled sufficient men to march out to the drift, the Zulu were already in retreat towards the Tafelberg. Lacking enough mounted men to stage an effective pursuit, Tucker resigned himself to the mournful duty of burying the dead. The bodies were strewn across both sides of the river, most of them naked, the majority ritually stabbed and disembowelled. They lay in the mud among spilt and trampled mealies, the corpses of camp dogs, the remains of shredded tents and all the pathetic debris of camp life. Tucker's men collected them together and buried them on the southern bank. In the aftermath of the attack, the behaviour of the senior British ranks at Ntombe was called into account; while Moriarty's death saved him from censure, it was widely believed that the disaster was due to his own laxness, while Harward was later court-martialled for abandoning his men. He was found not guilty, but publicly censured. Sergeant Booth, on the other hand, was deservedly awarded the VC.

In the aftermath of the attack, the Luneburg garrison made frantic efforts to improve its defences, convinced that a major Zulu assault was imminent. In fact, however, the Zulu forces had split after the battle, expecting British reprisals. Manyanyoba departed westwards up the Ntombe valley to the shelter of his caves, while Mbilini retired to Hlobane, taking many of the captured rifles and ammunition with him. Something of a stalemate lasted for nearly a fortnight after the battle, until on the 25th a mounted patrol from Khambula rode through the Ntombe valley, destroying Manyanyoba's abandoned homesteads and crops.

By that time, the war was in any case about to enter a new phase. In the immediate aftermath of Isandlwana, King Cetshwayo had squandered his chance to invade Natal. From the first, he had been committed to a defensive war, waged only to drive the invader off Zulu soil, and in any event his army had needed several weeks to rest and recover after their costly victory. Each day that passed strengthened the British position, however, so that by the end of March Chelmsford was able to plan fresh offensive operations. His first invasion plan had collapsed completely, and he would need to start from scratch, but in the meantime his first priority was to extricate Colonel Pearson's coastal column, which had been besieged in Eshowe since the end of January. By the third week of March, Chelmsford had begun to assemble a relief column at the Lower Thukela Drift, and sent orders to garrisons along the border asking them to make diversionary attacks, in the hope of drawing part of the Zulu force away from Eshowe.

This British build-up was only too obvious to the king and his council, and in the middle of March the Zulu, too, reassembled their army. They were faced with something of a strategic dilemma, for although the British movements on the Thukela were apparent, Mbilini and the Qulusi had repeatedly sent messages to the king asking for the support of the royal regiments against Wood's column. On 24 March, therefore, the main Zulu striking arm – the same regiments that had triumphed at Isandlwana – set out from oNdini, heading north between the White and Black Mfolozi rivers, aiming for Khambula.

Intelligence of this move reached Colonel Wood, but he seems to have disregarded it, perhaps because Chelmsford's instructions to create a diversion allowed him to mount an audacious attack which he had been hoping to do for some time. Ever since Wood had stood on the shoulder of Zungwini mountain at the end of January, and watched the abaQulusi manoeuvring on the slopes of Hlobane opposite, he had been eager to drive them off. His determination had been heightened by the fact that over several weeks of skirmishing, both Mbilini and the Qulusi had repeatedly fled to Hlobane to escape British pressure, and by the fact that the Zulu regularly sheltered large numbers of cattle on the summit – as many as 2000 head, as British reports greedily noted. Wood's men had developed into first-class cattle-rustlers, largely because the Irregulars, the Boer contingent from the Utrecht district, and many of Wood's black auxiliaries all came from farming stock; not only did they appreciate the blow that loss of cattle represented to their Zulu enemy, they hoped to enrich themselves from the loot. Furthermore, on 10 March, the British had secured one of their few diplomatic successes of the war, when, after weeks of dithering, Prince Hamu kaNzibe, an immensely important isikhulu from the north, a member of the Royal House who resented Cetshwayo's ascendancy, had surrendered to Wood, bringing his followers with him. The disaster at Ntombe, coming just two days later, can hardly have reassured Hamu, nor encouraged further surrenders, and Wood was probably keen to provide more tangible proof of the advantages of defection, by supplying Hamu with captured Qulusi cattle.

Accordingly the British set out from Khambula on the night of 27 March in what was little more than a glorified cattle raid. They were divided into two parties, and Wood's plan was that one group, under the command of Lieutenant Colonel J. C. Russell, should block the western end of the mountain, while another, led by Redvers Buller, should circle round and assault the far – eastern – end. Buller's men were to climb to the summit, and drive across the plateau, rounding up the cattle sheltered there, before effecting a junction with Russell's men, and returning to Khambula that same evening. Because Hlobane was just too far from Khambula for infantry to reach and return within a day, Wood employed only his mounted men and black auxiliaries. Wood himself accompanied the assault, but prefered to adopt no more than a supervisory role, leaving the immediate command decisions to his subordinates. To succeed, the plan depended heavily on the element of surprise, and Buller's men went to great lengths to conceal the line of their approach, deliberately shifting their bivouac after dark, and camping without fires and lights.

It is not clear whether the British achieved the degree of surprise they had intended. Certainly, the nature of the fast-moving war in the northern theatre meant that the Zulu commanders were constantly alert for the possibility of surprise attack, while years of insecurity had made Mbilini particularly watchful. Buller's party reached the eastern slopes of Hlobane before dawn, following a cattle track that wound up the shoulder of the mountain before narrowing to a steep, boulder-strewn path which cut up through the cliffs that ringed the summit. If their approach was spotted, the abaQulusi held their fire until Buller's party reached the cliffs, for it was not until then that the British came under a sudden heavy fire from warriors concealed among the rocks, and from behind a loose stone wall which had been built across the path. Most of the fire was ineffective, but two officers of the Frontier Light Horse were shot dead at close range, and several horses were killed, before Buller's men burst through the Qulusi cordon, and gained the summit.

The summit of Hlobane is a gently undulating plateau, a crazy-paving of low boulders, worn almost flat here and there by aeons of erosion. In those days, surface water drained off the summit via a number of shallow streams, and at various points in low-lying hollows the ground was soft, and marked by long, coarse marsh-grass. It is difficult terrain to walk on, and more so to ride across, though most of the Irregulars' horses were sure-footed local ponies, accustomed to rocky conditions. Buller directed several of his troops to dismount, and to take up positions around the plateau to secure the summit, while the auxiliaries set about rounding up the cattle grazing untended nearby, and driving them westwards. In the first light of dawn the British attack seemed to be going well.

This impression, however, was misleading. If Buller had reached the summit through luck and determination, Russell at the far end had been defeated by geography. At the western end, Hlobane mountain came to a point, and abutted a smaller plateau, Ntendeka, 200 feet below. The point where the two interconnected seemed, from a distance, to form a pass of sorts, a narrow, grassy slope framed on either side by impenetrable cliffs. Russell's command had ascended Ntendeka without difficulty, but on reaching the pass found that it was nothing more than a steep staircase of overgrown boulders, and quite impractical for mounted men. Unable to fulfil his orders, Russell halted his command to await Buller's arrival

Several miles away to the east, Buller was unaware that he was unsupported as he drove steadily across the summit. Indeed, he was largely unaware of events outside his immediate vicinity, because only at the very edges of the plateau does Hlobane afford any views of the country below. He was, moreover, coming under increasing Zulu pressure.

It is difficult to avoid the impression that Mbilini and the abaQulusi had lured Buller into a carefully prepared trap. Even if they had not expected to be attacked that morning, they must have been aware of the possibility, and to have made contingency plans. The cattle on the summit were a perfect decoy; once the British were up, they would have extreme difficulty in coming down. Sure enough, large numbers of Qulusi had already assembled below the northern face of the mountain, and were streaming up to harass Buller's rearguard. Another party, swinging round the western end of the mountain, rapidly swept across the foot of the cliffs where Buller had ascended, cutting the line of his retreat. Moreover, what Mbilini and the abaQulusi *izinduna* knew, but Wood had chosen to ignore, was that the great army from oNdini was in the vicinity. It was only a matter of time before it arrived to complete the destruction of the British.

While Buller skirmished on the summit, Wood himself had had an uncomfortable encounter. Accompanied by his staff and one of Cetshwayo's junior brothers, Prince Mthonga kaMpande, who had been a refugee in the Transvaal, Wood had started from his bivouac the night before, and followed Buller's trail towards the foot of the mountain. Here he came across part of Buller's command – Weatherley's Border Horse – who had served as Buller's rearguard, and at some time become lost during the ascent. As both groups reached the foot of the cliffs, they came under a sudden heavy fire from Zulu concealed among the jumble of huge boulders which lay there. The Border Horse took several casualties, and Wood's civilian interpreter, Llewellyn Lloyd, was shot and killed. Wood had been close to Lloyd, and seems to have been shocked and confused by his death. The Border Horse were pinned down among the ruins of a stone cattle kraal, and Wood's Staff Officer, Captain Campbell, offered to go forward and drive out the Zulu marksmen. One, in particular, was causing difficulties, firing from a natural stronghold, where a cleft between two enormous boulders had formed something of a cave. Campbell rushed forward across a few yards of open space, followed by Wood's young orderly, Lieutenant Lysons, and a group of Mounted Infantry from his personal escort. They reached the rocks safely, but as Campbell entered the cleft, he was struck by a bullet fired at close range, which blew the top of his head off, and he fell dead instantly. Lysons and one of the escort stepped across his body, firing into the cave together, killing one Zulu, and wounding another who fled back out through the crevice, and disappeared into the boulders beyond.

The escort carried Campbell's body down to Wood. Wood now seems to have been completely unnerved, losing any sense of wider involvement in the battle. Determined not to abandon the bodies of his friends to the Zulu, who were then skirmishing only a few hundred yards away, he ordered Mthonga's retinue to scrape a shallow grave with their spears, and presided over a hasty burial. He then retired down the mountain, abandoning any responsibility for the battle raging around him.

After the war, Wood's staff came to believe that Mbilini himself had killed Campbell. It is possible; certainly, he had a homestead in the region, and the rocky cleft dsplayed signs of being a carefully prepared refuge. And Mbilini was wounded about this time – two light wounds in the head and upper body – possibly inflicted by the shots fired by Wood's escort.

Elsewhere on the mountain, the British position was continuing to deteriorate. Weatherley's men succeeded in gaining the summit, only to find that much of Buller's rearguard had been forced to abandon its position by the Zulu pressure, and that the summit was alive with small groups of Qulusi, who fired on the larger British groups, and tried to cut off stragglers. Most of Buller's command had retreated westwards, but Buller had detached one troop of the FLH, under Captain Barton, to retire down the original ascent, and bury the bodies of the officers killed on the way up. Barton's men met the Border Horse coming in the other direction, and were told that the path through the cliffs was now highly dangerous, due to the large numbers of Qulusi positioned among the rocks. Any qualms they might have had about following their orders were soon dispelled by the arrival of a messenger with a fresh order from Buller; the main Zulu army had been spotted, and Barton was to retire from the summit as quickly as possible.

The main army had spent the night bivouacked to the south of Hlobane, screened by a long ridge, known as the iNyathi. They had resumed their advance towards Khambula early on the morning of the 28th, marching in two wings, with several miles between them. While the left wing advanced slowly, crossing into the open country south of Hlobane several miles from the mountain, the right wing advanced more rapidly, spilling over the ridge much closer to Hlobane. Here they were alerted to the fight by the sounds of distant firing, and as they rushed forward, Mbilini's men called out from the cliffs above them, directing their advance.

To the British parties at the western end of the mountain, the Zulu approach had been obvious; Russell moved down from Ntendeka on to a nek of land which connected it to Zungwini beyond, and Wood, too, retired to Zungwini. On the summit, however, the Zulus had not been spotted until they were much closer, and their arrival sealed the fate of Weatherley and Barton. The two groups had descended the mountain, and were riding south, when they came under heavy fire from Qulusi, carefully placed in cover on the flats below. Beyond the Qulusi, the right wing of the Zulu army – the uKhandempemvu, iNgobamakhosi and uVe *amabutho* – suddenly came into view, and the uKhandempemvu broke away to attack them. Weatherley and Barton promptly turned about face, and tried to escape round the eastern end of Hlobane, only to have their way blocked by a formidable line of cliffs opening up below them, and by Qulusi streaming down from the mountain. Caught against the cliffs, many were killed, and the uKhandempemvu, coming up behind, completed their destruction. The survivors slipped down through the cliffs and scattered in disarray across the open country beyond. Both Weatherley and Barton were among those killed.

On the summit, meanwhile, Buller was retreating towards the pass at the western end, unaware of its impracticality as an escape route. He was now severely harassed by large numbers of abaQulusi on the summit, and by groups who moved rapidly around the base of the mountain to cut him off. These were joined by the iNgobamakhosi and uVe *amabutho* from the right wing of the main army, and together they made any retreat on the southern side of the mountain impossible. Although the first men to reach the pass connecting Hlobane to Ntendeka – the auxiliaries – managed to clamber down, driving captured cattle with them, the retreat collapsed into rout as the Zulus pressed close upon the mounted men, following behind. Among the steep boulders horses slipped and fell, while the Zulu, hiding among the rocks on either side, darted out to stab or shoot at the riders. The British officers tried repeatedly to organise a rearguard, but most of the men were seized with panic, and simply scattered, trying to find their own way down. Across on Zungwini, Russell's command began to retreat towards Khambula. Many of the survivors fleeing the débâcle followed him, and were severely mauled by the iNgobamakhosi and uVe who pursued them. Small clumps of men and individuals rode pell-mell across country, with the victorious abaQulusi in pursuit. By nightfall, the British had been completely driven from the field.

The battle of Hlobane proved the most serious British reverse of the war after Isandlwana. Their losses amounted to fifteen officers, 79 Irregulars and over 100 auxiliaries killed. The Zulu losses were unknown, but whatever the cost, the battle was a great success. Despite his injuries, Mbilini himself emerged with his reputation further enhanced, since he was widely credited with being the architect of the defence, and it is certainly true that most of the damage had been done to the British by his followers and the abaQulusi; the royal *amabutho* had simply arrived in time to complete the trap.

Curiously, the only white prisoner-of-war taken by the Zulus during the campaign was captured at Hlobane. A trooper of the Border Horse by the name of Grandier, he was apparently separated from his unit during their disastrous retreat, and caught hiding among the rocks on the side of the mountain. He was taken that evening to Mbilini's homestead, where he was questioned by Mbilini himself. He was then sent to oNdini under guard. He was interrogated by the king, and according to his own account was later sent back to Hlobane, so that Mbilini might have the pleasure of killing him. On the way, he overpowered his guards and escaped, and made his way towards Hlobane, where he was later found by a British patrol. Quite why King Cetshwayo did not kill him on the spot he did not say, nor was his explanation of how he, a man exhausted by days of privation, was able to overcome his guard convincing; Zulu sources are unanimous that the king ordered him to be taken close to Khambula and freed unharmed.

That night, the main Zulu army camped to the west of Hlobane, and the following morning it advanced to attack Wood's camp at Khambula. Most of the abaQulusi joined it, but it seems that Mbilini, perhaps because of his wounds, led his own followers north towards the Ntombe instead. The main army was, after all, under the command of senior *izinduna* appointed by the king, and Mbilini's handful of followers were unlikely to affect the outcome either way. In the event, this proved a wise decision, for the main Zulu army was severely defeated at Khambula on the 29th. After several hours of heavy fighting, it was driven away from Wood's camp with heavy losses, and the ensuing British pursuit was so severe that many of the *amabutho* disintegrated. The abaQulusi were chased all the way back to Hlobane, and suffered heavily as a result.

The British victory at Khambula was a serious blow, not only to Zulu fortunes in the northern sector, but in the war as a whole. The Zulu lost any advantage they had won at Hlobane, while the royal *amabutho* were greatly disheartened by the realisation that they could not always triumph as they had at Isandlwana. Within a few days, Khambula was followed by the defeat at Gingindlovu; from the beginning of April, the tide of war turned inexorably against the Zulu kingdom.

The abaQulusi abandoned Hlobane in the aftermath of Khambula. Some went north to the Ntombe, where Mbilini seemed unshaken, and still determined to carry the war against soft targets. Within a day or two of the battle he is said to have attacked the dependents of men known to have joined Wood's auxiliaries, and on 4 April he was one of the leaders of a combined force of 1200 warriors which again ravaged the amaKholwa settlements on the outskirts of Luneburg.

At last, however, his luck ran out. On the 5th, a patrol of seven mounted men of the 80th Regiment, led by Captain Prior and Second Lieutenant Ussher, and accompanied by H. Filter son of Luneburg's Lutheran pastor – and a handful of levies, set out from Luneburg to investigate a report that a handful of Zulus were still lingering in the vicinity, looting cattle and horses. They caught up with a party of four mounted Zulus, driving away cattle, and opened fire at about 400 yards' range, before giving chase. Two Zulus were killed immediately, and another was shot as he fled. This man slipped from his horse, and was speared on the ground by the auxiliaries; he turned out to be Tshekwane kaSihayo, a brother of the famous Mehlokazulu, and an associate of Mbilini. The fourth rider managed to escape, but as his horse descended into the bed of a river, he was seen to stagger in the saddle as he was shot at from above by an auxiliary known as 'Sinnaquie'.

The fourth man proved to be Mbilini. The bullet entered his back above his right shoulder, and came out at his waist. Despite this awful wound, he managed to rejoin his followers, who took him back towards his homestead on Hlobane. Whether he reached it or not is unknown, for within ten days the British were confidently able to report that he had died of his injury.

The defeat at Khambula and the death of Mbilini shifted the focus of the war away from the northern sector. Mbilini's followers were disheartened by his death, while the abaQulusi and Manyanyoba remained largely on the defensive. By the end of May, Lord Chelmsford was ready to begin his fresh invasion of Zululand, and early in June Wood's column moved out from Khambula to join the advance on oNdini. On 4 July the last great battle of the war was fought in plain view of the king's great residence itself, and the Zulu army once more scattered. Cetshwayo retired into the bush country of the Black Mfolozi, while the British razed his great *amakhanda*. To Lord Chelmsford, freed from the ghost of Isandlwana at last, it seemed that the war was over.

And yet, ironically, it was in the northern sector that the last resistance flickered on. The abaQulusi refused to submit until it was confirmed that the king had been captured, while Manyanyoba, and the survivors of Mbilini's retainers, were reluctant to surrender for fear of retribution. Skirmishing spluttered on until September, when the British, exasperated at their inability to winkle the Zulus out of their caves, finally lost patience and blew several up, with the defenders still inside. Manyanyoba himself finally surrendered on the 22nd, and the British relocated him in an area controlled by one of their client chiefs.

The story of the northern theatre is often overlooked in the wider history of the Anglo-Zulu War, but Mbilini's victories at Ntombe and Hlobane qualify him to be regarded as one of the most successful commanders of the war. His guerrilla tactics, heavily influenced by his Swazi origin, offer a glimpse of what the main Zulu army might have achieved had it possessed the imagination to abandon its tradition of frontal assaults in the open. His early death robbed the Zulu of a dynamic and imaginative commander, who, had he lived, might yet have played a significant role in the latter stages of the war.

7

MEHLOKAZULU kaSIHAYO

'He liked a fight now and then ...'

Among the British in the war of 1879, the names and deeds of many of the middle- and junior-ranking Zulu *izinduna* remained almost entirely unknown. British knowledge of their enemy was limited to the king, his family and his senior councillors. Even by the end of the war, when British troops had marched across the country and accepted the surrender of dozens of important chiefs and thousands of their retainers, they made little attempt to interest themselves in the experiences of the ordinary warriors who had striven so valiantly to resist their invasion.

One exception was a young man whose notoriety among the British dated not to the war – where his exploits would prove commendable enough – but to an incident which took place in the tense months before the British invasion, and was, indeed, cited by the British authorities as one of their pretexts for it. Mehlokazulu kaSihayo was a junior commander of the iNgobamakhosi *ibutho* in 1879, but he had achieved notoriety in British eyes in June 1878, when he had led a Zulu force across the border to arrest two runaway wives of his father, Chief Sihayo kaXongo Ngobese.

The Ngobese family had risen to prominence in the 1850s, during King Mpande's attempts to rebuild the kingdom following the disastrous war of 1838–40. The costly struggle against the Voortrekkers, the split in the Royal House, and subsequent civil war had threatened to shake the kingdom apart, and Mpande had been able to retain the allegiance of many of the regional *izikhulu* only at the expense of relinquishing some of his own powers. Furthermore, the Anglo-Zulu accord of 1843, which had followed the British military occupation of Port Natal, had finally limited the Zulu kingdom's borders to the Thukela and Mzinyathi borders in the south, and put an end to the attempts by successive Zulu kings to control various groups in Natal. And with the subsequent influx of white settlers into Natal came increased economic pressure, as Zululand was inexorably drawn into the periphery of the settler economic framework. The 1850s were the golden years of the Zululand hunter and trader, and Mpande was constantly pestered by whites seeking to gain access to the lucrative markets his people represented, or to his rich hunting grounds.

As a result, Mpande's reign was a long and subtle struggle to restore royal authority in the face of rapidly changing circumstances, and it was to this that the Ngobese family owed their ascendancy. In the 1850s, Mpande placed Mfokazana kaXongo as *induna* over the upper Mzinyathi border. Mfokazana brought a number of his people, the Qungebe, with him, and took control over the groups already living there in the king's name. Mfokazana had close links with both Mpande and the Royal House, and was one of the king's most trusted officials, and his appointment was an indication of the importance Mpande placed on the Mzinyathi border. This is scarcely surprising, since the area straddled the crossing at Rorke's Drift, one of only two main entry points into the kingdom, and one already extensively used by white traders. In general, Mpande's policy was to control white access to the kingdom as much as possible, and through Mfokazana he was able to monitor and manipulate white activity in the area.

Mfokazana apparently died without issue, and his estate passed to his brother, Sihayo. In the 1850s, when the Royal House was split by a bitter succession dispute, Sihayo had been astute enough to back Prince Cetshwayo before the latter's comprehensive victory at 'Ndondakusuka in 1856, and was allowed to continue in his post as a result. Indeed, Sihayo and Cetshwayo became close personal friends, and their destinies remained linked for the rest of their lives. When Cetshwayo became king in 1873, he confirmed Sihayo's post as royal representative on the Mzinyathi border.

The importance of that role had grown steadily with the increase in white traffic over the years. Although he was dependent on Cetshwayo's patronage, Sihayo's position had afforded him considerable autonomy, and his personal power and prestige had grown through the links he had cultivated with the white world on his own account. He had acquired guns, horses and several wagons, enjoyed dressing in European clothes, and was known to visit missionary friends and dine at their table. His affluence was evident in his personal homestead, kwaSokhexe, which was wryly named after a game in which the participants scratched a maze in the dust, then tried to trace their way out – a comment on its size and complexity – and which nestled in a hollow on the slopes of the Ngedla hill, overlooking the Batshe stream. The Batshe was a shallow tributary of the Mzinyathi, and its valley was renowned for its fertility. When British troops ravaged the area in 1879, they commented on the number of mealie fields bordering the stream, and the richness of their crop.

Mehlokazulu was born to Sihayo sometime in the mid-1850s. Little is known about his early life, except that he was enrolled into the iNgoba-makhosi *ibutho*, which Mpande had begun to collect together as cadets in the last years of his reign. The iNgobamakhosi were not formally enrolled as a regiment until after the old king's death, and indeed, because they were the first regiment formed by Cetshwayo, he always had a particular affection for them.

Cetshwayo, a more vigorous man than his father, had little time for the subtle policies of regeneration which Mpande had pursued, and his attempts to establish his authority were more forthright. Like Mpande, Cetshwayo disapproved of young men seeking excuses to avoid service in the *amabutho*, or of being kept home by their local chiefs, and this was reflected in the size of the iNgobamakhosi, which some British sources estimated was as much as 6000 strong. When Cetshwayo built his new *kom'khulu*, or great place, oNdini, on the Mahlabathini plain, he appointed the iNgobamakhosi as one of those regiments privileged to be quartered there. This was an honour resented by the more senior regiments, such as the uThulwana – in which the king himself had served – which were also based there, and which were composed of much older men. Friction between the two regiments was commonplace, and the uThulwana complained frequently to the king that the insolent youngsters of the iNgobamakhosi failed to show them the respect their age and status afforded them.

Of course, the *amabutho* were only summoned in their entirety for a few months of the year, and for the most part only a few companies of the iNgobamakhosi were called up to serve the king. It is no coincidence, however, that Mehlokazulu was one of a handful of individuals picked out from among them to attend the king in person. Mehlokazulu and a few of his companions – all the sons of important chiefs – were charged with fetching water for the king from a particularly pure stream on Hlopekhulu mountain, several miles away from oNdini, and then assisting the king at his ritual ablutions in his most private quarters. They even carried out this service when the king performed cleansing ceremonies in the hut of the *inkatha yezwe ya'kwaZulu*. To attend the king under such circumstances was a position of enormous trust, and reflected the regard which Cetshwayo retained for Mehlokazulu's father, Sihayo.

Mehlokazulu also held a command within his regiment. Although the senior commanders of new regiments were appointed from older men selected by the king, junior officers were generally selected from among young men within the regiment itself who showed initiative and daring. Mehlokazulu certainly possessed those qualities, and his standing would undoubtedly have counted in his favour. The extent of his authority is uncertain, but he probably commanded at least a company, and possibly a section of several companies, who had served together at one of the regional *amakhanda* as cadets.

Almost certainly, therefore, Mehlokazulu was involved in a famous clash between his regiment and the older uThulwana, which took place at the annual umKhosi, or harvest ceremonies, at the end of 1877. The initial reason for the clash was a result of the lingering tension between the two regiments, but reflected wider rifts within the country. The uThulwana were married men, and frequently had their wives visit them in huts they shared with the 'boys' of the iNgobamakhosi. As a result, the younger warriors were often expected to wait outside the huts while the uThulwana were entertaining. When the iNgobamakhosi taunted the uThulwana about this, the uThulwana complained to the king. At a meeting of the royal council, the senior commander of the uThulwana, one of the king's most senior advisers, Mnyamana Buthelezi, passed dismissive comments about the iNgobamakhosi, prompting the iNgobamakhosi's commander, Sigcwelecwele kaMhlekehleke, to mutter, 'You shall see when we go out!'

Later, when the two regiments were formed up in the great central space of the royal homestead, and about to march out to take part in the ceremonies, congestion erupted at the gateway. A section of the uThulwana, the iNdluyengwe, was just leaving when the uVe, a young regiment incorporated into the iNgobamakhosi as their vanguard, came up and tried to push their way through. A stick-fight broke out, and both regiments rushed to support their comrades. The news was immediately carried to the senior commanders, including Hamu kaNzibe, Cetshwayo's brother, who was also a commander of the uThulwana, and who was not entirely reconciled to Cetshwayo's rule. Hamu was deeply insulted that Cetshwayo's favourite regiment had dared to attack his men, and he gave the order for the uThulwana to take up their spears. It was forbidden for regiments to take spears to the umKhosi, because in the heated atmosphere of the ceremonies stick-fights were common, but the uThulwana, who spent a good deal of time at oNdini, had their spears in their huts. The iNgobamakhosi, however, had left theirs at home. The uThulwana quickly dispersed to collect their weapons, and advanced out of the gate towards the iNgobamakhosi, singing a war-song. The unsuspecting iNgobamakhosi, not realising the uThulwana were fully armed, rushed to attack them, but soon discovered their mistake. They broke up into groups and scattered across the Mahlabathini plain, trying to find refuge in the royal homesteads there, which were already full of men from other regiments. The fighting continued for most of the day, despite attempts by the king's messengers to stop it; the iNgobamakhosi attacked every man wearing a headring, and the uThulwana every man without. It was not until nightfall that the uThulwana were called off. By that time at least 70 iNgobamakhosi had been killed, and some accounts put the figure as high as 200.

The incident caused a sensation within the kingdom, but most of the country sided with Hamu, and judged the matter the king's fault for trying to 'shove in' the iNgobamakhosi with the uThulwana, to whom oNdini belonged by rights. The king was forced to fine each individual member of the iNgobamakhosi a beast, and Sigcwelecwele was also fined. Since it was no longer possible for the two regiments to share the same *ikhanda*, the iNgoba-makhosi were moved to kwaHlalangubo, a homestead nearer the coast.

The incident had a number of important long-term consequences, not the least of which was a further deterioration in the relationship between Hamu and Cetshwayo. Significantly, Hamu was the only important member of the Zulu Royal House to defect to the British during the course of the 1879 war. Moreover, it exaggerated the gulf between the most senior men in the kingdom, the councillors and commanders, like Mnyamana, who had risen to prominence in Mpande's reign, and the younger generation of men such as Sigcwelecwele, who were favourites of the king. This tension was to have no small impact on the fortunes of Sihayo and his sons. On the whole, however, although shamed by the king's censure, the iNgobamakhosi emerged with its regimental pride enhanced by this demonstration of its reckless and aggressive spirit.

Mehlokazulu himself does not seem to have suffered as a result. Indeed, as a young man, he apparently enjoyed the advantages which his father's position afforded him. Sihayo's trading network allowed Mehlokazulu access to horses and guns, and he was apparently a good shot. He had something of a bad reputation among the Natal border traders, and this probably reflected the fact that he was not intimidated by white skins, and would not be cheated. He belonged to a generation fast losing the awe in which their fathers held the white world, and who regarded the economic activities of the whites as merely another aspect of Zulu life, to be met with on an equal basis. Moreover, Mehlokazulu was undoubtedly conscious of the prestige of the Ngobese family, and was prepared to act vigorously to defend it. More than family honour was at stake, since the economic wellbeing of the Qungebe was dependent on a degree of respect, and reflected wider aspects of economic rivalry on the borders. On one occasion a group of Transvaal Boers complained to Cetshwayo that Mehlokazulu had been responsible for the theft of some of their stock; Mehlokazulu refused to return it, denying the Boer claim, and pointing out that the Boers were grazing on Zulu land. Cetshwayo supported Mehlokazulu, and the matter was dropped.

Such undercurrents may well have formed a backdrop to the incident which first brought Mehlokazulu to the Natal authorities. In July 1878, while the chief himself was attending the king at oNdini, two of Sihayo's wives fled from kwaSokhexe, and took refuge among the people living beyond the Mzinyathi river, across the border in Natal. Both women had been unfaithful, and one was indeed pregnant by her lover. Moreover, she was also accused of trying to bewitch Sihayo. These were heinous offences according to Zulu custom, and the women had clearly decided to take advantage of Sihayo's temporary absence to escape the consequences. They had, however, underestimated the anger and determination of his household, for they had moved only a mile or two beyond the river.

On the morning of the 28th, the people of a household of a black Border Policeman by the name of Mswagele, situated a few miles below Rorke's Drift, found themselves surrounded by a force of 30 mounted Zulu, mostly armed with firearms, and up to 200 others on foot, armed with shields and spears. The Zulu were led by Mehlokazulu, his brothers Bhekuzulu and Mkhumbikazulu, and their uncle Zuluhlenga, and they informed Mswagele that they had come looking for one of Sihayo's wives. Mswagele's people showed some inclination to resist, but were overawed by the Zulu, and the woman was dragged out and across the river to Zululand, where she was put to death. The following day, Mehlokazulu again crossed the Mzinyathi, and arrested a second woman, this time at the homestead of another border guard, Maziyana. She, too, was taken back across the river and killed.

Settler society in Natal was outraged. Hot pursuit actions, in which officials on either side hunted and apprehended suspects seeking sanctuary across the border, were not unknown; but although Mehlokazulu was not accused of harming any Natal citizens during these incidents, his actions were unduly harsh. Whereas adultery among a chief's household was liable to be punished by death, it was more usual for offenders to be disgraced and turned out. Mehlokazulu's uncompromising response may well have been the result of a desire to maintain a strong stance in the light of a dispute over *ilobolo* – the so-called 'bride-price' payments – and his family's wider involvement with those living on the other side of the river.

Whatever the real cause, the incident came at a time when tension between the British authorities and the Zulu kingdom was running high, and Mehlokazulu's raid confirmed British suspicions that any peaceful accord with the Zulus was impractical.

The Natal authorities had demanded Mehlokazulu be surrendered to them for trial shortly after the incident, and when the British later presented their ultimatum to King Cetshwayo, Mehlokazulu enjoyed the distinction of being one of only two men whose deeds were cited by name as the cause of the crisis (the other was Mbilini waMswati).

The Natal demands placed Cetshwayo in a quandary. It seemed absurd that the British would be prepared to go to war over such a trivial issue, but the concentration of British troops on the borders suggested otherwise. Many of the king's more senior advisers, including Mnyamana and Hamu, were indignant that the kingdom stood at risk from the actions of Sihayo's 'foolish boys', and argued that Mehlokazulu should take the consequences of his own actions. Some went so far as to jostle and abuse Sihayo in the king's council itself. Mehlokazulu found it expedient to flee his home and take refuge with Mbilini, in the remote northern part of the kingdom. Yet Cetshwayo felt that he could not abandon Sihayo, a long-standing friend and supporter, whose son was himself a royal favourite. Moreover, any move to do so would surely be seen as a tacit acknowledgement of British authority. The iNgobamakhosi *ibutho*, in any case, were outraged that one of their own should be handed over without a fight, and refused to give him up. Although Cetshwayo therefore offered to pay a fine in cattle as compensation for the incidents, he could not give in to the British demand to surrender Mehlokazulu himself.

It is doubtful whether it would have made much difference, even if he had. Frere was, by this time, determined on armed confrontation, and other aspects of the British ultimatum were equally – and deliberately – unacceptable.

The British ultimatum expired on 11 January 1879, and the Anglo-Zulu War began.

When the king assembled his army in the second week of January, Mehlokazulu returned to join his regiment. Sihayo, too, had reported to the king at oNdini, but since kwaSokhexe lay directly across the line of any British advance from the Rorke's Drift road, he left another son, Mkhumbikazulu, to organise his adherents in defence of their homes and crops.

Sihayo's suspicions of British intentions were well-founded. The British Centre Column, accompanied by Lord Chelmsford himself, crossed the Mzinyathi at Rorke's Drift on 11 January. Chelmsford felt that some demonstration against Sihayo was necessary, given the terms of the ultimatum, and on the 12th he mounted a foray against kwaSokhexe. Mkhumbikazulu commanded a Zulu force which took up a position among the boulders lying at the foot of the Ngedla mountain, a mile or two below the homestead, but after a stiff fight, they were driven out. Mkhumbikazulu himself, and 30 or 40 of Sihayo's followers were killed, for negligible British loss. Once the skirmish was over, the British ransacked Sokhexe in a leisurely way, then set it on fire, before returning to Rorke's Drift.

Chelmsford's attack on Sokhexe was to profoundly influence the course of the war. Although the king had assembled the *amabutho*, he and his councillors were still undecided as to how to proceed. They hoped that the war might still be averted by last-minute negotiation, but when Chelmsford began attacking homesteads, it was immediately clear that the British could not be placated. Moreover, it confirmed the council's suspicion that the Centre Column was the greatest threat. As soon as news of the incident arrived at oNdini, therefore, the assembled regiments were instructed to perform the necessary rituals to prepare them for war. Once these were finished, the king called out pairs of regiments composed of men who were close together in age, and directed them to challenge one another to determine who would achieve the most in the coming fight. The iNgobamakhosi were ordered to challenge the uKhandempemvu, and later the uNokhenke the uMbonambi, and it is no coincidence that these regiments all played a prominent part in the coming campaign.

The army left oNdini on 17 January and moved slowly westwards, taking several days to reach the front. Since the theatre of operations included Sihayo's territory, Sihayo was present with a handful of mounted scouts. Lord Chelmsford's advance, too, had been slow, hampered by the weather, and it was only on the 20th that he had advanced to establish a new camp, some twelve miles from Rorke's Drift, beneath a distinctive rocky outcrop known as Isandlwana. By the 21st, the two armies were manoeuvring within twenty miles of each other, but whereas the Zulu high command knew of Chelmsford's whereabouts, the latter had only the vaguest impression of Zulu movements.

At about 12 noon on the 22nd, a troop of cavalry from the camp at Isandlwana gave chase to a group of Zulu herdboys driving cattle, and, on cresting a rise, suddenly found themselves staring down at the assembled mass of King Cetshwayo's army. Mehlokazulu himself left a very vivid account of the subsequent battle, and captured the shock of that first encounter:

> The Zulu regiments were all lying in the valley ... but the [uKhandempemvu] made their appearance under the Ngutu range, and were seen by the mounted men of the English forces, who made at the [uKhandempemvu], not seeing the main body of the army. They fired, and all at once the main body of the Zulu army arose in every direction, on hearing the firing ...

It was immediately clear to every warrior who glimpsed the British incursion that there could be no further waiting. The uKhandempemvu rushed out of the Ngwebeni valley, drawing the rest of the *amabutho* behind it. There was no time for the last-minute pre-battle rituals, nor for any advice from the senior commanders. In those first few minutes, it was left to regimental commanders to shake their forces into some sort of order, and even before they came in sight of the camp, they had taken up the traditional 'chest and horns' formation. The iNgobamakhosi, and the young regiment incorporated with them, the uVe, streamed out to form the left horn of the army. As they moved across the iNyoni heights, descending on to the plain and in clear sight of the British camp, the iNgobamakhosi encountered an isolated British rocket battery, and easily overran it. Beyond, closer to the camp, was a piquet of mounted Natal Volunteers:

There the iNgobamakhosi ... came in contact with two companies of mounted men. This was on the left ... we were on the heights looking down. Some of these mounted men had white stripes up their trousers (carbineers), there were also men dressed in black ... The English force kept turning and firing, but we kept on; they could not stop us. But on the side of this little hill there is a donga, into which the mounted men got, and stopped our onward move there: we could not advance against their fire any longer. They had drawn their horses into this donga, and all we could see were the helmets. They fired so heavily we had to retire; we kept lying down and retiring again ...

As Mehlokazulu's account suggests, the speed of the Zulu attack had taken the garrison by surprise, and the British had advanced some way from the camp, forming up in extended order, and covering a wide front. Nevertheless, for a while, the intense British fire caused both the chest and the left horn to stall in their attack. Gradually, however, the Zulu began to outflank the British right, and the British position became too extended. Mehlokazulu himself described the British collapse:

On seeing us retire towards the Buffalo [i.e. attempt to move around the British flank], they retired on the camp, fearing lest we should enter the camp before they could get to it, and that the camp would not be protected. All the troops had left the camp to come and attack us, but on seeing us retiring on the camp as we did so, they also retired on the camp...
... When the soldiers retired on the camp, they did so running, and the Zulus then intermixed with them, and entered the camp at the same time. The two wings then met in the rear of the camp, and those who were then in the camp were blocked in, and the main body of the Zulu army was engaged in chasing and killing all the soldiers ...

The British collapse was sudden and devastating. Individual companies tried to draw together to make a stand below Isandlwana, but the press of Zulus was too great. Mehlokazulu described the desperate nature of the fighting:

When the carbineers reached the camp they jumped off their horses, and never succeeded in getting on them again. They made a stand, and prevented our entering the camp, but things were getting very mixed and confused; what with the smoke, dust, and intermingling of mounted men, footmen, Zulus, and natives, it was difficult to tell who was mounted and who was not. The soldiers were at this time in the camp, having come back from the front ... They were firing on the wings of the Zulu army, while the body of the army pushing on the wings also succeeded, and before the soldiers knew where they were, they were surrounded ... They were all killed, not one escaped ...

... Some Zulus threw assegais at them, others shot at them; but they did not get close – they avoided the bayonet; for any man who went up to stab a soldier was fixed through the throat or stomach, and at once fell. Occasionally when a soldier was engaged with a soldier in front with an assegai, another Zulu killed him from behind ...

To add an apocalyptic touch to the last dreadful moments of the camp, the moon passed across the face of the sun in a partial eclipse, and an eerie half-light fell across the battlefield.

Mehlokazulu himself was clearly in the thick of the fighting, though his own long and detailed account includes surprisingly few references to his own activities. Indeed, when he was interviewed by the writer Bertram Mitford a few years after the war, Mitford found Mehlokazulu too polite to dwell on his own heroism. 'As to whether he had killed many men at Isandhlwana,' recalled Mitford, 'he supposed he must have killed some one, but there was a great deal of confusion.' Nevertheless, Mehlokazulu emerged from the battle with his reputation as a warrior enhanced among his fellow Zulu, a sure sign that he had been heavily involved. Indeed, in later years Mehlokazulu would occasionally allow himself to tease the BaSotho chief Hlubi about their respective roles in the battle. Hlubi had commanded a troop of African horsemen, fighting for the British, which had been part of the force holding the donga against the iNgobamakhosi; Mehlokazulu enjoyed the recollection of the sight of Hlubi's horsemen in retreat, and sometimes claimed that he had chased the chief personally – and almost caught him. This must indeed have been a memory to savour, for after the war the British set Hlubi up as one of their appointed chiefs to rule Zululand – and the chief he displaced was Sihayo.

The battle of Isandlwana proved an extraordinary victory, but the price paid by the ordinary warrior was brutally high. Over a thousand Zulu were killed in the immediate vicinity of the camp – 'Zulus died all around Isandhlwana,' commented Mehlokazulu – and at least as many were wounded, some sustaining terrible injuries from the heavy-calibre British rifle fire and shellfire. The dead were dragged into the grain pits of nearby homesteads, or into dongas, and covered over, while the wounded faced long and agonising journeys back to the friends and relatives who would tend them. Once the last resistance in the camp was overcome, the Zulu ransacked the tents and wagons, carrying away anything of military value, smashing open crates of supplies, and cutting the tents into useful lengths of canvas. The British dead were stripped of some of their clothing, as those who had killed in battle were required to wear something of their victim's until they had undergone cleansing rituals. By late afternoon, the army was retreating slowly towards the Ngwebeni valley. When Lord Chelmsford and his force returned that night, they found nothing but devastation.

It took several days for the army to return to oNdini, and many of the exhausted warriors did not trouble to report to the king, but simply went home. Those who did arrive at oNdini could not be reviewed by the king until they had been cleansed of the polluting effect of blood. When at last the king reassembled the army to discuss the campaign, there was earnest argument among the *izinduna* as to which regiment had been the first to penetrate the British line. The iNgobamakhosi jealously claimed this honour, but after weighing the facts, the king recognised that it had been the uMbonambi *ibutho* who had been first into the tents, and those men of the uMbonambi who had killed an enemy in the fight were permitted to wear the coveted *iziqu* necklace, made of small, interlocking wooden beads, which signified particular courage in battle.

In the aftermath of Isandlwana, the army needed to rest, and the king allowed the *amabutho* to stand down. It is not clear if Mehlokazulu returned to the ruins of kwaSokhexe, and in any case most of Sihayo's dependants had withdrawn from the border, and taken refuge in caves, out of reach of British patrols. Nevertheless, in the weeks after the battle, there was occasional skirmishing, as both sides crossed the river in small parties to loot and burn deserted homesteads on the other bank. Several British patrols were sent out towards Isandlwana to investigate the possibility of burying the dead, but they were carefully watched by Zulu scouts, and on several occasions fired upon. Perhaps Mehlokazulu was involved in the incidents, or perhaps he was among the trickle of Zulus who braved the terrifying spectacle of the dead to visit Isandlwana, and pick over the remains of the camp. Certainly, his family recalled that in later years Mehlokazulu's homestead contained an interesting selection of European items.

By March, it was clear that the war was about to enter a new phase. Isandlwana had effectively scotched Chelmsford's original invasion plan, and of his three offensive columns, one had been repulsed, another was besieged at Eshowe near the coast, and only the third – Wood's column, in the north – remained active. Nevertheless, by the middle of the month, it was clear to Zulu scouts that the British were assembling new forces on the border.

The king's response was to summon the *amabutho* again, and on 24 March, the same army which had triumphed at Isandlwana set out to 'eat up' Wood's column.

The army marched slowly, apparently in two columns, with the younger regiments – the uVe, iNgobamakhosi and uKhandempemvu – forming the right wing. On the night of the 27th, it bivouacked at the headwaters of the Black

Mfolozi, masked from Wood's camp at Khambula hill, less than 30 miles away, by a high ridge known as the iNyathi. Early on the morning of the 28th, the right wing was alerted by the sound of distant shots to a skirmish taking place beyond the iNyathi. The young *amabutho* moved forward, crossing the ridge, to see fighting going on along the summit of a flat-topped mountain in front of them. This was Hlobane, the stronghold of a local Zulu group, the abaQulusi, and Colonel Wood had decided to assault the mountain that morning.

The left wing of the Zulu army seems to have been too far off to be drawn into the fight, but the right wing, with the typical recklessness of the young *amabutho*, ran forward to join the battle, which was already by that time far advanced. The British troops had been drawn on to the mountain, and then cut off by the abaQulusi, and had scattered into small groups, trying to find a way down. As the right wing approached, Zulu on the sides of the mountain called out to them, directing their approach. One regiment, the uKhandempemvu, split off to the right, to attack groups retreating down the eastern end of Hlobane, while the uVe and iNgobamakhosi moved across the foot of the mountain towards the western end. The uVe, in the van, arrived in time to kill some of the British stragglers fleeing pell-mell across country, but the iNgobamakhosi took little part in the fight. Nevertheless, Mehlokazulu recalled proudly that 'they had beaten the Maqulusi, and succeeded in getting all the cattle in the whole neighbourhood which were there, and would have taken away the whole had we not rescued them'.

That night, the Zulu army moved a few miles west of Hlobane, and bivouacked for the night. The following morning, it moved off in an ordered manner to attack Khambula.

Even before it began, both sides were acutely aware of the importance of the coming battle. Certainly, the British could not afford another defeat of the magnitude of Isandlwana, while the king and his advisers realised that, with the British again mustering on their borders, their only hope of bringing the war to a successful conclusion lay in achieving just such a victory, and as quickly as possible. Moreover, both sides had learned a good deal from Isandlwana and Rorke's Drift. While the king had instructed his men under no circumstances to attack entrenched positions, Wood's hopes of success rested on them doing exactly that.

When the army was still some miles away from Khambula, the commanders brought it to a halt, and the men were ritually prepared for battle. Even as they formed up once more and began to advance, there was still the possibility that it might bypass Khambula, and strike instead at the exposed frontier towns along the Transvaal border. For a while Wood feared it was doing just that, until the great columns suddenly shifted their line of advance, and swung towards Khambula. Quite why they did this, in flat contradiction of the king's orders, remains a mystery, but it had much to do with the perception of regimental and junior commanders that it was their duty to attack the enemy wherever they encountered them. As at Isandlwana, the grand intentions of the senior Zulu generals counted for little when the enemy was in plain sight in front.

Wood's position consisted of a series of interconnected redoubts and laagers, lying across the top of a ridge. When the army was still several miles away, it split, one wing moving out to form the right horn, circling round to the north of the camp, while the left horn and chest manoeuvred into position to the south and east.

The uVe and iNgobamakhosi made up the right horn, and again Mehlokazulu was with his regiment. Once they had encircled the camp, the two regiments halted about a mile from it, to the north, apparently waiting for the rest of the army to come into position, out of sight, on the southern side of the camp. Then, at about 1.30 p.m., the right horn suddenly moved forward, throwing out skirmishers to screen what appeared to be a full attack. Afterwards, Wood's African scouts suggested that this was the result of the rivalry between the younger regiments, born at Isandlwana, and that the iNgobamakhosi was reluctant to lose the prestige of being the first to attack to its great rivals, the uKhandempemvu, who were on the opposite horn. Perhaps this was so; Mehlokazulu lamely explained that 'we thought the Zulu army was not far off, but it appears that the main body had not yet got up'.

Whatever the cause, that first move cost the Zulu the battle, and probably the war. Watching the awe-inspiring sight of the regiments deploying, Wood had been worried that his firepower would be inadequate to meet a co-ordinated attack on all sides. When he saw the right horn advance unsupported, however, he spotted his chance, and immediately ordered his mounted men to sally out and provoke the iNgobamakhosi and uVe into a full-scale attack. By doing so, he hoped to be able to direct his fire – particularly his artillery – at each thrust in turn, rather than being assailed on all sides.

And he achieved just that. Mehlokazulu's account of the subsequent fighting is heavy with the shock of defeat:

> The horsemen galloped back as hard as they could to camp; we followed and discovered ourselves almost close to camp, into which we made the greatest possible efforts to enter. The English fired their cannon and rockets, and we were fighting and attacking them for about one hour. I mean the Ngobamakosi regiment. Before the main body of the Zulu army came up, we, when the Zulu army did come up, were lying prostrate – we were beaten., and we could do no good. So many

were killed that the few who were not killed were lying between dead
bodies, so thick were the dead ...

The sound of the repulse of the right horn brought the rest of the army
forward to attack, and for over four hours the Zulu tried to force a way into
the camp. On several occasions they came close, capturing one of Wood's
outlying laagers, but they were never able to co-ordinate their attacks properly
after that first disaster. Despite their losses, the iNgobamakhosi rose up from
their cover at one point, and made another determined assault, but to no
avail. Each attack was greeted by a hail of shrapnel and rifle fire. By late afternoon the army was exhausted, and began an orderly retreat. Wood was determined to make the most of his success, and ordered his mounted men to
drive the Zulu from the field. In one of the most ruthless actions of the war,
the mounted men cut down the Zulu without mercy, and the retreat collapsed
into a rout. As Mehlokazulu observed: 'At the conclusion of the fight we were
chased by the English forces over three ridges, and were only saved from
complete destruction by the darkness. I myself only just escaped.'

Khambula would prove a mortal blow to the Zulu army, and its morale
would never recover. Mehlokazulu had a realistic appreciation of where the
fault lay:

> It was unfortunate for the Zulus that the Ngobamakosi regiment should
> have marched quicker than was expected; we had no intention of
> attacking the camp, but were drawn on to do so by the mounted men
> before the main body of the Zulu army came up. The regiments were
> anxious to attack, but we went there cross, our hearts were full, and we
> intended to do the same as at Isandhlwana [sic] ...
>
> We acted contrary to instructions at Isandhlwana, and were
> successful; and then we acted contrary to instructions at Kambula [sic].

The night after the battle was a miserable one for the army. The survivors
drifted through the dark countryside, avoiding British patrols, and carrying
those wounded they could. Nearly a thousand bodies lay around the laager,
many badly mutilated by shellfire, while hundreds more lay out on the line of
retreat. Perhaps 2000 had died in all, and as many as a thousand more escaped
with terrible wounds that would prove fatal over the following days and
weeks. Mnyamana Buthelezi, the senior *induna* present, tried to rally the
men, and keep them together, but most simply refused, abandoning any sense
of discipline, and drifting away to their homes.

It was three months before the king was able to reassemble the army, and
during that time the war passed inexorably into the hands of the British. Lord

Chelmsford relieved Eshowe, defeating the king's coastal forces at Gingindlovu just days after Khambula. By May, the British were reorganising to make a new thrust, stronger than anything the Zulu had yet faced, straight into the heart of Zululand. As the king reflected dolefully to his councillors, 'What is there to stop them?'

The British invasion began afresh in June. This time Chelmsford employed two columns, both larger than anything he had put into the field in January. One, the 1st Division, moved slowly up the coast, burning deserted homesteads as it did so, while the other, the 2nd Division – commanded by Chelmsford himself, and supported by Wood's column – advanced through central Zululand. For two months after Khambula, King Cetshwayo was unable to reassemble his army, for the warriors were exhausted, and reluctant to obey his commands, Instead, the king tried with increased desperation to open negotiations with the British, to ward off the impending catastrophe. But Chelmsford had nothing to gain by diplomacy now, and by the end of June the 2nd Division had reached the heart of the Zulu kingdom.

By this time, the regiments had at last responded to the king's summons, realising that the war had reached a climax. On 4 July, Chelmsford took most of his fighting men across the White Mfolozi, and formed them up in a large square on Mahlabathini plain, less than two miles from oNdini itself. Once again, the Zulu army took up the challenge, and the *amabutho* streamed out from the surrounding *amakhanda*, or rose up from the long grass all around, to attack him. For the first few minutes the attack was as spirited as ever, but it soon faltered when exposed to the full weight of Chelmsford's firepower. Although the warriors were as brave as ever, there were few among them now who had not experienced the terrible hail of fire before, and they no longer attacked with the recklessness of Isandlwana and Khambula.

Nevertheless, there were still several determined attacks, and one, in particular, caused Chelmsford some concern. Part of the Zulu left – the uVe and iNgobamakhosi *amabutho* – rushed into the kwaNodwengu military homestead, which lay only a few hundred yards from Chelmsford's square. Using this to mask their preparations, they charged out to attack the right rear of the British formation. The assault was so fierce that Chelmsford had to move his reserves to support the corner, and the attack wilted under a storm of fire.

Most of the Zulu attacks ran out of steam before they got within 50 yards, however, and once Chelmsford judged that they had lost momentum, he ordered his cavalry, including the recently arrived 17th Lancers, out from the centre of the square. The Lancers mounted an impressive charge which drove the Zulus back to the hills surrounding the plain, where artillery fire broke up any attempt to rally. The cavalry then rode across the plain, killing the wounded, and setting fire to the great royal homesteads, including oNdini itself. By nightfall, Chelmsford had marched back to his camp on the southern side of the Mfolozi.

Once again, the Zulu casualty figures had been high; perhaps 1500 men had been killed and unknown numbers wounded. Many of those who had been wounded close to the square were killed during the pursuit, before they could get away. Mehlokazulu had been present at the battle, and survived, but hardly mentioned it in his account of the war, merely admitting that 'at the Ondine battle, the last, we did not fight with the same spirit, because we were then frightened. We had had a severe lesson, and did not fight with the same zeal.'

The Zulu army dispersed quickly after the battle, while the king himself went into hiding. Lord Chelmsford was convinced, with some justification, that the Zulu were thoroughly beaten, and resigned his command, leaving it to his successor, Sir Garnet Wolseley, to accept the surrender of the chiefs, and to impose terms for peace. Over the next few weeks, *izikhulu* across the country made their way to meet Wolseley, and formally surrender. Only in the northern districts did resistance continue until after Cetshwayo was captured in August.

Both Mehlokazulu and Sihayo were recognised by the British, and arrested. Sihayo was imprisoned at one of the British posts, Fort Cambridge, while Mehlokazulu was sent down under guard to Pietermaritzburg. Since he had been mentioned by name in the British ultimatum – indeed, he was the only man so mentioned who survived the war, since Mbilini had been killed in action – it was felt that the colonial authorities might prefer charges. In fact, although he was held for a while at Pietermaritzburg gaol, and questioned about his role in the war, no charges were forthcoming, and he was released, 'as anyone who gave the matter a moment's thought', the traveller Mitford commented, 'might have foreseen would be the case'.

Sihayo's district had suffered heavily during the war from its proximity to the British base at Rorke's Drift, across the river, and most of the Qungebe had fled away from the border, to take refuge in caves, to avoid the constant British raiding, which had burnt their homes and destroyed their crops. They had begun to return in August, and Sihayo himself was set free by the British and took up residence at Nusu, one of his homesteads that had escaped the torch, to see what remained of his authority.

The Ngobese family were not, however, to be allowed to rebuild their lives undisturbed. Wolseley's post-war settlement, driven by a need to destroy the institutions of the monarchy while at the same time avoiding the expense and responsibilities of outright annexation, was based on the principle of replacing Cetshwayo with thirteen district chiefs, chosen from men who were thought to be sympathetic to British interests. Some were established Zulu *izikhulu*, like Hamu kaNzibe, who had been smart enough to change sides while the fighting was still going on, while others were outsiders. The most notable of these was Hlubi, the chief of a section of the baTlokwa BaSotho, who had fought alongside the British at Isandlwana. Hlubi was given control of a band of land running along the Zulu bank of the Mzinyathi, to serve as a buffer between Natal and the Zulu chiefs beyond. This was, indeed, the very district which had once been ruled over by Sihayo, and the British were happy to see a man they had cast as a notorious enemy dispossessed.

The arrival of Hlubi inevitably caused tension with the Qungebe, who were now his subjects. Hlubi established his homestead in the Batshe valley, near kwaSokhexe, and set about courting the support of local white missionaries and traders. While Sihayo continued to enjoy the backing of the Qungebe, Hlubi was reluctant to act openly against him; but neither could Sihayo afford to antagonise the baTlokwa, endorsed as they so conspicuously were by British authority.

In the event, the issue had been resolved in August, when Mehlokazulu was still in Pietermaritzburg. Mnyamana Buthelezi, who was still regarded as the king's chief minister, sent an *impi* to the border which rounded up and carried off between 400 and 600 head of Sihayo's cattle. Mnyamana had always strongly been opposed to the war, and held Sihayo to blame for allowing his sons to provoke the British. The raid was a punishment for this transgression, and by the time Mehlokazulu arrived back in October, in the hope of rebuilding kwaSokhexe, he found the Qungebe destitute, and his father's authority in tatters. Hlubi, realising that they were now utterly unable to resist, ordered Sihayo and Mehlokazulu to leave the Batshe valley, and resettled them on the borders of his territory, on the slopes of Qudeni mountain, near the junction of the Mzinyathi and the Thukela.

Sihayo and Mehlokazulu lived there for at least two years, until Hlubi again forced them to move on. In 1882, the traveller, Bertram Mitford, found them living just beyond the eastern border of Hlubi's lands, in the uPhoko valley. Mitford provided a vivid picture of Mehlokazulu's philosophical acceptance of their changed fortunes:

> To my inquiries as to how he was getting on since the war, Mehlo-ka-Zulu replied that it hadn't made much difference to him individually; his father had been a powerful chief but now was nobody, and had been driven out of his former country. Still, they managed to live.
> 'Did he regret having fought?'
> 'No, he couldn't exactly say that; he was a young man and he wanted to prove himself as a warrior. He had fought in all the principal

engagements: Isandhlwana [sic], Kambula [sic], and Ulundi, and now he wanted to "sit still".'

'Always?'

'Well, that he couldn't say either; he liked a fight now and then; there was no mistake about it ...'

Indeed, by 1882, fighting was once again brewing. Wolseley's settlement had thrown the tensions which existed within the kingdom into high relief, and Zululand was fast dissolving into pro- and anti-royalist factions. King Cetshwayo himself was held in exile under guard at the Cape, but as clashes between rival factions in Zululand threatened to escalate, the Colonial Office began to consider the possibility of returning Cetshwayo to at least part of his old territory. Both Sihayo and Mehlokazulu remained staunchly loyal to the king; given the antipathy with which the colonial authorities regarded them, they were scarcely likely to be otherwise.

Cetshwayo returned to Zululand in 1883. The British deprived him of a huge chunk of territory along the Thukela and Mzinyathi rivers – known formerly as the British Reserve – on the pretext of providing a sanctuary to the king's political opponents, while in the north, Zibhebhu kaMaphitha, who since the war had quarrelled bitterly with the Royal House, was allowed to retain his territory. The king was at once surrounded on two sides by his enemies, and at the same time prevented under the conditions of his restoration from reviving the *amabutho* system.

Cetshwayo, nevertheless, returned to oNdini, where he rebuilt a new homestead, only slightly smaller than the one destroyed by the British less than four years before. Chiefs with royalist sympathies from across the country began to visit him to pay their respects, and immediately his followers took encouragement from his return to attack their enemies. At the end of March a royalist army advanced against Zibhebhu, only to be utterly routed at the battle of Msebe valley. An open confrontation seemed inevitable, and Cetshwayo decided to throw caution to the wind, and to call up his followers who still recognised their allegiance to their old *amabutho*. Throughout May and June, the king assembled many of his former chiefs and councillors at oNdini, together with several thousand warriors. Sihayo was among those who answered the call; it is not clear whether Mehlokazulu did so, but the iNgobamakhosi had responded in large numbers.

Then calamity struck. On the night of 20/21 July 1883 Zibhebhu made a dramatic night march through the Mfolozi thornbush, and appeared at dawn the next morning over the crest of the hills overlooking oNdini. The royalists were completely taken by surprise, and their regiments collapsed. The Mandlakazi chased them from the field, falling particularly on the middle-aged *izin-*

duna who could not run so fast. The slaughter among the royalist notables was appalling, and afterwards Cetshwayo was able to list no less than 59 *izikhulu*, chiefs and *izinduna* who died that day.

Among them was Sihayo, whose lifelong loyalty to his king had brought him humiliation, destitution, and finally death. He had helped Cetshwayo to escape from oNdini, but was overtaken and killed.

The king fled to the sanctuary of the Reserve Territory, and before he could devise a new policy, the final tragedy struck: on 8 February 1884 he died.

Cetshwayo's heir was his young son, Dinuzulu, who was only fifteen at the time of his father's death. Yet Dinuzulu was a confident and energetic youth, and he immediately took up his father's cause with a fierce determination that disconcerted many of his father's surviving advisers. Indeed, the deaths of so many senior men had opened the way for a younger generation of uSuthu supporters to seize the initiative. They were free of some of the great weight of tradition which made many of their elders, who had grown to adulthood in the days of the country's independence, over-cautious, and they were hardened by years of exposure to the hardships of civil war. They lacked their fathers' awe for the white world, and saw the whites as a political tool, like any other, to be used to advantage. Within a few months the uSuthu had made approaches to the Transvaal Boers to intercede on their behalf. Significantly, one of those who acted as intermediary was Mehlokazulu.

Zululand had not yet been opened to white settlement, and the Boers responded with alacrity, tempted by the prospect of new access to rich grazing lands. In May a Boer commando presided over a ceremony which formally installed Dinuzulu as king, and on 5 June a combined Boer–uSuthu force defeated Zibhebhu's Mandlakazi at Tshaneni mountain, in northeastern Zululand.

After years of defeat, the victory vindicated the aspirations of the Royal House, but the price Dinuzulu would pay was terrible. The Boers laid claim to a huge stretch of Zululand, stretching almost to the sea. The uSuthu protested, but were powerless to resist. Paradoxically, it was the British who came to their aid. After some frantic negotiations, Britain agreed to recognise Boer claims in northwestern Zululand in return for their abandoning their claims towards the coast. In May 1887, Britain formally annexed what remained of independent Zululand.

The final assumption of British authority did little, however, to reassure the Royal House. The new British administration had accepted the guiding principle of the Natal authorities, that the Royal House was the most dangerous threat to peace and security in Zululand. Further attempts to reduce the influence of Dinuzulu merely antagonised the uSuthu, and when, in November 1887, the British allowed Zibhebhu to return to his old lands in northern Zululand, in a deliberate attempt to nullify uSuthu influence, violence broke out within weeks. Dinuzulu and the uSuthu leaders raised their supporters, and took to their strongholds across northern and central Zululand. In a daring attack in May, Dinuzulu routed Zibhebhu under the walls of the British magistracy at Nongoma. Troops were once more rushed into Zululand.

In the confusion, Mehlokazulu, still an ardent royalist, attempted to restore his fortunes. Since the death of his father at oNdini, his position had become desperate. The British refused to acknowledge him as Sihayo's heir, and Hlubi had driven him from his traditional lands. Nor was he particularly welcome among other pro-British chiefs, who were wary of his reputation, and accused him of offences such as cattle theft. Given his straitened circumstances and the need to rebuild his wealth and influence, he may well have been guilty. At the time of the rebellion he was living in the territory of Chief Faku, which lay inside the Boer New Republic, just to the east of Hlubi's territory. When the rebellion broke out, the British called upon their old ally, Hlubi, to support them. Hlubi raised a unit of horsemen, and went to the front to assist the troops, leaving his territory largely undefended. Mehlokazulu promptly gathered some armed followers, and threatened to cross the border and drive Hlubi's people out. In the event, the attack failed to materialise, perhaps because the extent of British support made it a deeply dangerous move, and perhaps because the uSuthu rebellion soon collapsed. By July the British had stormed the uSuthu strongholds, and Dinuzulu and the senior uSuthu leaders had fled to the Transvaal. The Transvaal authorities refused to give them sanctuary, however, and they were handed over to the British, who subsequently tried them for treason, and exiled them to St Helena.

Paradoxically, the defeat of the uSuthu at last allowed the royalists some relief. The British began to question some of the assumptions about their methods of control, and gadually moved away from their catastrophic policies of divide and rule. Instead, they began to subvert traditional means of authority by adopting them as part of their own administration. Instead of supporting only those chiefs who were bitterly opposed to British rule, they set about exploiting those whom the majority of ordinary Zulu still accepted as their traditional leaders. The greatest beneficiaries of this important shift were the uSuthu leaders, who were returned to Zululand in 1894, although Dinuzulu – significantly – was not recognised as king, but as 'government induna'.

Mehlokazulu, too, at last achieved the recognition he yearned for as chief of the Qungebe. He was, in any case, increasingly unwelcome in the New Republic, where a Boer farmer had accused him of insulting his wife, and he had been tried and imprisoned as a result. In 1893 the British offered him the chance to return to his old districts, and take charge of the Qungebe, in the hope that this would ensure his future loyalty.

Mehlokazulu accepted the offer, and for several years the British policy seemed to work. Yet the world of the Zulu was changing rapidly in the last decade of the nineteenth century. With the extension of European control came European taxes, and the pressure on young Zulu men to work, not for their chiefs as they had in days of old, but to travel into Natal or the Transvaal to sell their labour to the whites, to raise the cash necessary to pay the taxes. With the erosion of economic independence came the undermining of traditional forms of authority. In 1897 Britain passed over control of Zululand to Natal, raising the spectre of the country being opened to white settlement. This move was delayed by the outbreak of the Anglo-Boer War, but the Zululand Land Delimitation Commission, which met between 1902 and 1904, opened up almost a third of the Zulu country for white settlement. Inevitably, this land included some of the best farmland in the country, and thousands of Zulu were obliged to abandon lands they had lived upon for generations and to move into overcrowded and impoverished reserves.

Moreover, a series of natural calamities struck Natal and Zululand in the last years of the old century. In 1895 the area had been devastated by a plague of locusts, and the resulting food shortages were compounded by several seasons of drought. Worst of all, however, cattle disease swept through southern Africa, reaching Zululand in 1897, and destroying countless thousands of cattle. To many Africans in the region, it seemed that the very basis of their society was on the point of collapse. Many of them looked nostalgically to traditional leaders, like Dinuzulu, for comfort, and saw the advent of white rule as the source of their misfortune.

Against this background the Natal authorities implemented a poll tax in August 1905, in an attempt to balance their books in the aftermath of the Anglo-Boer War. For many Africans, particularly those who were most exposed to the colonial system in Natal, this was one burden too many to bear. Some groups refused to pay, and when the Natal authorities tried to force them, violence flared. In April 1906 the chief of the Zondi people, Bambatha kaMancinza, living on the Natal side of the Thukela, attacked a police patrol, and fled to take refuge in Zululand, calling upon Dinuzulu and the Zululand chiefs to support him.

While many Zulu sympathised with Bambatha, however, few were willing to risk the wrath of the authorities by openly backing him. Dinuzulu himself had, by this time, accepted the inevitability of European military superiority, and was reluctant to expose his people to further onslaughts. To those chiefs who sent secretly to him for advice, he told them to pay the tax, and 'sit still'. On the other hand, mindful of his responsibility to a man who had offered him allegiance, Dinuzulu was reluctant to act against Bambatha and those who supported him.

The absence of a clear signal from Dinuzulu placed the rebel sympathisers in a quandary. The rebels deliberately invoked the symbolism of the old Zulu kingdom as a rallying cry, and appealed to chiefs who had a long history of support for the Royal House and resistance to European rule. Bambatha took refuge in the inaccessible Nkandla forest, where he managed to persuade the aged Chief Sigananda of the Cube people to assist him. Sigananda was closely associated with the Zulu kings; his father had been a friend of King Shaka, nearly a century before, while Cetshwayo had taken refuge in Cube territory after his defeat at oNdini. Indeed, Cetshwayo's grave lay in Cube territory, and the rebels had made it their rallying point.

The support of Sigananda added huge prestige to Bambatha's rebellion. Sigananda was one of only two significant Zulu chiefs to back the uprising; the other was Mehlokazulu kaSihayo.

Although Mehlokazulu seems to have been pushed into rebellion by circumstance, he had undoubtedly been unsettled by the activities of the Land Delimitation Commission. For long a champion of Zulu independence, he appears to have bitterly resented the final loss of so much territory to the whites, and in 1904 had written to Dinuzulu, warning him that this was just the first step in a British attempt to deprive him entirely of his birthright. When Mehlokazulu was called upon to pay the poll tax in 1906 he failed to comply, pleading ill-health. Already, by that stage, colonial troops were moving on the borders of Mehlokazulu's district, manoeuvring to surround Bambatha in the Nkandla bush, and Mehlokazulu began to fear that he would be attacked. Certainly, his reputation seemed to count against him, and many whites believed he was poised to rebel. Although reluctant to go into armed revolt, Mehlokazulu's position became increasingly desperate, and in the climate of fear and suspicion which followed Bambatha's arrival in Zululand, Mehlokazulu seemed to be pushed towards rebellion. It was about this time that a young missionary, the Reverend A. W. Lee, blundered into a meeting between Mehlokazulu and another local chief, Makafula kaMahawuka, and his account suggests something of the tense atmosphere of the time. Lee called on Makafula to inquire after his health:

> I found that he had a gathering of some kind on his hands. The kraal was crowded with young men, all looking rather war-like in their feathers and beads, and all behaving in a truculent manner. I entered his own hut to find myself confronted by the big chief of the Nqutu area, Mehlokazulu ka Sihhayo [sic] of the Maqungebeni people. We were both taken aback, I, because I had not expected to thrust myself in such distinguished company, and he, because the last thing he wished to see there was a person with a white face. Mehlokazulu was a

Zulu of the old school, a fighting man with a distinguished record ... He glared at me out of his prominent, rather blood-injected eyes, and, turning to Makafula, he asked, 'Who is this white boy? Why does he come here? What does he want?' ... It was an uncomfortable moment. I felt I had blundered into a secret meeting between the two chiefs at which they had been discussing the situation. After-events showed plainly that Mehlokazulu had already made up his mind to rebel against the Government, and that he had visited Makafula in order to gain his adherence to some plan of action.

Whether Mehlokazulu had already decided to rebel is a moot point; probably, he hoped to avoid any involvement in the looming confrontation. The authorities would not allow him to sit on the fence, and he was ordered to supply levies for a force which was being assembled to attack Bambatha. Instead, he fled into the bush with his wives and cattle. When a local magistrate sent messages encouraging him to surrender, he replied simply, 'I can't go back now, I have been surrounded by troops. I don't know what harm I have done.' In early May, he apparently took the precaution of assembling his fighting men in a homestead near the Mangeni gorge – the same area that Lord Chelmsford's forces had searched on the day before Isandlwana, 27 years previously. Here they were joined by disaffected groups from other local chiefdoms. Although Mehlokazulu proceeded to have the men ritually prepared for war, he announced to the assembly that his policy was to wait and see what the white troops would do; he would not go on to the offensive, but would respond if attacked.

Mehlokazulu's fate was sealed in the third week of May. On the 28th, some of his followers, working their way along the foothills of the Qudeni mountain, and in the company of other rebels setting out to join Bambatha in the Nkandla, were intercepted and dispersed in a sharp action at Mpukinyoni. The rebels launched a spirited attack in traditional Zulu style, surrounding the colonial bivouac in the usual 'chest and horns' formation, but suffered heavily in the face of rapid rifle and machine-gun fire.

Mehlokazulu himself was not at Mpukinyoni. Probably, he had stayed behind to see what the colonial troops were doing in his own districts, for on the 27th a column had moved down from Helpmekaar, crossed into Zululand at Rorke's Drift, and advanced towards Isandlwana. After a night camped near the old battlefield, they proceeded to search the Malakatha and Hlazakazi range for signs of rebel activity. The heavy-handedness of the troops on such occasions – they were determined to intimidate waverers into submission – probably forced many of the uncommitted to join the rebels. Mehlokazulu's principal homestead was set ablaze, and the cattle belonging to any homestead which the troops suspected of disloyalty were confiscated. Many people fled to the bush at their approach, which the troops interpreted as proof of their sympathies. Rumours that Mehlokazulu was about to sweep down and attack the column were rife. When the troops spotted several unidentified groups lingering on the Malakatha hillsides, they promptly shelled them for good measure. According to Zulu sources, Mehlokazulu was among one of these groups, with his attendants. The chief was mounted, and the concussion from a shell bursting nearby knocked him off his horse. Although he was unhurt, he was badly shaken; any doubt he may have harboured about the attitude of the colonial forces towards him must have been rudely dispelled. They had knocked him off the fence in no uncertain terms.

Mehlokazulu was now in his fifties, and facing the final crisis of his life. By adopting the rebel cause, he brought to it the considerable weight, not only of his personal reputation as a warrior, but something of the old kingdom's heroic tradition of defiance. Yet he was by this time perhaps not best equipped to take to the field. He had grown stout, and the strain of the previous few months, of living in hiding, of seeing his homesteads destroyed once more by white troops, his cattle taken and his followers scattered, appears to have affected his judgment. While he had never been taken in by European pretensions, he seems to have become bitter towards the whites in old age, and to have been dismissive of the threat they posed. This would prove a fatal misjudgement.

In the aftermath of Mpukinyoni, Mehlokazulu concentrated his followers in the Nkonyeni forest, closer to the Nkandla forest. Colonial troops had been repeatedly sweeping the Nkandla, however, and although it had been difficult, in the extremely harsh terrain, to pin the rebels down, Bambatha's supporters had suffered a number of losses in the ensuing skirmishing. This had been enough to cause Bambatha to abandon Sigananda, and to slip away west, towards the Nkonyeni. Here he managed to effect a junction with Mehlokazulu. The rebel force now apparently numbered 23 *amaviyo*, or companies; although such companies varied considerably in size, this amounted to a significant body, between 1200 and 1500 men. The rebels, however, were reluctant to give up the Nkandla entirely, partly because the colonial forces found it so difficult to track them in it, and partly because old Sigananda's support was of considerable propaganda value. On 9 June, therefore, Mehlokazulu and Bambatha, at the head of the largest rebel concentration of the rising, began to move back towards the Nkandla. Their intention was to slip quietly into the Mome gorge, a refuge so steep and narrow that it was considered almost impervious to assault by white troops.

The rebels reached the mouth of the gorge that evening, after a difficult march. They were reluctant to enter it that night, because of the difficulty of the terrain. Mehlokazulu himself was tired, and insisted that the bulk of the *impi* camp on an open space, nestling among the hills which gave access to the gorge. During the night, the rebel leaders were awoken by a herd-boy, who claimed to have heard the sound of wagon wheels, moving far off in the darkness. Mehlokazulu was convinced that no troops could approach the gorge under cover of darkness, however, and contemptuously dismissed the report. According to the bitter account of one rebel *induna*, Mehlokazulu refused to enter the gorge 'because he was very stout and wore boots and was tired'.

This was a fatal mistake. By good intelligence work, the colonial forces had received news of the rebel approach, and had set out to intercept them, converging from different directions on both the mouth and the head of the gorge. Somehow, keeping good order over impossible terrain, they managed to surround the mouth of the gorge without being detected. Dawn on the morning of the 10th saw a mist hanging at the foot of the gorge. As the rebels began to stir, Mehlokazulu and Bambatha became suspicious, and sent scouts up on to one of the ridges which overlooked their position. The scouts returned to report that there were white troops in position there. Immediately the rebel leaders ordered their men to form into an *umkhumbi* – a circle – to receive last-minute preparations and instructions; but just as they did so, the mist lifted, and their movement was spotted by the troops on either side.

The ensuing action was more of a massacre than a battle. Machine-gun fire and shells suddenly rained down on the rebels from three sides. Bambatha himself apparently panicked, and it was left to some of his junior *izinduna* to try to seize the initiative. Some of the men were formed up under fire and attempted to rush towards the troops, but they were met with a storm of machine-gun fire which broke up their formations, and sent them streaming into the gorge. Within minutes the rebel position collapsed completely. The gorge offered no refuge, however, for while one portion of the colonial troops lined the ridges overlooking the mouth, another had reached the head, and sealed it off as a means of escape. The rebels were now trapped in the dense bush which lined the banks of the Mome stream. Some tried to fight their way out, and were killed; others hid in the bush, only to be flushed out as the troops descended to sweep through it.

Both Bambatha and Mehlokazulu were reported killed. While there are suggestions that Bambatha actually escaped, Mehlokazulu's fate is certain enough. As the troops swept through the bush, he was seen trying to get away; he was dressed in European clothing, and followed by an attendant who was carrying for him a new pair of riding boots. Mehlokazulu was shot dead.

The action at the Mome gorge cut the heart out of the rebellion in Zululand. Over 600 rebels were killed, and the loss of Mehlokazulu was especially dispiriting. Within a few days Sigananda emerged from hiding to surrender to the troops, and the revolt north of the Thukela collapsed. There would be fresh outbreaks, on the Natal side of the border, but they lacked the intensity of the fighting in Zululand.

Mehlokazulu's death was sadly appropriate to a life that had been characterised by a dogged but unequal resistance to white authority. As a junior commander in 1879, Mehlokazulu embodied the spirit of defiance which had taken the old Zulu army to victory at Isandlwana, but he paid the price of his reputation in the post-war years. He suffered persecution, dispossession and hardship as a result of his allegiance to the Royal House, but remained at the forefront of its continued struggle to reassert itself in the face of bitter opposition from the British and their agents. While Dinuzulu himself came to realise that the struggle could never be won in military terms, Mehlokazulu had responded to the impossible conditions of 1906 in characteristic manner.

— 8 —

ZIBHEBHU kaMAPHITHA

'White horse that checks the vanguards'

In September 1882, a meeting was held at Rorke's Drift between British and colonial officials and representatives of some of the great chiefdoms of Zululand. It was one of many such meetings that took place against the background of anarchy which characterised the post-war settlement of Zululand. Afterwards, one of the distinguished participants, the Lieutenant-Governor of Natal, Sir Henry Bulwer, gave a very flattering appraisal of one of the Zulu dignitaries who had been involved in the talks. Bulwer formed the impression that Chief Zibhebhu kaMaphitha of the Mandlakazi was 'beloved by his own people, he is also popular with the Zulus generally. He is a man of energy, courage and strength of mind. He can bring into the field not less than 3000 fighting men, and probably more.'

Years later, another Natal administrator recalled that Zibhebhu 'is regarded as the greatest Zulu general since Shaka. In fact, he was probably Shaka's equal.' Other white traders and officials spoke in admiring terms of Zibhebhu's courage, resolute character, his 'progressive' outlook, and the military skills which led them to call him the 'Napoleon of the North' (i.e. northern Zululand).

Of the many ironies which characterise the history of the Zulu kingdom in the nineteenth century, the colonial attitude towards Zibhebhu is among the most poignant. While King Shaka was vilified by successive generations of white commentators, Zibhebhu was praised for sharing the same military attributes – notwithstanding the fact that Zibhebhu himself had been an imaginative and daring opponent of the British in 1879. The key to understanding this apparent contradiction lay in Zibhebhu's emergence as a military and political force in Zululand in the 1880s. Where once he had been a loyal commander under King Cetshwayo, he later assumed authority with the support of the colonial administration, and became implacably opposed to any re-emergence of the Royal House.

Zibhebhu understood and shared the motives that drove settler society – the European concepts of trade and profit – and to colonial Natal he became a bastion of settler values and aspirations, forward-looking, enlightened, progressive. He was the perfect counter-balance to the dark days of savagery, barbarism, and political and economic self-reliance represented by the old Zulu order; and white Natal therefore saw much to admire when he repeatedly and spectacularly defeated the adherents of the Royal House. Despite his extraordinary personal qualities – courage and a remarkable military flair, tempered with steely ambition and ruthlessness – it remains true that much of Zibhebhu's remarkable career was only made possible by the open support of the colonial and British authorities.

In the bitter years after 1879, of course, there were many in Zululand for whom Zibhebhu's opposition to the Royal House and his obvious alliance with white interests earned him rather less flattering descriptions. Among the supporters of the exiled King Cetshwayo, Zibhebhu and his followers were known contemptuously as *amambuka* – renegades. One of King Cetshwayo's *isigodlo* girls, who later became a Christian, damned him simply as 'a real Judas'.

Although the origins of Zibhebhu's feud with the royal family can be traced directly to the destructive effects of colonial policies, they did nonetheless reflect long-standing tensions within pre-colonial Zululand.

Zibhebhu's followers, the Mandlakazi (*great power*) were a branch of the chiefly line of the Zulu clan itself, and their significance within the kingdom was therefore a reflection of the power and influence of the Royal House itself. The Mandlakazi emerged a generation before Shaka, and Zibhebhu's grandfather, Sojiyisa, was considered a brother to Shaka's father, Senzangakhona. Whether this was a blood relationship or a genealogical one is not entirely clear; in some versions of the story Senzangakhona's father, Jama, adopted Sojiyisa as an orphan, and when Sojiyisa died without children, the Zulu 'raised up' children to be his heirs. In all events, the relationship was a close one, and when Shaka created the Zulu kingdom by a mixture of military force and diplomacy in the 1820s, Sojiyisa's son, Maphitha, was given control of a large tract of central northern Zululand in the king's name.

It was to Maphitha's success in this regard that the Mandlakazi owed their fortunes. The Mandlakazi territory was of great strategic importance in Shaka's new kingdom. Partly this was because it included the traditional lands of the Ndwandwe people, who had proved Shaka's most resilient enemies, and who had only recently been defeated, and partly because Maphitha's northern reaches abutted the Lebombo mountains, which were the gateway to a wider world beyond. It was Maphitha who exercised control of the groups beyond the Lebombo range, who were not closely incorporated into the Zulu kingdom, but gave their allegiance to it. Perhaps more importantly, it was Maphitha who acted as the king's representative with the Mabhudu-Thonga groups who lay to the north-east, between Zululand and the Portuguese enclave at Delagoa Bay, and who therefore exercised effective control over the trade routes from the bay to the interior.

Maphitha's loyalty to the Zulu monarchy seems to have survived Shaka's assassination, and Dingane's conflict with the Boers. Indeed, the Mandlakazi continued to support Dingane even after Mpande had 'broken the rope which tied the nation together', and defected to the Boers; and it was not until after the battle of Magqonqo in 1840 that Maphitha recognised the inevitable, and gave his allegiance to Mpande. It was a move that left Dingane isolated – with only a handful of loyal followers, he was murdered shortly afterwards – and at the same time confirmed the importance of Mandlakazi support.

The civil war of 1840 had opened great rifts within the kingdom, and throughout his reign Mpande tried to restore the central role of the Royal House while tacitly recognising the enormous power exercised by his regional chiefs. Maphitha, in particular, was allowed a good deal of independent authority which reflected not only the physical distance between his territories and the centres of Mpande's administration, but also the fact that Mpande could not afford to alienate him. Although the young men of the Mandlakazi were still required to serve in the king's *amabutho*, Maphitha enjoyed the privilege of being able to appoint his own *izinduna* – state officials – and to try local disputes without recourse to the king. Moreover, the king was careful to discover Maphitha's views before embarking on any major course of action, and would often withhold important policy decisions for days until Maphitha could be consulted.

Zibhebhu was born as the senior son of Maphitha's great house in 1841, and in due course was enrolled in Mpande's uMxapho *ibutho*, formed about 1861. From an early age, Zibhebhu showed himself to be shrewd, ambitious and aggressive. As a young man, he enjoyed his father's involvement in the European trade, is said to have visited Delagoa Bay, and learned to ride and shoot. This gave him an insight into the European world that was uncommon in Zulus of his generation. In later years, despite a quiet and controlled manner, he also proved to be both ruthless and unusually acquisitive.

Both Mpande and Maphitha, as they grew to be old men, found themselves troubled by sons who were growing impatient of their inheritance. King Mpande refused deliberately to nominate an heir, with the result that his two senior sons, the Princes Cetshwayo and Mbuyazi, fought with each other, while Maphitha grew increasingly suspicious of his heir, Zibhebhu. Ironically, given later events, circumstances contrived to forge a sympathy between the two young men, and when civil war broke out between the princes in 1856, many Zulu attributed Cetshwayo's success to the support of the Mandlakazi at the decisive battle of 'Ndondakusuka. While Zibhebhu himself was too young to take a commanding role in the battle, he probably served with the Mandlakazi forces as a mat-carrier. Years later, Cetshwayo remembered his support when Maphitha, increasingly convinced that Zibhebhu was plotting against him, appealed to Mpande for permission to kill him. Cetshwayo intervened on Zibhebhu's behalf, and Mpande refused Maphitha's request.

Both Mpande and Maphitha died at last in 1872, within a few months of each other. The official mourning ceremonies for the king lasted almost a year, and it was not until August 1873 that the nation gathered to install Cetshwayo as his successor. By that time, Zibhebhu had already been installed as the new chief of the Mandlakazi. The installation was not without its tensions, for even after Cetshwayo's victory in 1856, Mpande continued to torment him with the possibility that he would nominate some other heir, and even as he made his way to the emaKhosini valley – the sacred valley of the ancestors – at the head of a procession of thousands of his followers, Cetshwayo was nervous that a new challenger might emerge from within the kingdom. When Cetshwayo's scouts reported that Zibhebhu was approaching at the head of a column of fully armed Mandlakazi, a rumour spread through Cetshwayo's entourage that they were about to be attacked. As the two parties drew together, the Mandlakazi suddenly halted and formed up in battle order. Panic spread among Cetshwayo's followers, who prepared to flee, but Cetshwayo kept his head, and sent forward some of his attendants to greet the Mandlakazi. Whatever Zibhebhu's intentions, the moment passed, and the installation passed off peacefully enough.

Indeed, Zibhebhu seems to have thrived in the early years of Cetshwayo's reign. Like his father, he worked to keep royal influence in his district to a minimum, and now that he was chief he extended his trading connections, cultivating contacts in colonial Natal, strengthening ties with Delagoa Bay, and forming a partnership with John Dunn – Cetshwayo's white *induna*, who controlled the southern approaches to the kingdom – to recruit labourers in the Mabhudu-Thonga chiefdoms, and march them across country to work for white farmers in Natal.

It may have been this lucrative involvement with the white economy outside the country which led Zibhebhu to advise caution as the settler states and Cetshwayo moved towards confrontation in the 1870s. For many within the Zulu kingdom, the markedly aggressive tone which characterised British attitudes following their decision to adopt the Confederation policy came as something of a shock. The king and the *izikhulu* understood that the British were pursuing deeper aims than their complaints about border issues implied, but were at a loss as to how best to respond. Some were indignant at British attempts to interfere in purely Zulu issues, and advised the king to reject out of hand the increasingly strident British demands. A significant party within the council urged the king to do whatever he could to placate the British, however, for fear of the consequences. Among these were Mnyamana Buthelezi – who had served Mpande as a councillor, and was Cetshwayo's most senior and respected adviser – and Hamu kaNzibe and Zibhebhu kaMaphitha. It is no coincidence that both Hamu and Zibhebhu's territories lay in northern Zululand, where they exercised a good deal of autonomy, and that both were heavily involved in trade which they could expect to be severely disrupted in the event of war.

In fact, the British offered King Cetshwayo little choice, and the ultimatum of December 1878 was specifically designed to be almost impossible for the king to accept. Despite their misgivings, both Zibhebhu and Mnyamana whole-heartedly committed themselves to the war once it became inevitable, while Hamu entered secret negotiations with the British, and would prove the only *izikhulu* of note to desert to them while hostilities were still in progress.

Once it became clear that British forces were actually crossing into Zulu territory, the king mustered his army. While local forces were directed to harass the British flanking columns, the main army – almost 25,000 men – was directed to attack the British Centre Column, which had crossed into Zululand at Rorke's Drift. Among them was Zibhebhu, who had been appointed chief *induna* of the uDloko *ibutho*, but was also given charge of the scouts during the coming campaign.

While the honour of the Zulu victory which ensued at Isandlwana on 22 January 1879 must go to Ntshingwayo – and to the regimental and junior commanders who led their men so skilfully and courageously during the attack – Zibhebhu's role should not be overlooked. Arguably the greatest Zulu master-stroke of the campaign was to manoeuvre the Zulu army to within five miles of the British camp, without being detected by British scouts, and for this Zibhebhu deserves some praise. The army was particularly vulnerable on 21 January, when it moved from its bivouac at Siphezi mountain – only fifteen miles from Isandlwana, and visible from it – into the Ngwebeni valley, north-west of the camp. Although the valley itself is sheltered, the country in between is undulating and open, and despite the careful Zulu efforts to move in small regimental groups, rather than dense columns, the danger of discovery was very real. And in fact, a mounted patrol from Isandlwana did come close to revealing the movement. Before it was quite in sight of the army, however, it was suddenly and vigorously attacked by Zibhebhu's scouts, and driven off. The British concluded that this was nothing more than an encounter with a small party of Zulus who lived locally, and withdrew without the slightest suspicion of what they had so nearly stumbled upon.

Indeed, there is a story that Zibhebhu himself entered the British camp at Isandlwana, passing himself off as a member of the Native Contingent, and that he climbed the mountain itself, noting every detail of the British camp from above. Needless to say, this story is apocryphal – not only is it intrinsically unlikely, but most of the British dispositions were clear enough from nearby hilltops in any case – but it does indicate the extent of Zibhebhu's reputation among the Zulus as a thorough and daring scout.

When the British finally blundered into the Zulu forces at about noon on the 22nd, Zibhebhu seems to have been leading his *ibutho*, the uDloko, which formed part of the reserve. Together with the *amabutho* associated with the royal homestead at oNdini – the uThulwana, iNdluyengwe and iNdlondlo – the uDloko followed behind the right horn, which swept into the valley behind Isandlwana hill, cutting the British line of retreat. Whereas the right horn turned to attack the camp in the rear, however, the reserve cut across country, to deny the British the road to Rorke's Drift, and to harry survivors who began to flee across country as the British position collapsed. While the uThulwana, uDloko and iNdluyengwe crossed the Mzinyathi river closer to Rorke's Drift, Zibhebhu appears to have accompanied the iNdluyengwe *ibutho*, which cut across the summit of Mpethe hill, to strike the survivors as they attempted to cross the river at Sothondose's Drift, further downstream. The arrival of the iNdluyengwe effectively sealed the drift as a means of escape, and the iNdluyengwe descended into the Mzinyathi valley, combing the bush to flush out survivors who were still hiding there. Zulu stories which credit Zibhebhu with having personally shot Lieutenants Melvill and Coghill of the 24th Regiment are unlikely, and simply reflect the prominent part he played in the hunt for survivors.

At some point during the pursuit, however, Zibhebhu suffered a gunshot wound to the hand, and retired from the field. This probably occurred at the drift, at a time when the battle was largely over. The army had, after all, completely overrun the British camp, and elements had pushed forward as far as the river, which formed the boundary with Natal. King Cetshwayo had ordered his warriors not to cross the border, and Zibhebhu was far too cool an individual to be prompted by the heat of the moment to ignore the king's express orders.

Zibhebhu's withdrawal left Prince Dabulamanzi kaMpande as the senior commander with the reserve. Dabulamanzi was a more rash man than Zibhebhu; the reserve crossed the river, of course, and was defeated at Rorke's Drift. It is interesting to speculate as to how that battle might have gone had Zibhebhu been in charge.

In the aftermath of Isandlwana, Zibhebhu retired to his personal homestead at Bangonomo, in north-eastern Zululand, to recover. The injury cannot have been a serious one, for he once more responded to the king's call to reassemble the army in early March. This time the army was directed to attack Colonel Wood's column, in north-western Zululand. On 28 March, while still some miles from Wood's camp at Khambula, the army stumbled on Wood's troops, who were in the process of attacking the abaQulusi stronghold of Hlobane mountain. The right wing of the Zulu army rushed forward to support the attack, but there is no indication that either Zibhebhu, or the uDloko, were involved in the action, probably because they formed part of the left wing, which remained uncommitted.

The following day, the main army attacked Khambula. Once again, it was under the direct command of Ntshingwayo kaMahole, and Mnyamana Buthelezi was present as the king's personal representative. The army assaulted Wood's entrenchments for some four hours, but, despite some successes, was unable to make a significant breakthrough, and was forced to retreat. Zibhebhu seems to have been no more able to distinguish himself than other commanders, although during the retreat he cautioned Mnyamana against attempting to rally the army, realising that it was spent, and any such attempt would only expose it even further to the ruthless British pursuit.

The disaster at Khambula was deeply discouraging to both the king, his commanders and ordinary Zulus who had endured the firestorm, and suffered appalling casualties, all to no effect. The army dispersed in something akin to despair, and the king was unable to reassemble it until June. By that time, Lord Chelmsford had reorganised his forces, and had begun a fresh invasion.

Despite increasingly desperate peace overtures from the king, and stiff resistance from Zulus living across Chelmsford's line of advance, the British had reached the south bank of the White Mfolozi river by the end of June. Here Chelmsford paused for a few days, ostensibly to offer Cetshwayo a chance to surrender, but in fact to make his final preparations. He established his camp on the southern bank of the White Mfolozi; across the river lay the Mahlabathini plain, and the cluster of royal homesteads, including oNdini itself, which constituted King Cetshwayo's capital.

The river was wide but shallow, with two good crossing points a mile apart. On the opposite bank, these were overlooked by a long stony ridge, which ended abruptly in a steep bluff which commanded the river. Although the king was reluctant to provoke a final confrontation before every chance of negotiation had been exhausted, Zulu troops had been posted along this ridge to watch for any signs of a British crossing. Commanding this detachment was Zibhebhu – a rare independent appointment that gave him the opportunity to display some of his natural tactical flair.

Despite the king's orders that the Zulu should not fire the first shot, Zibhebhu took it upon himself to harass the British watering and bathing parties which came down to the river. As usual with Zulu marksmen, his men were poorly trained and carried obsolete weapons, but they were skilfully placed, and their fire was enough to send the British fatigue parties scurrying back to their camps, and to bring pickets up from the rear to return the fire. These fire-fights continued sporadically for several days, until all pretence at negotiation came to an end, and hostilities began in earnest. At one point, the king, increasingly desperate to ward off a defeat he now considered inevitable, sent a herd of his famous white royal cattle to the British as a peace offering, but it was met at the drift by the young warriors of the uKhandempemvu *ibutho*, who were indignant that the king should thus humiliate himself and refused to allow the cattle to pass.

Hostilities resumed in earnest on 3 July. Chelmsford was keen to demonstrate that the period allotted for negotiations was over, and he wanted to scout out the Mahlabathini plain to find a good position for the coming battle. As a result, he ordered a reconnaissance to be carried out by some 500 mounted men under the command of Colonel Redvers Buller.

Buller's men crossed in two parties early in the afternoon, covered by shellfire from Chelmsford's camp. One party swept around the bluff, catching the Zulus posted there by surprise, and scattering them with casualties. The other, commanded by Buller himself, made for the centre of the plain. Passing the great *ikhanda* of kwaNodwengu, Buller deployed part of his force to act as a reserve to cover his retreat while he led the rest further on to the plain. A group of scouts suddenly appeared in the long grass before them, and Buller's men gave chase. The scouts melted away, but the pursuers were distracted instead by a small party of goatherds. These, too, fled before their approach, and a group of mounted *izinduna* suddenly appeared, shouting taunts and firing shots. To these, too, Buller gave chase, until he realised that all of these groups had been leading him in the same direction – towards the banks of the Mbilane stream, which lay between him and oNdini itself. Buller called his men to a halt, and as he did so, a double line of warriors suddenly rose up from the grass only 50 yards in front of him. Buller had been led into a skilful trap; some 4000 warriors, among whom the uMxapho regiment was represented in force, had been lying in wait for him.

Zibhebhu himself had been among the *izinduna* who had lured Buller on, and he had prepared the ground well. Just a few yards beyond the spot where Buller had halted, the long grass had been carefully plaited to trip the horses; had he blundered into it, there would have been little hope of extricating himself. As it was, it was a close-run thing. As the warriors in front of him fired a heavy but inaccurate volley, Buller turned his men about and began to gallop back towards the river. As they did so, the horns of the waiting Zulu force rose up on either side, and rushed forward to cut him off. Buller's men narrowly managed to slip through the gap before the horns closed, although several men were killed, while others distinguished themselves by rescuing unhorsed men in the teeth of the Zulu pursuit. Even so, the Zulu might have caught him had Buller not had the foresight to leave his reserve, who now rode out to open a heavy fire on the pursuing Zulu. The British retreated in good order towards the river, but the Zulu continued to chase them, only breaking off their pursuit when they reached the banks of the Mfolozi itself.

Although the British were exhilarated by the adventure, and encouraged by the heroism of their own men, the true honours in the incident had gone to Zibhebhu. The Zulu trap was well conceived and carefully executed, and Zibhebhu himself had behaved with a cool and purposeful daring which would prove typical of his later career. Only Buller's equally sharp instincts had prevented the British group from being overtaken by disaster.

The British patrol had given Chelmsford the information he needed, however, and at first light the following morning he stood his command to, and, leaving his baggage wagons under guard on the southern bank, crossed the White Mfolozi with his fighting men. As they marched out on to the plain, he formed them into a large rectangle, the men in ranks four deep, with field guns and Gatlings at the corners and interspersed along the sides. In this formation he moved slowly out to take up his selected position in the centre of the plain. As he did so, the *amabutho* began to emerge from among the *amakhanda* on the hills around him, or to rise up from the dongas where they had established temporary camps. Chelmsford sent out his irregular cavalry to provoke the Zulu to the attack, and the last great contest of the war began.

In the first few moments of the battle, the Zulu attacked with the same determination they had showed at Isandlwana and Khambula. Yet the British firestorm which greeted them was awesome, a rolling thunder of cannon and volley-fire which rippled the square. Most of the Zulu attacks were driven to ground more than a hundred yards from the British position. Here and there, some particularly courageous *izinduna* led rushes which reached to within 50 yards before being cut down, but on the whole most Zulu proved reluctant to risk a charge across the last few yards which separated them from the British.

Zibhebhu's role in the battle remains uncertain. Some reports suggested that he was in command of the left wing of the Zulu army – the uVe, iNgobamakhosi and uKhandempemvu regiments – which poured into the kwaNodwengu *ikhanda* at the height of the battle. KwaNodwengu was only a few hundred yards from the right rear corner of Chelmsford's square, and after pausing to form up, the Zulu rushed out to mount a charge of such intensity that Chelmsford had to move his reserves within the square to meet it. The Zulu came so close that the field guns placed at the corner fired several rounds of case shot, and the infantry officers drew their revolvers ready for hand-to-hand contact. At the last moment, however, the charge melted away, and the survivors retired, still under heavy fire, to the meagre shelter of kwaNodwengu.

The attack of the Zulu left proved the most determined of the day, and once it had been repulsed Chelmsford realised that the Zulu were spent. He had been keeping his cavalry safe inside the square for just such a moment, and he now ordered them out to charge the Zulu and drive them away from his position. Although the Zulu attempted to rally here and there, they could not stand up to the charge, and they retired from the field, pursued no less ruthlessly than at Khambula or Gingindlovu. The battle had lasted just 90 minutes, and Chelmsford had inflicted as many as 1500 Zulu casualties for the loss of a dozen of his own men killed, and 70 wounded.

Triumphantly, the British rode across the plain, setting fire to the great royal homesteads, including oNdini itself. By mid-afternoon, Chelmsford had retired across the Mfolozi, and had begun plans to withdraw from Zululand.

In the immediate aftermath of the defeat, the Zulu kingdom seemed on the point of collapse. The army dispersed, exhausted and dejected warriors scattering across country. King Cetshwayo had not stayed to watch the defeat himself, but retired towards the Black Mfolozi, accompanied by his household and attendants. Most of his commanders made their way to their own homes; many would now find themselves under pressure from the British to abandon the king and make their own terms.

Paradoxically, it was an act of loyalty on Zibhebhu's part in these dark days which sowed the seed for his bitter conflict with the Royal House. The British had not penetrated Zibhebhu's territory, and he offered Cetshwayo refuge at one of his homesteads. The king refused for himself, but took advantage of the offer for his young heir, Dinuzulu, and some of the women of his household. He also sent with them some of the royal cattle for safekeeping. Once it was clear, however, that the British were not threatening Zibhebhu, Cetshwayo's full brother, Ndabuko, objected to this arrangement. Ndabuko was a headstrong and proud man who insisted that he was Dinuzulu's rightful guardian, and he insulted Zibhebhu by declaring that it was not proper for the heirs of the House of Senzangakhona to eat off the meat-tray of the House of Sojiyisa. The presence of Dinuzulu within Mandlakazi territory conferred a good deal of prestige on Zibhebhu, and he only handed him over to Ndabuko with reluctance. He refused, however, to give up Cetshwayo's cattle, and the issue became a point of contention which would ultimately poison the relationship between the Mandlakazi and the royalists, with catastrophic results for Zululand as a whole.

The king was eventually captured by the British in the Ngome forest towards the end of August, and taken under guard to the coast, where he was put on board a steamer, destined for exile in the Cape. Lord Chelmsford's successor, Sir Garnet Wolseley, was then faced with the task of disposing of Zululand in a way that was favourable to British interests. The British government had set its face firmly against direct annexation, and Wolseley's solution was to divide the country up among thirteen appointed chiefs. In selecting these chiefs, Wolseley was guided by the need to select men who were considered sympathetic to British interests, and who would oppose any reassertion of royal authority. Some, like Hamu kaNzibe and John Dunn, were members of the old order who had defected to the British during the hostilities, while others were representatives of lines which had been significant before Shaka's day, and whom Wolseley hoped would welcome the chance to reassert their independence from the House of Senzangakhona. And then there were men who were considered 'progressive', who understood and shared something of the European economic system, and were happy to work with European traders and labour-recruiters. Such men, who appreciated the significance of the developing cash economy, and realised that cattle had a commercial value in the broader world which went beyond their specific associations in Zulu culture, were still rare in Zululand, and the colonial authorities in Natal saw them as a means of undermining what remained of Zulu economic independence.

Foremost among such 'progressive' Zulu was Zibhebhu kaMaphitha, and despite the fact that he had taken such an active part in the recent war, Wolseley confirmed him as an independent chief in northern Zululand.

At the time of his appointment, Zibhebhu was in his late thirties, a short man with broad shoulders whose physique was powerful, despite a tendency to fat. He was married, and wore the *isicoco* headring, which his enemies noted contemptuously was thin and lopsided. His ambition was clear to everyone who met him, but his manner was quiet, controlled and forthright. He was in the prime of life, and the British had freed him from any obligation he felt towards the Royal House. No sooner had his position been confirmed than he began vigorously establishing his authority over the people in his territory. He revived his trading routes, and one white contact in Natal, a young adventurer by the name of Johan Colenbrander, moved to take up residence at Zibhebhu's principal homestead at Bangonomo, where he set about buying up guns, and training some of Zibhebhu's adherents to ride and shoot.

Trouble with the royal family followed soon after. Ndabuko's dismissive remarks about the inferiority of Sojiyisa's House rankled with Zibhebhu, and he was determined to make royalist supporters acknowledge his authority. In his view, Cetshwayo had been brought down by the British, who had established Zibhebhu as one of his replacements; he no longer acknowledged that the Royal House held any authority over him. This view was bound to antagonise the royal princes, who still considered that they were the legitimate authority in Zululand, and who worked to restore the king to his rightful position. To make matters worse, when the British had drawn the boundaries for Zibhebhu's territory, they had included within it the homesteads of a number of the king's brothers, including Ndabuko himself, and Ziwedu kaMpande, who was regarded as the most senior member of the Royal House after the king himself. To ensure that such men fully accepted their new status, Zibhebhu confiscated any cattle which had formerly belonged to the king, and harassed and humiliated members of the royal family, attacking any who offered overt resistance.

In their ignominy, the king's supporters, the uSuthu, appealed for support outside Zululand. Their plight won them the sympathy of the Bishop of Natal, John Colenso, a tireless libertarian whose views were largely out of step with his settler congregation. When the uSuthu attempted, however, to appeal to the colonial authorities, or directly to the British government, they found their complaints rejected out of hand. The colonial authorities were unashamedly partisan, believing it to be their duty to support chiefs like Zibhebhu, Dunn and Hamu, whom they saw as bastions against the resurgent evil of the old Zulu order. Zibhebhu and Hamu, in particular, were encouraged by this official sanction, and reacted even more harshly to any form of uSuthu protest within their boundaries. Homesteads were raided, people evicted, and cattle confiscated.

Although the authorities steadfastly refused to answer the uSuthu appeals, the increasingly disturbed conditions in Zululand did raise some concern in the Colonial Office. Whatever the success of Wolseley's settlement at turning the power of the kingdom against itself, and nullifying any threat against its white neighbours, the escalating violence itself was threatening to affect the border regions, and to destabilise the area as a whole. It was against this background that the British government had come under increasing pressure from King Cetshwayo and his supporters. Cetshwayo, exiled in Cape Town, proved an energetic and astute campaigner, who had managed to muster a wide range of supporters. The king presented himself as the only means of restoring order to Zululand, and after an extraordinary visit to London in July 1882, the British government was inclined to agree.

Clearly, however, to restore Cetshwayo to his entire kingdom would have squandered the lives and money wasted in defeating him in 1879. Nor could the British in all conscience set him up over chiefs whose authority they had created, and who had often only accepted their position on the understanding that Cetshwayo would never return. As a solution to this dilemma, the British decided to split Zululand into three. A large stretch of territory lying north of the border with Natal would be placed under British protection, and would become known as the Reserve Territory, while Zibhebhu, who had emerged as the most resolute opponent of the Royal House, would be allowed to retain his independence.

When Cetshwayo landed back on Zulu soil in January 1883 his position was impossible from the start. Hemmed in on either side by his enemies, he could neither fulfil his followers' expectations – he was prevented by the terms of his restoration from reviving the *amabutho* system – nor restore his authority. Many of his supporters lived either in the Reserve or in Zibhebhu's territory, and while they refused to move, they continued to visit the king to give him their allegiance, and deny the authority of their appointed chiefs. This, of course, provoked Zibhebhu to retaliate against them, and aroused the latent hostility of the colonial authorities towards the king. In such circumstances violence was inevitable; although the authorities in Natal put the blame squarely on Cetshwayo's shoulders, the king himself wryly admitted that his position had been impossible from the first: 'I did not land in a dry place,' he said, 'I landed in the mud.'

Encouraged by the king's return, those leading royalists who had suffered most at Zibhebhu's hands, including Prince Ndabuko and Mnyamana kaNgqengelele, began to assemble forces at Mnyamana's homestead on Zibhebhu's borders. It is not clear whether the king approved their action; perhaps he did not, but the grievances felt by his supporters were too deep to be ignored. The uSuthu force numbered some 5000 men, organised in *amaviyo* – companies – by chiefdom, rather than in the old *amabutho*. It was commanded by Ndabuko himself, and by Makhoba kaMaphitha, one of Zibhebhu's brothers with whom he had quarrelled, and who knew Mandlakazi territory well.

The uSuthu force set off on 29 March in a straggling column several miles long. It was accompanied by hundreds of young boys, who drove cattle and carried sleeping mats and weapons for their fathers or elder brothers. As was usual in Zulu warfare, the commanders followed behind the fighting men. No sooner had the uSuthu crossed into Mandlakazi territory, advancing on Zibhebhu's principal residence of Bangonomo, than they began to burn the homesteads of Zibhebhu's supporters, and carry off their cattle. Although revelling in their first taste of victory for three years, the uSuthu force was suffering from a dangerous lack of discipline. According to Zulu sources, Zibhebhu had watched their progress from horseback for most of the day, occasionally trading shots with the uSuthu advance guard; that evening, he returned to his forces and reported, 'I have been testing the enemy. It has no competent leader, and you will beat them tomorrow.'

When the sun rose on 30 March, the uSuthu force was breakfasting near one of Zibhebhu's gutted homesteads. Ahead of them, their route lay up a shallow valley known as the Msebe. Although the Msebe was only thinly scattered with trees and bush, the hills running down on either side were deeply scored with watercourses, so that the valley sides in between were ribbed with low ridges. This restricted visibility, and it was impossible to get a true impression of the lie of the land from the bottom of the valley. Just as they were forming up for the day's march, the uSuthu were surprised to see a group of half-a-dozen horsemen ride into view down the Msebe; among them was Zibhebhu himself. The Mandlakazi chief rode to within a few hundred yards of the enemy, taunting them, and he and his escort fired off several shots before retiring back up the valley. The sight was too much for the uSuthu, who immediately hurried after him, without waiting to take up battle formation.

Although Zibhebhu was heavily outnumbered, his 1500 men were mostly experienced warriors who had served under him in one small success after another. They had absolute faith in his leadership, and they were, moreover, supported by Johan Colenbrander, and a handful of white adventurers. The Mandlakazi were concealed in the dongas on either side of the valley, and when the uSuthu were effectively trapped, Zibhebhu suddenly rode into sight, shouting out, *'Ya lunga! Shayani ikhanda layo!'* – 'It is now favourably placed! Strike its head!' Immediately, his warriors rose out of the ground on either side of the head of the uSuthu column, and charged down upon it. They struck the emGazini contingent on the left first, who were so surprised that they collapsed without standing. The tight nature of the ground, and the cacophony at the head of the column, spread confusion among those in the rear, who also broke as those from the front fell back through them. Within a few minutes, the whole uSuthu army was retiring in despair. Zibhebhu himself rode ahead of his force with his mounted men, and personally shot down a number of *izinduna* whom he recognised in the uSuthu ranks. Only the uSuthu rearguard attempted to make a stand, and they held up the Mandlakazi long enough for most of the uSuthu generals, who had been in the rear, to get away. Beyond that, it was a rout; the uSuthu dead amounted to thousands, more than the Zulu had sustained in any battle against the British, and their bones littered the line of retreat for decades to come. Many of the principal uSuthu leaders lost sons in the battle, while Zibhebhu saw to it that Makhoba kaMaphitha – his brother, who had led the uSuthu forces – was hunted down and killed. The battle went on till nightfall as the uSuthu scattered towards the Nongoma ridge. Many were seized by utter panic; the astonished Mandlakazi found one warrior standing with his shield in front of his face, blindly stabbing out at imagined foes all round him. The Mandlakazi watched him in awe for a minute or two, then stabbed him to death.

The battle was undoubtedly a defining moment in Zibhebhu's career. It marked the point at which the friction of the preceding years broke out into open civil war, while Zibhebhu's personal reputation soared. Drawing on the tactics he had developed in 1879, Zibhebhu had proved himself one of the most dynamic and innovative generals in Zulu history. By the same token, royalist fortunes sunk to a new low in the aftermath of Msebe. USuthu supporters across northern Zululand fled to their strongholds, abandoning their homes to the victorious Mandlakazi. Other enemies of the uSuthu – including Prince Hamu kaNzibe, the king's half-brother who had defected to the British in 1879, and had been a bitter opponent of Cetshwayo's return – joined the Mandlakazi, driving out the uSuthu from their lands, and plundering their stock.

The defeat left the uSuthu leadership in dismay. Prince Ndabuko, hitherto an over-confident and rash man, seemed weighed down by the responsibility of the losses. Abandoning any attempt to live by the conditions imposed by the British, Cetshwayo assembled his supporters at oNdini, and in June some 3000 men were doctored for war at the king's homestead, and led north against the Mandlakazi by Dabulamanzi. They had scarcely crossed the Black Mfolozi, however, when a Mandlakazi army confronted them, and Dabulamanzi's force ignominiously retired without standing to fight.

The situation was clearly becoming desperate for the uSuthu. Although Cetshwayo had not instigated the attack on the Mandlakazi, his prestige in the restored territory depended on his ability to protect his followers, and he could hardly abandon his supporters in the north. Over the following month, he continued to receive his followers at oNdini, and it was clear that a major clash was brewing. In fact, the uSuthu leadership had decided on a new strategy; rather than confront Zibhebhu directly, they had decided to attack Hamu, whom they considered the weaker of the two. In fact, however, Zibhebhu did not wait for them to gain the initiative, but struck first.

On 20 July Zibhebhu mustered his forces at his ekuVukeni homestead, in the southern reaches of his chiefdom. In all, he commanded perhaps 3000 warriors, including a contingent of Ngenetsheni – Hamu's followers – and was supported by five whites, including Colenbrander. The army was prepared for war, and that evening Zibhebhu himself led them out to the attack. His object was typically audacious; he was planning to attack oNdini itself. That night his men marched 30 miles through the thick bush of the Black Mfolozi valley, stopping only once to rest briefly, and to light fires to warm themselves. Before dawn they had reached the hills overlooking oNdini to the north. Here Zibhebhu allowed them another short rest, timing their advance so that they came over a ridge, within sight of oNdini, as the sun rose behind them. It was the classic time for the Zulu attack – 'the horns of the morning' – and Zibhebhu guessed that their menacing silhouette against the sunrise would demoralise the uSuthu before they even attacked.

And so it did. The uSuthu forces were only just rising when the news arrived of the Mandlakazi approach. Many of the young warriors were forming up by the gate, saying farewell to members of their families who had brought them food, and who were about to depart. Most of the senior men had not yet joined them, however, and instead had rushed to attend the king. The king indignantly refused to consider flight, and ordered his army out to attack the Mandlakazi. But in the confusion, many of the *amabutho* set off without their appointed *izinduna*, or without any clear idea of their objectives. Moreover, since Msebe, Zibhebhu's reputation had achieved terrifying proportions, and the young uSuthu warriors showed a marked reluctance to face him.

The two armies met only a mile or two from oNdini. Despite their exhausting march, the Mandlakazi approached in such a determined manner that the uSuthu collapsed before them. Some of the king's regiments opened fire on Zibhebhu's men with a half-hearted fusillade, but when this produced no obvious effect, they turned and ran. Only the uSuthu centre, composed of more senior men and stiffened by the presence of a number of senior *izinduna*, made any attempt to stand, but they could not hold their line unsupported. The uSuthu fell back on oNdini, where members of the old uThulwana *ibutho* rallied. The Mandlakazi streamed into the royal homestead by the side-gates, and fighting spread throughout the complex. The uThulwana were soon overwhelmed, and the Mandlakazi set fire to some of the huts; for the second time in its history oNdini went up in flames. The remaining uSuthu scattered across the Mahlabathini plain, with the Mandlakazi in hot pursuit. Many of the young uSuthu warriors were fit and agile enough to escape, but the more senior men, overweight and slow, were caught and killed. At least 59 of the great men of the kingdom, *izikhulu, amakhosi* and councillors whose experience stretched back to Mpande's time, were killed, and the king himself was wounded. Zibhebhu's warriors thoroughly looted what remained of oNdini, carrying away the cattle and trinkets of the royalists, and retired in triumph to Bangonomo.

The battle of oNdini marked the real end of the old Zulu order. King Cetshwayo's attempt to revive the structures of the old state lay in ashes, and the bonds which had held Shaka's kingdom together were shattered. The king himself was in despair, and his fortunes were never to recover; on 8 February 1884, he suddenly collapsed and died. A British doctor pronounced the cause of death as a heart-attack; many Zulus believed he had been poisoned.

The death of the king ushered in a new era for the royalists. The king's son and heir, Dinuzulu, was just a teenager, but he was a strong and ambitious youth, and was supported by many of the old royalist establishment, including Mnyamana Buthelezi, and most of the king's surviving brothers. Realising that the situation required desperate measures, Dinuzulu, and the clique of younger, more cynical and ruthless men in whom he confided, appealed to an outside agency to intervene on their behalf. Promising farms as a reward, the uSuthu reached an agreement with a number of farmers in the Transvaal border regions. On 21 May 1884 the Boers proclaimed Dinuzulu king of the Zulus, much as Andries Pretorius had once done to Mpande, his grandfather, over 40 years before. No sooner was the pact sealed than a combined Boer and uSuthu force set out to settle the issue with Zibhebhu. Johan Colenbrander, Zibhebhu's white adviser, rode down to Natal to try to raise a mercenary force to counter the Boer threat, but found that few whites were prepared to support him. Moreover, as Colenbrander tried to return through Zululand to join

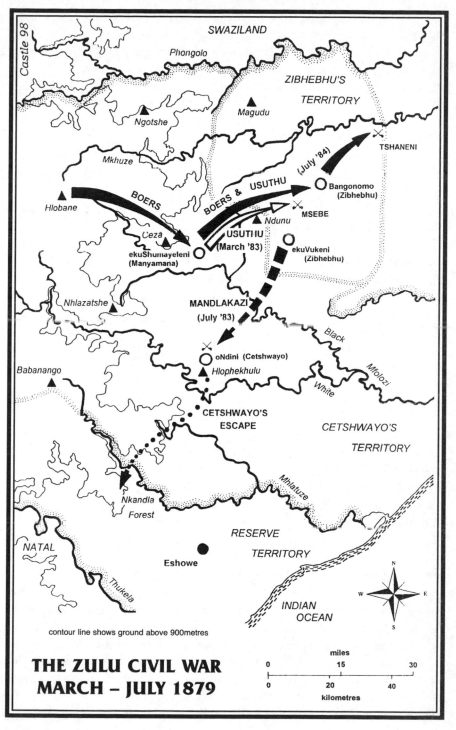

THE ZULU CIVIL WAR
MARCH – JULY 1879

Zibhebhu, he found his way blocked by uSuthu sympathisers; Zibhebhu would have to face his attackers alone.

By early June the uSuthu succeeded in mustering about 7000 fighting men, supported by 150 Boers. Advancing westwards from the Boer camp near Hlobane mountain, they cautiously entered Zibhebhu's territory, only to find that he had abandoned his homesteads before them. The Mandlakazi had retired down the Mkhuze river, and the uSuthu followed them until they reached the point where the Mkhuze flows through a narrow gap in the Lebombo mountains. This spot, overlooked by the twin peaks of the Tshaneni and Gaza mountains, was such a perfect spot for an ambush that the royalists approached with some caution.

And rightly so. Zibhebhu, outnumbered and – more significantly – outgunned by the Boers, realised that he stood little chance of defeating the invaders in the open. Instead, he had carefully concealed his men in broken ground on the southern bank of the Mkhuze. Here a deep donga flowed across the front of the uSuthu approach, and Zibhebhu had hidden in it his vanguard. He expected the uSuthu to blunder into these men, and had instructed them to make only a short stand, and then to flee back down the river, into the hills. From past experience he knew that the uSuthu – undisciplined and lacking strong leaders – would give chase, and would become disorganised among the broken terrain. His main body, therefore, he had concealed further back, on the slopes of Tshaneni, from where they could rush down and attack the uSuthu as they pursued his vanguard, catching them in the flanks and rear, and pinching them against the river.

It was a typically well thought-out ambush, and would probably have succeeded but for the presence of the Boers, and one stroke of misfortune. The royalist force tentatively advanced up the river towards the hills on 5 June, with the uSuthu at the front and the Boers supporting them in the rear. As it did so, the uSuthu left, thrown out in advance, stumbled across the Mandlakazi in the donga. Before the Mandlakazi could fall back, drawing the uSuthu after them, a solitary shot from the foot of Tshaneni – apparently an accidental discharge – warned the uSuthu of the presence of Zibhebhu's men. The main Mandlakazi body, realising the trap had been sprung prematurely, rose up and charged down on its enemies. It struck the uSuthu right, which was only just coming up, with such force that it pushed it back on the rest of the uSuthu body. The battle might still have gone Zibhebhu's way, but at this point the Boers to the rear opened fire, shooting over the heads of the uSuthu in front of them, and into the struggling mêlée. They shot down many of their own side in the confusion, but the Mandlakazi suffered so heavily that they drew back. Under cover of a heavy Boer fire, the uSuthu returned to the attack, and the Mandlakazi began to retreat down the river towards the hills. Here they were caught in the very trap they had planned for the uSuthu, for the rough ground broke up their formations, and the uSuthu cut them up piecemeal. Suddenly freed from the dread which had demoralised them for months, the uSuthu fell on their enemy with a vengeance, driving the Mandlakazi warriors back among their non-combatants, sheltering in the hills behind, until the entire Mandlakazi force was in full flight. The numbers of Mandlakazi dead were unknown, but their bones littered the battlefield for a generation to come. The elated uSuthu rounded up between 40,000 and 60,000 head of cattle and hundreds of Mandlakazi women and children.

Zibhebhu himself did not play his usual conspicuous part in the fight, probably because the battle had begun before he intended. After it was over, the uSuthu spotted him on his distinctive white horse, flanked by two white mercenaries who had stuck with him, on the rocky slopes of the Lebombo hills. Zibhebhu apparently took his defeat philosophically. 'I wonder I have lived so long,' he is supposed to have said, 'but oh! My poor children!'

The Mandlakazi scattered after the defeat, most seeking sanctuary in the Nyawo chiefdom of Chief Sambane, north of the Lebombo. King Dingane had once taken refuge here, too, and the Mandlakazi were no more welcome than he had been, for the Nyawo feared retribution from their enemies. Within a few days, Zibhebhu had assembled a core of his followers – about 7000 men, women and children – and made another daring march, this time out of desperation. Somehow he slipped through the uSuthu forces ranging across northern and central Zululand, and entered the British Reserve in the south, appealing to the Resident for protection, much as Cetshwayo had done only a year before. To Zibhebhu's disappointment, the British – who had always supported and encouraged him in his opposition to the Royal House – refused to intervene on his behalf. They declared that Zibhebhu had never been an official British ally, and had undertaken war against the uSuthu on his own account; his misfortunes were therefore of his own doing. This must have been a bitter blow to a man who had borne the brunt of the colonial administration's quarrel with the royal family, but the British did not abandon him entirely; he was offered sanctuary in a reserve on the banks of the Thukela river, near Middle Drift.

Indeed, the battle of Tshaneni might have spelt the end of the Mandlakazi, had it not been for continued suspicion of the Royal House among colonial administrators in Natal and the Reserve Territory. Zibhebhu had been forced to leave a number of his followers in hiding in the north, while many chiefs who had joined him in his glory now retired to their own strongholds for fear of royalist reprisals. Zibhebhu's allies, particularly Prince Hamu and John Dunn, were now on the defensive. Although Zibhebhu remained defiant, and determined to return to his old territory at the first opportunity, the chances of him doing so seemed slim.

His opportunity came as a result of the final assumption of British authority in Zululand. In the aftermath of Tshaneni, the Boers claimed their reward for their services. The extent of the land claimed by the Boers was so outrageous that even Dinuzulu and the uSuthu objected. They tried to restrict the Boers to the north-western portion of the country, which abutted the Transvaal. In the face of the military superiority demonstrated so effectively at Tshaneni, however, Dinuzulu was powerless to resist.

The prospect of a new Boer republic north of the Thukela did, however, provoke a response from the British. For a decade, Britain had stood aloof from the consequences of its intervention in Zulu affairs. Reluctant to bear the cost of direct control, it had watched as the effect of its policies had shaken the country apart, manipulating events through trusted agents such as Zibhebhu, yet affecting to deplore the bloodshed its own policies had engendered. Ironically, it was not the prospect of the Zulu nation being dispossessed which finally induced Britain to intervene; it was the possibility that the Boers might open a line of communication with rival European powers through outlets on the Zululand coast. Since the Great Trek of the 1830s, Britain had been reluctant to abandon its authority over the Boer republics, and British policy had been to isolate the Boers by denying them direct access to European trade and sympathisers. The British informed the Boers that their claims in Zululand represented a threat to British interests, but offered to recognise the Boer position provided it was limited to the north-western districts. Faced with the prospect of a direct confrontation with the British, the Boers backed down, and abandoned their claims to the coastal district. In February 1887 the British recognised the existence of a new, independent Boer state, the New Republic, whose capital, Vryheid – freedom – was laid out not far from Hlobane mountain. Three months later the British formally extended their authority over the remainder of Zululand.

The extension of British control inevitably brought friction with the Royal House. While Dinuzulu sought ways to extend his control over his followers, the British were committed to a policy of denying his authority. A struggle of wills developed, during which the British took the fatal decision to restore Zibhebhu to his territory as a counterweight to the influence of the Royal House.

Zibhebhu had been fretting in exile in the Reserve since his defeat at Tshaneni. Asked how soon he could go, Zibhebhu replied, 'I would like to go at once.'

Zibhebhu returned to his old lands in northern Zululand on 1 December 1887, at the head of just 700 fighting men. He had anticipated opposition and, ominously, had left his women and children in the Reserve until he could establish himself. Inevitably, he found that many uSuthu groups had occupied his lands during his absence, and he set about rigorously driving them off. Encouraged by his apparent success, his scattered supporters across northern Zululand emerged from hiding to join him. The situation was further complicated because Zibhebhu's borders had never been properly defined, and in any case included at least two chiefdoms who were staunch supporters of the uSuthu. Moreover, both Dinuzulu and Ndabuko had built homesteads in northern Zululand, which lay only a few miles west of the land claimed by Zibhebhu.

Indeed, the sight of Zibhebhu driving hapless uSuthu from their lands almost on his doorstep drove Dinuzulu to fury. Towards the end of 1887, a British magistrate, Richard Addison, arrived to establish a post at Ivuna, on the top of the Nongoma ridge, which separated the uSuthu from the Mandlakazi; almost immediately he came under pressure from both sides to intervene. At various times, both Dinuzulu and Zibhebhu appeared outside the fort at the head of a fully armed *impi*, demanding that Addison curb the activities of the other. Addison shared the prevailing colonial sympathy for Zibhebhu, and when this became clear, Dinuzulu again entered secret negotiations with the New Republic, encouraging them to intervene. When Dinuzulu returned to Zululand, he made preparations to occupy Ceza mountain, one of the traditional Zulu strongholds in northern Zululand. Supporters from across Zululand rallied to him, and began raiding the nearby homesteads of Zulu they considered hostile to the Royal House, rounding up cattle and sheep with which to sustain themselves. The British, worried that they had insufficient troops in Zululand to protect their officials, ordered Zibhebhu and his fighting men to muster to support the exposed garrison at Ivuna. If this move was intended to intimidate Dinuzulu, however, it had precisely the opposite effect.

On 2 June Addison marched out from Ivuna to arrest Dinuzulu and Ndabuko on charges of cattle-raiding. When he arrived at Ceza, however, he found an *impi* waiting for him, and after a brief skirmish he was forced to withdraw. British prestige in northern Zululand promptly collapsed. Young uSuthu warriors felt safe to attack the homesteads of their enemies, and several white traders – who had generally been regarded as neutral throughout the civil war – were murdered. Moreover, Dinuzulu's quarrel with the British administration rapidly assumed the character of a sideshow compared with his long-standing feud with Zibhebhu.

At Ivuna, Zibhebhu had proved a difficult ally for the British. Despite their injunctions to the contrary, he had sent men to plunder the homesteads of uSuthu supporters whose owners had abandoned them for the safety of Ceza mountain. In the meantime, however, uSuthu supporters in his own territories had taken advantage of his absence to attack some of his followers. Outraged, Zibhebhu promptly rode out from Ivuna to attack the homesteads of the chief he believed responsible.

To Dinuzulu, it seemed obvious that Zibhebhu was waging his old war on the uSuthu under the cloak of British protection. This seemed intolerable, and throughout the middle of June the uSuthu assembled supporters at Ceza. In all, Dinuzulu managed to raise a force of 4000 men, who were doctored for war, and on the evening of 22 June set out to attack Zibhebhu at Ivuna.

Zibhebhu's forces were encamped in temporary shelters on a rise known as Ndunu hill, about half a mile from the fortified magistracy which constituted the British post at Ivuna. In between lay the marshy bed of the Mbile stream, which fell away into the valley behind the hill. The uSuthu attack, at first light on the morning of 23 June, caught even Zibhebhu by surprise. The uSuthu suddenly appeared on the ridge from beyond the northern slopes, sweeping rapidly down on their objective. Zibhebhu had at most 800 men available, and only a few minutes' warning of the attack. With typical energy, he immediately formed them up in battle array, with his young iNyonemhlophe *ibutho* in the centre, and the more senior ekuVukeni and Bangonomo regiments – named after his principal homesteads – on either side. His personal courage was undaunted, and as the uSuthu advanced rapidly towards him, he rode along the front of his own warriors, encouraging them by calling out, *'Bayinhlananisela nje, ngaba xosha ngenduku!* 'They are a mere rabble, you could chase them off with sticks!' As he reached the end of his line, he turned back, and pointing at the enemy, said, *'Naku lapa kunzima kona Maiye! –* 'It is here where the difficulty lies. To the attack!' Shouting the Mandlakazi war-cry, 'Washesha!', the iNyonemhlophe charged forward. The uSuthu centre was screened by some 30 or 40 horsemen, carrying firearms, but the iNyonemhlophe drove them back with flung spears. Following closely behind the horsemen, however, were the uSuthu uFalaza regiment, who advanced rapidly to close with the Mandlakazi. For a while the Mandlakazi held, but the uSuthu, with their superior numbers, extended to their left, and soon outflanked Zibhebhu's position. At this the older men on the Mandlakazi flanks began to give way; Zibhebhu was driven back from the summit of the hill, and down the slope beyond, where his line collapsed. Some of the Mandlakazi attempted to retire towards the British fort, but the uSuthu right swiftly cut between them and their objective, driving them down the banks of the Mbile stream. Zibhebhu himself managed to avoid his pursuers in the bush at the foot of the hill, but many of his men could not, and as many as 300 were killed. The victorious uSuthu thoroughly looted Zibhebhu's camp, then retired from the field, leaving no more than 30 dead behind them. The garrison at the fort could do no more than send a sortie after them, to shadow their retreat.

Zibhebhu emerged from hiding later that day, furious at his defeat, and blaming the British for not having allowed him free rein on his return six months earlier. In fact, he had handled his troops well during the fight, but his men were heavily outnumbered, and the uSuthu had caught him completely by surprise. The battle of Ndunu hill would prove the last great battle of the old warrior's career, and the odds had been stacked too heavily against him.

Addison abandoned the exposed position at Ivuna after the fight. With Dinuzulu and the triumphant uSuthu in open rebellion, Zibhebhu had little choice but to join him, taking refuge for a second time among the British.

The battle at Ivuna was the start of a short-lived uSuthu rebellion. Once again, British troops were hurried into Zululand, but the resulting battles were small affairs compared to those of 1879. The Zulu kingdom was hopelessly divided, exhausted by decades of internecine conflict, and had neither the manpower nor the will to launch the spirited attacks of old. For the most part, the uSuthu were confined to their strongholds, until the British and their allies drove them out. Dinuzulu and his uncles fled to the New Republic, but the Boers were far too astute to risk a confrontation with the British when the rebellion was clearly already lost, and refused their support. Instead, Dinuzulu and Ndabuko crossed into Natal and surrendered to the British authorities in November. Within the month Dinuzulu, Ndabuko and Shingana had been found guilty of high treason, and sentenced to exile on St Helena.

They had no sooner departed than Zibhebhu slipped back to his old territory. Defeat had not dimmed his fierce determination to restore his authority, and he immediately orchestrated an attack upon a number of uSuthu supporters in his domain.

Yet, as Zibhebhu would discover, there had been a marked change in British attitudes towards Zululand. The British government had at last begun to question the assumptions of the colonial officials who had shaped their policies since 1879, and had begun to recognise that it was their own fiercely divisive approach which had created the climate for the rebellion. While Zibhebhu could still count on the support of many officials in Natal, he found that the British were no longer prepared to excuse his every action. He was ordered to Eshowe to account for his latest attacks, and promptly put on trial. While he was found not guilty of the charges – largely due to the influence of his white friends – the Colonial Secretary in London refused to sanction his return to his former territory until that had been properly surveyed. Throughout 1891 a new commission addressed the problem of contesting land claims between the uSuthu and Mandlakazi, seeking – for the first time – to find a workable solution that would be accepted by both parties.

It was not until 1898 that Zibhebhu was actually allowed to return to the Mandlakazi heartlands. By that time, the political world had further shifted, for administration of Natal had passed from the British government to the colony of Natal, while the uSuthu exiles on St Helena had been pardoned. Ironically, Zibhebhu and Dinuzulu returned to their homelands at the same time, and the

Resident Commissioner insisted that both of them should appear before him at Eshowe. They were told that peace between them was a condition of their restoration, and both solemnly agreed to set aside their differences.

Yet the bitterness between them could not be dispelled by a symbolic reconciliation. Zibhebhu kaMaphitha had been the greatest Zulu general of his age. But if his military flair had been apparent in the war of 1879, it had been the Royal House who had most keenly felt its edge. To the uSuthu, Zibhebhu would remain a traitor, a man who struck his own king, and who, quite possibly, had him murdered. Yet to Zibhebhu, in his turn, it was the Royal House who, through their refusal to accept the British settlement at the end of 1879, had sought to undermine his legitimate authority, and it was in their haughty pretensions that the Mandlakazi saw the cause of so much bloodshed. Wherever the truth lay, more people had died in the civil war than had ever been killed by the British, and their blood would poison the relationship between the uSuthu and Mandlakazi for generations to come.

Yet fate intervened to prevent another clash. Zibhebhu worked to consolidate his position at Bangonomo, but in the aftermath of the Anglo-Boer War a fresh dispute arose with Dinuzulu over the question of King Cetshwayo's cattle. Zibhebhu, however, was now nearly seventy, an old man whose health was failing, and on 27 August 1904 he died at Bangonomo. After his death, the Mandlakazi divided among themselves in a succession dispute between his sons, Msenteli and Bokwe.

Zibhebhu's legacy was certainly an ambivalent one. The great split between the House of Sojiyisa and the House of Senzangakhona continued to trouble Zululand throughout much of the twentieth century, occasionally flaring into violence. When King Dinuzulu died in October 1913, his successors invited the Mandlakazi to send representatives to the funeral ceremonies, but only a few junior *izinduna* did so, while as late as 1917 Msenteli kaZibhebhu declared, 'I know it is the intention to bring about a reconciliation ... that will never be. We must clean our guns ... the paths will soon run red with blood if we are forced into a reconciliation.' Nevertheless, Dinuzulu's successor, his son Solomon Nkayishana, placed great emphasis on healing the rift, and appointed both Bokwe kaZibhebhu and Mathole kaMnyamana Buthelezi as his advisers, thus emphasising the role of both within the kingdom. Yet even today there are many in Zululand who recall the civil war of the 1880s as the real struggle for survival of the old kingdom, and retain bitter memories of the role played by either side.

For all that, the achievements of Zibhebhu were remarkable. Truly, as his praises recalled, he was 'Quick to arm and undeterred by war. With a spirit fearsome, brave and undaunted.'

KING DINUZULU kaCETSHWAYO

'He who strikes hard like a lion; the swift one like lightning ...'

With the death of King Cetshwayo at Eshowe in February 1884, the struggles of the Zulu Royal House entered a new phase. Not since the end of the war of 1879 had the fortunes of the king's supporters sunk so low. While the royal family had doggedly refused to accept the limitations placed upon them by the post-war settlement, by the restoration, and by the civil war itself, the reality of those dark months was that royal authority counted for very little in Zululand in 1884. All the great props that had sustained the king in the days of Zululand's independence were gone, the herds of royal cattle plundered, the great *amakhanda* destroyed, the *amabutho* turned against one another. The *izikhulu* and *amakhosi* – the great men of the nation – were divided against themselves, and Zibhebhu kaMaphitha, who had been one of the king's greatest commanders in 1879, was now the Royal House's most bitter opponent. Moreover, the king was dead, his councillors in hiding, while the Mandlakazi and Ngenetsheni raided royalist supporters across the country with impunity.

This was the birthright inherited by Dinuzulu kaCetshwayo, who, in the eyes of his supporters, became the fifth Zulu king upon the death of his father in 1884.

Dinuzulu was still a young man at the time of his succession, not yet sixteen, but his life had already been one of hardship and suffering. He had been born in 1868 to Cetshwayo's first wife, Nomvimbi, at the emaNgweni homestead near the coast. Since, in the hierarchy of an important polygamous household, the position of first wife was generally considered an inferior one, Dinuzulu's claim to follow his father was not great, but the fate of Cetshwayo's other sons reflected the troubled time; his second son, Nyoniyentaba, was killed in his mother's arms during Zibhebhu's sack of oNdini, while his last son, Manzolwandle – who was born to his nominated 'great wife', and therefore might have had a superior claim – was born a few months after his death. Any division among the Royal House would have proved disastrous in the circumstances of 1884, however, and it is possible that Cetshwayo realised this even as he lay dying, for according to his brothers he nominated Dinuzulu as his successor, almost with his last breath. In any case, the royalist establishment, led by Prince Ndabuko and Mnyamana Buthelezi, were quick to proclaim their acceptance of Dinuzulu as the new king.

Despite his youth, Dinuzulu was a good choice. Intelligent and forceful in his manner, he was, as one African observer commented, 'clever with the qualities of the young lion'. Although he had grown up among the panoply of the kingdom in the last days of its glory – he was old enough to have been presented to his grandfather Mpande, though he did not remember him – he was to prove equally at home in the white world, and had already learned to ride and shoot. Indeed, in the troubled years that followed he would prove both brave and daring, and always accompanied his armies into battle whenever he could – the last king of the Zulu to do so. Like his father, he was fiercely proud of his birthright, and bitterly resentful of those who failed to recognise it. Because of this, he shared the deep hatred felt by the uSuthu for Zibhebhu. When Cetshwayo had accepted Zibhebhu's offer to send his family to sanctuary among the Mandlakazi at the end of 1879, Dinuzulu had been old enough to take offence at Zibhebhu's presumptuous manner, and had been aware that Zibhebhu had appropriated many of his father's cattle. Dinuzulu had slipped away to take refuge among the Buthelezi, much to Zibhebhu's irritation, with the result that their political differences were already exaggerated by personal animosity, even before Zibhebhu's sack of oNdini in 1883. Dinuzulu had only just managed to escape the slaughter on that occasion, and was led to safety on horseback by the *induna* Sitshitshili kaMnqandi.

The death of Cetshwayo therefore found Dinuzulu desperate to avenge the tragedies and indignities inflicted on his family by Zibhebhu. Moreover, he was not prepared to be restrained by the councils of older men, such as Mnyamana, who were conservative and cautious, and instead sought out the company of a new, more cynical and ruthless generation. It is no coincidence that among his father's brothers he was closest to Ndabuko, who was perhaps the most reckless and aggressive among them, and who had not only urged the Zulu army to cross into Natal after the battle of Isandlwana, but had also taken the lead in the campaign against Zibhebhu.

Yet in truth the desperate plight of the uSuthu required desperate measures, and the options available to them were limited. The uSuthu fighting men had scattered across Zululand, while their families hid in caves and strongholds, away from the Mandlakazi, who rampaged unchecked through the king's former territories. There was no possibility of a military solution without outside intervention, while the British steadfastly blamed the Royal House for its own problems, and refused to intervene. In April 1884, therefore, Dinuzulu began secret negotiations with the Transvaal Boers.

This was a policy rich in irony and fraught with danger. Several times in its history the Royal House had appealed to outsiders for help against internal enemies, and on each occasion the price had been heavy. Mpande had only been able to defeat Dingane with the support of the Voortrekkers, and had almost forfeited half the kingdom as a result; only the advent of British authority in Natal, which drove many of the Trekkers out, had saved him. Mbuyazi had attempted to secure the support of the Natal authorities in his struggle against Cetshwayo, but had been refused and, pinned against the border, was wiped out. Cetshwayo had allowed the same Natal authorities to give their support to his coronation, only to have this used against him during the crisis of 1878. Indeed, Cetshwayo had been adamant that his followers should not ask for Boer help during the civil war, saying simply that 'if you once get them into the country you will never get rid of them'. Moreover, while the British refused to become embroiled in the turmoil of northern Zululand, there was every possibility that they would object to the Boers becoming so, and that this would bring further trouble on the uSuthu.

In the autumn of 1884, nevertheless, there seemed to be little choice, and Dinuzulu was prepared to take the consequences. In essence, Dinuzulu was prepared to offer land to anyone who would support him, and although the Transvaal Republic was at pains to distance itself officially from the uSuthu approach, many border farmers could not believe their luck. The Boers established a committee to raise a commando to support Dinuzulu, and hundreds of frontier farmers and adventurers flocked to join them.

The pact was sealed on 21 May. Some 9000 Zulu and 350 Boers gathered on a farm near Hlobane mountain to proclaim Dinuzulu king. Two wagons were drawn up side by side to form a platform, and Dinuzulu was led up on to it, where he knelt as four Boers placed their hands on his head, and swore to protect him. One of the Boers then anointed him with castor oil, in imitation of the European act of consecration, and the Zulu roared out the royal salute – 'Bayethe!' A week later, a joint Boer–uSuthu army took to the field to attack Zibhebhu.

The uSuthu managed to muster about 7000 fighting men near Mnyamana's ekuShumayeleni homestead. Only about 120 Boers rode south from Hlobane to join them – though nearly 800 would eventually claim farms as a reward. From their rendezvous they advanced eastwards towards Zibhebhu's Bangonomo homestead. The exact role played by Dinuzulu in the coming fight is uncertain, but Zulu sources are unanimous that he was present, and indeed such was his hatred of Zibhebhu that he always took to the field against him when he could.

The combined uSuthu/Boer force blundered into the Mandlakazi below the slopes of Tshaneni mountain on 5 June. The uSuthu crumpled in the face of a stiff attack, but the Boers, firing over their heads, halted the reverse, and the Mandlakazi broke.

For the uSuthu, the battle of Tshaneni proved an exhilarating victory, dispelling the air of defeat and despair that had dogged them since Msebe the previous year. Although it had been the presence of the Boers that had undoubtedly turned the battle in their favour, Dinuzulu nevertheless emerged from the action with his personal prestige considerably enhanced. For a while it seemed that he might yet repair the damage inflicted on the Royal House over the preceding years, and restore something of the old order.

Yet there was a price to pay for the victory, and when the Boers presented their bill, the uSuthu were stunned. The Boers demanded so many farms that their claims extended clear across Zululand to the sea. Almost all Zululand not yet claimed by the British would be forfeit, including the emaKhosini valley, the most sacred spot in the country. Dinuzulu and the uSuthu leadership tried to protest, but after Tshaneni they knew that it was in vain. In August Dinuzulu formally agreed to the Boer demands. The Boers declared the establishment of a New Republic, independent from the Transvaal, with a new a capital called Vryheid.

It was a deeply humiliating moment for Dinuzulu. Instead of emerging from the conflict as king, he now found himself regarded as little more than a puppet of the Boers. Boer farmers began to spread out across the heartland of Zululand, marking out farms, and evicting Zulu who had occupied their lands for generations. Weakened by years of civil war, reduced to poverty and hunger by the constant fighting, and overawed by the Boers' impressive fire-power, there seemed to be nothing that the Zulu could do to resist.

Yet it was at this point that fate took another twist, and the British intervened. Worried by the prospect of a Boer republic on their doorstep, the British reversed the policies of the previous decade, and formerly annexed most of what remained of free Zululand, confining the Boers to the north-western sector.

The uSuthu leaders regarded the advent of British rule with mixed feelings. While it freed them from their debt to the Boers, all the evidence suggested that the British were no more willing to recognise Dinuzulu's claim to king-ship than had their predecessors. Indeed, the British continued to operate on the basis that the claims of the Royal House were the principal cause of unrest in the country, and that the aspirations of the royal family should be firmly contained.

It was inevitable, therefore, that friction between Dinuzulu and the British would follow swiftly on the advent of British rule. Indeed, a few days before the Union flag was hoisted in Zululand, Dinuzulu had punished one of his *izinduna* for attacking the family of a chief on the grounds of witchcraft. This was a deliberate assertion of his royal prerogative, and the British immediately recognised it as such. To make the point that Dinuzulu had exceeded his authority, they insisted that he make reparations to the punished *induna*, and pay a fine in cattle to the British. Dinuzulu responded by pointedly ignoring all British attempts to impose their authority over him, snubbing official meetings, and refusing to pay the fine. The physical manifestations of British authority were sparse enough – a handful of magistrates, a unit of locally raised Zululand Police, and no more than a company or two of redcoats; Dinuzulu felt confident in defying them. When a particularly energetic magistrate surrounded his homestead with police, Dinuzulu's warriors faced them out, until, outnumbered and increasingly exposed, they had to withdraw.

The British were not prepared to allow Dinuzulu's continued defiance, however, and instead they adopted another course, one which in fact brought about the very collision they had hoped to avoid. In November 1887 they allowed Zibhebhu to return to his old territory. Zibhebhu had been brooding over his defeat at Tshaneni from the Reserve Territory, and officials in Natal, loyal to the man who had served them well in the past, urged that he be returned to his old lands as a counterweight to the influence of the uSuthu. The British administrator in Zululand agreed, and Zibhebhu and his followers were escorted back to northern Zululand under escort of British troops. No sooner had he returned that Zibhebhu began to evict uSuthu supporters who had occupied his lands in his absence.

The return of Zibhebhu was regarded as highly provocative by the uSuthu, and Dinuzulu in particular burned with an implacable fury. To him the Mandlakazi were *amambuka* – renegades – and Zibhebhu the man who had killed his father; for the British to expect them to live together was absurd and insulting. The position was made all the worse by the physical proximity of their respective homesteads. Both Dinuzulu and Ndabuko had established themselves in the open Vuna valley, in the north of the country; while they were bordered to the west by Chief Mnyamana's pro-uSuthu Buthelezi, only the Nongoma ridge now separated them from the restored Mandlakazi territory.

The British were well aware that this area could prove a flash-point, and to keep the two sides apart a small British presence was established at Ivuna, below Ndunu hill, on the Nongoma ridge. This consisted of a magistracy, and a small circular earthwork fort. The magistrate, Richard Addison, was expected to prevent trouble between the uSuthu and Mandlakazi with the aid of a contingent of Zululand Police.

For several months the situation remained extremely tense. Dinuzulu complained bitterly that Zibhebhu was oppressing the uSuthu, but Addison and his superiors remained convinced that Dinuzulu's pretensions lay at the heart of the conflict. Dinuzulu had still not paid the fine levied on him earlier, but when Addison attempted to enforce the order, he, too, found himself outmanoeuvred by Dinuzulu's warriors. Armed bands of both Mandlakazi and uSuthu roamed the northern districts, rustling cattle, falling on homesteads and settling old scores. By May the British were losing patience, and increasingly determined to enforce their authority by military means. Zibhebhu, as a government ally, was ordered to Ndunu hill with his warriors, to support a move against Dinuzulu. Dinuzulu himself retired on Ceza mountain.

Warrants were issued for the arrest of Dinuzulu and Ndabuko, and on 2 June a force of British dragoons and Zululand Police set out from Ivuna for Ceza. The troops remained at the foot of the mountain while a small detachment of police wound up a rocky path towards the summit. Half-way up, they stumbled upon a force of 200 warriors of Dinuzulu's uFalaza ibutho, who were surprised by their presence and immediately formed up across their front. This the police commander considered an act of aggression, and opened fire. The sound of the shooting promptly brought Dinuzulu himself, at the head of the imBokodwebomvu regiment, running down the mountain in support. The police were ordered to withdraw, but the uSuthu advance was so rapid that the troops were sent forward to secure their retreat. Realising that they were greatly outnumbered, the entire British force fell back, with the victorious uSuthu in pursuit. At one stage the British commander had to deploy two troops of Inniskilling Dragoons in line to charge the uSuthu, to prevent them from closing with the stragglers, and several warriors were cut down with sabres. Despite this, British losses still amounted to two dead and three wounded before the uSuthu called off their pursuit at the Black Mfolozi.

The affair at Ceza was little more than a skirmish, but its effect was electric. Dinuzulu had made an irrevocable break with British authority and, as at Tshaneni, he had chased his enemies from the field. Across Zululand, chiefs and commoners who sympathised with his cause began to prepare for war. White traders, who had largely been regarded as neutral in former fights, were suddenly seen as agents of white imperialism, and several were attacked and killed in isolated places about the country. British prestige was close to collapse, and more redcoats were marched into Zululand. Dinuzulu's uncle, Shingana, occupied Hlopekhulu mountain, another renowned stronghold, this time near oNdini, with a large *impi*, and also began to attack local waverers.

The full force of the uSuthu wrath, however, was reserved for Zibhebhu. He was still camped with his men on Ndunu hill, and, despite the efforts of the British magistrate to contain him, he raided and harried uSuthu homesteads within his reach. Confident that his reputation was enough to overawe the uSuthu leadership, he had taken no particular precautions against a counterattack. The folly of such carelessness became apparent at first light on the morning of 23 June 1888, when an uSuthu *impi* suddenly crested the Nongoma ridge to the north, and swept down to attack him.

Dinuzulu had assembled an army of nearly 4000 men on Ceza mountain in mid-June, and they had been carefully prepared for war, using a Mandlakazi spear captured at oNdini to achieve supernatural ascendancy over their enemy. Ironically, Dinuzulu's tactics might have been influenced by Zibhebhu's daring overnight march on that occasion, for his men accomplished a similar feat on the night of 22 June. Moving out from Ceza in the dusk, they had followed a route which led them down the Sikhwebezi valley and across the rising country west of Nongoma, before circling round to find a more accessible path up the heights to the north. They had achieved this without being spotted by either the Mandlakazi, or by patrols from the British fort.

The first the British garrison and Mandlakazi knew of their presence was as they came into sight about half a mile away. They were already in battle formation, with a chest and flanking horns screened by a line of skirmishers. The British garrison – mostly black Zululand Police, with Addison himself in overall command – naturally assumed that they were the prime target of the Zulu attack, and this seemed to be confirmed as the uSuthu right horn raced out in their direction. Addison ordered the police to open fire, but to his surprise the uSuthu suddenly veered to their left, away from the fort. The reason for this soon became apparent as the uSuthu advance carried them down into the bed of the Mbile stream, which separated the fort from Zibhebhu's camp on Ndunu hill beyond.

It had never been Dinuzulu's intention to attack the British, and before the battle he had warned his men against doing so unless under the greatest provocation. Dinuzulu's target was Zibhebhu; the purpose of the right horn had been to cut between Zibhebhu and the fort, to deny the Mandlakazi the support of their protectors.

Although the uSuthu strategy had been devised in consultation with the veteran *induna* Hemulana kaMbagazeni, the battle of Ndunu hill, more than any other, was Dinuzulu's. The plan was characterised by the daring which had become his trademark, and it was his courage and resolution which carried it to success. While the uSuthu right neutralised the threat from the fort, Dinuzulu himself led a force of 30–40 horsemen to attack in the centre. Most of these men were armed with rifles, and among them were a handful of Boer freebooters, who had painted their hands and faces black, to prevent the British from identifying them. Immediately behind the horsemen were the iNgobamakhosi and uFalaza *amabutho*, forming the chest, with the imBokodwebomvu forming the left horn. About 200 yards from the Mandlakazi camp, the uSuthu yelled their war-cry, and broke into a charge.

Yet Zibhebhu was not a man to be easily intimidated, despite the fact that his men were heavily outnumbered, and had been caught offguard. He hastily drew them into a battle line, riding along their front, calling out encouragement, and heaping contempt on the uSuthu. As Dinuzulu's horsemen came within a few yards of the Mandlakazi line, they were met with a hail of spears which wounded and frightened the horses, driving them back. Nevertheless, the uFalaza and iNgobamakhosi, coming close behind, pressed through the horsemen to join with the Mandlakazi centre hand-to-hand. As one Zulu account put it:

> Then the uSuthu who were on foot closed in, and there were no more questions. Before it was quite light they started stabbing, and then the 'sparks' [skirmishers] on both sides flashed orward, and it was dudlu dudlu, thump thump. When the whole of the uSuthu army reached Ndunu, in a very short space of time it got among the Mandlakazi and destroyed them ...

While the Mandlakazi centre held its ground, the imBokodwebomvu extended to its left, and slipped round the Mandlakazi right. Taken in the rear, the Mandlakazi right flank began to give ground, and encouraged by the sight of this, and urged on by Dinuzulu who was in the thick of the fighting, the uSuthu surged forward. Suddenly the Mandlakazi line broke, and fell back off the hill, with the uSuthu in hot pursuit. Zibhebhu himself attempted to rally his men until it was too late, then he slipped off his horse and took refuge in the bush. Many Mandlakazi tried to head towards the fort, but most were already cut off by the uSuthu right, who pushed them down the valley of the Mbile, slaughtering them as they ran. In the fort, Addison tried to make a sortie with some of his police to divert the uSuthu, but Dinuzulu ordered a number of his horsemen to ride up on to the summit of Ndunu hill, and open fire on them. This fire was largely ineffectual, but it was enough to persuade the police to retire on the fort.

Free from the worry of intervention by the garrison, the uSuthu gleefully exacted their revenge on Zibhebhu. The Mandlakazi were scattered over several miles of countryside. Moreover, on the lower slopes of the hill, the uSuthu came across the camp of the followers of Prince Ziwedu kaMpande. Ziwedu had declined to join Dinuzulu's rebellion, and fearing that he might be attacked himself as a result, had taken refuge within sight of the fort. While his followers scattered in panic, the uSuthu swept down and carried off Ziwedu's cattle. Once they had finished looting and killing off the fugitives, the uSuthu regrouped, and marched back past the fort, the way they had come. All Addison could do to make his presence felt was send out a small patrol of police to harry the uSuthu rearguard.

The battle of Ndunu was a spectacular uSuthu victory, and much of the credit was due to Dinuzulu himself, who was still scarcely twenty years old. About 30 uSuthu had been killed, while the Mandlakazi had lost as many as

300 men. Moreover, Dinuzulu had dealt a telling blow to the pride and prestige of both the British and the garrison. The post at Ivuna was abandoned in favour of a more secure post further south.

Yet the uSuthu triumph was short-lived. While the uSuthu considered that Zibhebhu's humiliation was richly deserved, the British could not countenance such open defiance of their authority. British troops – chiefly the Inniskilling Dragoons and Mounted Infantry, supported by local auxiliaries – were marched to assist the beleaguered magistracies, and for the second time in a decade, the Zulu found themselves facing British redcoats.

With the country north of the Black Mfolozi abandoned to the uSuthu, the British instead determined to make a demonstration against Prince Shingana, who had been using Hlopekhulu mountain, near oNdini, as a base to raid anti-uSuthu groups nearby. On 2 July a British force attempted to arrest Shingana. The prince attempted to make a stand on the lower slopes of the mountain, but after a stiff skirmish was overrun. His followers scattered across the mountain and down into the White Mfolozi bush, with the British auxiliaries in hot pursuit. One British officer was shot dead during the battle, and over 60 auxiliaries killed or wounded, but 300 uSuthu had died, and Shingana himself had only just managed to escape.

The action at Hlopekhulu had a salutary effect on the course of the rebellion. Most uSuthu had taken up arms to exact their revenge from the Mandlakazi and their supporters, and now that was done, they were reluctant to take on British regulars in a war that they knew ultimately they could not win. Over the following weeks, uSuthu forces across the country began to disperse, and even Dinuzulu realised he could not remain secure at Ceza indefinitely. While British troops marched through the country, putting down any signs of resistance and intimidating waverers, Dinuzulu and the remainder of his army slipped across the border into the New Republic. Here he appealed to the Boers to support him, as they had done before Tshaneni, but the New Republic's leaders were too astute to risk a war with the British, and instead insisted that Dinuzulu's followers lay down their arms. Over the next few weeks, both Ndabuko and Shingana – the two uncles who had most actively supported Dinuzulu – surrendered to British troops. With his following melting away, Dinuzulu decided to give himself up, but, rather than surrender to the military, he took a typically bold step, slipped across the border into Natal, and took the train to the colonial capital at Pietermaritzburg. He hoped to stand trial away from the charged atmosphere in Zululand, but it did him no good; he was promptly placed under arrest and taken to Eshowe under guard.

Dinuzulu, Ndabuko and Shingana stood trial in February 1889 on charges of high treason and public violence. In truth, there was little their counsel could offer in defence, beyond the extenuating circumstances of the persecution of the Royal House, and all three were found guilty. Dinuzulu was sentenced to be jailed for ten years, Ndabuko fifteen, and Shingana twelve. The authorities wanted to remove them from Zululand in case their presence incited unrest, and instead they were sentenced to be exiled – like other enemies of the British Empire, before and after them – on the remote Atlantic island of St Helena.

When Dinuzulu and his uncles stepped on board the ship destined for St Helena in February 1890, it marked the end of an era, both for the young prince, and his country. For this surely marks the true end of the hopes and aspirations of the Royal House to turn back the clock to the days of their pre-colonial glory. Dinuzulu had proved an able and courageous warrior in the cause of the old Zulu kingdom, but that cause had been lost long before he took it up. He had restored to the uSuthu something of the pride they had lost in the dark days of Cetshwayo's defeat, and he had taken his revenge upon Zibhebhu, but in the end all this had counted for nothing in the face of the harsh reality of colonial rule. Zululand was broken, divided against itself, its traditional economy undermined, and its lands open to appropriation by covetous white settlers beyond the border. Perhaps, after the divisive Wolseley settlement of 1879, there had never been a chance that a king would emerge to unite the nation once more against the threat from outside; after 1888 even Dinuzulu knew it was hopeless. All that remained to him was to insist on the respect that was due to his birthright.

The rebellion had shown that there could be no military solutions in the struggle against colonialism, and Dinuzulu never took to the field again. On St Helena, he and his uncles were housed in comfortable lodgings, and Dinuzulu whiled away the time by developing an interest in European culture. He learned to speak, read and write English, and to play the piano, and he developed a taste for European clothes. Since he was not yet married, he had been allowed to take with him two of his female attendants, and during his time on the island he fathered no less than six children by them.

While Dinuzulu was away, the way of life of his people began to change forever. The British at last abandoned their support for Zibhebhu, and attempted to adopt a more even-handed approach to Zululand's problems. Yet the very extension of colonial control brought with it the undermining of the traditional Zulu way of life. The imposition of a hut tax inevitably forced young Zulu men to travel outside the country's borders in search of work which paid cash wages, and within a generation the tradition of giving service in the *amabutho* had been subverted to the needs of the expanding settler economy. With the absorption of Zululand into the colony of Natal in 1897, the Natal system of African administration was extended to Zululand, with the result that traditional chiefs effectively became local agents of colonial admin-istration, a position that increasingly placed them at odds with the needs of their people, and undermined their credibility.

At the same time that traditional forms of authority declined, so too did the traditional economy. After 1888 large numbers of white traders established themselves in Zululand, and there was increased pressure to open up Zulu-land to white settlement. The great herds of cattle which had once been the basis of Zululand's economic power, and which had already been devastated by a decade of war, dwindled still further, extracted by traders, or weakened by exposure to European-introduced diseases. When, in 1904, Zululand was officially divided up between lands to be made available to white farmers, and those reserved for African 'locations', the Zulu found themselves deprived of much of the country's best grazing lands.

Dinuzulu did not serve out his sentence. Rather than treat the Royal House as pariahs, the British had decided instead to harness the authority and respect they still commanded among their supporters to their own ends. Dinuzulu was offered the chance to return to Zululand, provided he renounced his claim to be Cetshwayo's successor, and instead accepted the post of a government-sponsored regional chief. His authority would be confined to his immediate followers only, the uSuthu adherents who had settled west of the Nongoma ridge. The erstwhile champion of pre-colonial independence would effectively be turned into an agent of imperial adminis-tration, yet in truth Dinuzulu had little choice but to accept. It was that or forsake any claim to power in Zululand forever.

Dinuzulu and his uncles returned to Zululand in January 1898, accompa-nied by an impressive baggage of western goods they had acquired in exile. While the authorities kept a wary eye out for signs of trouble, Dinuzulu was still met by crowds of several thousand Zulu who had gathered to welcome him. In something of a triumphal procession, he travelled north to his new territory, and established a new homestead, which he called oSuthu. It consisted of both a European dwelling and traditional huts, and reflected the increasing ease with which he straddled both cultures.

Yet in truth Dinuzulu's position was an impossible one. While the authori-ties regarded him as no more than one of many regional chiefs, the majority of Zulu regarded him as their king. Whereas there was no objection to Zulu from all over Zululand visiting the oSuthu homestead to pay their respects, Dinuzulu soon found that he could not fulfil his people's expectations of them. While he listened patiently to their grievances, he could do little to succour them, and this dilemma became all the more acute when, at the end of the century, Zululand suffered a series of natural disasters, and was brought almost to the point of famine.

Moreover, the attitude of the British continued to be ambivalent towards him. During the Anglo-Boer War, Dinuzulu was given increased powers, and allowed to enrol an *ibutho*, and train Zulu scouts for British service, in an attempt to counter Boer activity in the New Republic nearby. Once the war was over, however, these powers were removed, and instead of being rewarded for his loyalty, Dinuzulu found himself on the receiving end of complaints that he was trying to revive the old Zulu order and overthrow the power of the white man.

The difficulties under which he laboured became only too apparent when African society moved rapidly into crisis in the aftermath of the Anglo-Boer War. In an attempt to recover something of the cost engendered by the war, the Natal authorities levied a poll tax on the black population of Natal and Zululand. After years of impoverishment and humiliation, many groups regarded this as the last straw. When chiefs refused to pay, however, the Natal authorities reacted with heavy-handed measures, and violence flared. In April 1906 a minor chief of the amaZondi people, living on the Natal side of the Thukela, attacked a party of Natal Police, and precipitated an armed rebellion.

Some historians have argued that the name by which the disturbances are commonly known – the Zulu Rebellion – is a misnomer. Certainly, the rebellion both began and ended in Natal; only two Zulu chiefs of consequence openly joined the rebellion, while the rest submitted to the poll tax, and the fighting only touched the southern parts of the country. Yet in other respects, the term is entirely appropriate, for the rebels had come to regard the old Zulu kingdom with a nostalgic pride which offered them an ideal of power and independence that contrasted starkly with their present circumstances. While Bambatha was not a member of the Zulu kingdom, he sought to identify himself with it by the use of royalist symbols, and it was to Dinuzulu whom he turned for succour. Those chiefs who did support the rebellion were often men of prestige in the old kingdom, who had seen their authority whittled away, and their people impoverished by colonialism.

Yet Dinuzulu was among the first to realise that if the Zulu army had not triumphed in 1879, nor the uSuthu in 1888, there was no hope in 1906. The colonial authorities were too firmly entrenched, and the weapon technology at their disposal too awesome. The rebellion proved to be little more than an unequal succession of skirmishes, in which spears were matched against Maxim guns and quick-firing artillery. When Dinuzulu was called upon to join the rebellion by one indignant chief, his reply was instructive: 'He is *bodering* [talking nonsense] when he says that I am afraid. Who can fight the white man? I have been sent overseas by them. I do not want my children to suffer.'

Yet if Dinuzulu felt the futility of armed protest, he was also aware of his responsibilities to his people. While he ordered the chiefs to sit quietly and pay the tax, he also offered succour to those who had joined the rebellion. Given the extent to which the Zulu regarded him as their king, he could in fact have done little else, but this act in the end proved his undoing. In June 1906 Bambatha was killed in the action at Mome gorge, and the rebellion in Zululand collapsed. A separate outbreak south of the Thukela was ruthlessly suppressed. Once military operations had been brought to a successful conclusion, the Natal authorities began to examine Dinuzulu's role in the disturbances. Ironically, to many whites, too, he was the embodiment of everything that seemed threatening to them in the old Zulu order, and they were convinced he had instigated the rebellion. In December 1907 he was finally arrested on charges of high treason, sedition, public violence and murder. Dinuzulu understood the motives behind the charges well enough. 'My sole crime,' he said, 'is that I am the son of Cetshwayo.'

In the highly publicised trial which followed, the prosecution failed to prove over twenty serious charges, but Dinuzulu was nonetheless found guilty on three lesser charges, notably that he had given shelter to Bambatha's wife. He was sentenced to four years' imprisonment – a paltry sentence compared to the crimes with which he had been charged – but, more significantly, he was stripped of what remained of his authority. He was deprived of his position as government *induna*, his royal homesteads were destroyed, and his followers were dispersed among neighbouring chiefdoms.

Dinuzulu was taken first to Pietermaritzburg to begin his sentence, and later transferred to Newcastle, in northern Natal. In 1910, however, the formerly independent colonies and republics of South Africa came together in the Union, with Louis Botha as the first President. Botha had been among those Boers who had supported the uSuthu at Tshaneni, and he remembered Dinuzulu well. He offered to commute Dinuzulu's sentence if he would accept internal exile instead. Dinuzulu agreed, and was moved to a quiet farm in the Transvaal.

Yet the future had little to offer Dinuzulu kaCetshwayo, the last warrior king of the Zulu, and he died on 18 October 1913, from a combination of rheumatic gout and Bright's disease. His last words were 'Bury me with my fathers at Nobamba', and his body was taken back to Zululand, and given a traditional burial. He was 42 years old.

With his passing the last link with the glory days of the old kingdom was broken. To his son, Solomon Nkayishana, he bequeathed the painful legacy of trying to define a role for the Zulu monarchy in a world which was dominated by the harsh reality of white economic and political control.

— 10 —

BAMBATHA kaMANCINZA

'Happy are those who fought and are dead.'

By the early years of the twentieth century, African society in Natal and Zulu-land was in crisis, as it had been a century before, when Shaka was born.

By 1900, however, the triumph of colonialism was complete. Settler society in Natal, which had once been no more than a ramshackle enclave at Port Natal, entirely dependent for its existence on the goodwill of the Zulu kings, had risen to swallow its former patron. The old Zulu kingdom was no more; it existed only as a folk-memory, a symbol of power and African independence which was at once sinister to whites and nostalgic to blacks. Zululand was impoverished, divided against itself, and stripped of any means to protest. Moreover, the very way of life of the vast majority of Africans was under threat in a particularly subtle and damaging way. Rather than confront cultural differ-ences directly, it had always been a tenet of the colonial system in Natal that traditional practices should be subverted to the benefit of the settler commu-nity. Chiefs were only allowed to retain their positions so long as they accepted salaried posts as local administrators. Since chiefs then became responsible for implementing white laws and imposing white taxes, they found their duty to the government placed them at odds with the needs of their people, under-mining their credibility among the very people whom, traditionally, they were expected to represent. Taxation not only raised money for the colonial exche-quer, but also forced Africans to join the cash economy by selling their services, and therefore satisfied the enormous settler hunger for cheap labour. The burden of this fell most upon the young men in African societies; long used to serving the king in the *amabutho*, they now found themselves serving the white man instead. This was a process that often took them away from home, damaging the bonds which held traditional family life together, and encouraging an independent spirit among the workers, who came increasingly to resent the fact that the burden of raising the communities' cash resources fell entirely to them.

Moreover, these difficulties were exaggerated by an increase in white settlement at the end of the century, and by an increasingly autocratic and unsympathetic administration. In 1893 Natal had been granted responsible government – which meant in effect that it administered its own affairs, with a minimum of interference from Britain – and its policies came increasingly to reflect settler attitudes towards the majority African population. The Natal government was characterised by the belief that white settler claims to make best use of the land were entirely justified, that Africans needed to be forced into the developing capitalist economy, and that any protest should be rigorously suppressed. In particular, any attempt to revive the practices of the old Zulu kingdom were regarded as a threat to white supremacy. As a result, the government interfered ruthlessly in the politics of individual chiefdoms, rewarding favourites who supported them, and deposing chiefs who showed the slightest sign of opposition, often employing heavy-handed police tactics.

At the end of the nineteenth century, too, a series of natural disasters had swept across the region. In 1895, large parts of both Natal and Zululand suffered a plague of locusts, which destroyed crops in the fields, and promised the threat of famine. This was compounded by one of the area's occasional droughts. Worse, in 1897, the cattle disease rinderpest swept through South Africa from the north. While white farmers had been able to minimise the damage to their herds by isolating them and practising inoculation, the African groups, with their tradition of communal pasturage, were devastated, and as much as 85 per cent of stock in African ownership was destroyed.

The effects of these hardships profoundly unsettled the communities in both Natal and Zululand, but for slightly different reasons. In Natal, African groups had been exposed to the colonial system for a long time; they had supported it in its struggles against the Zulu kingdom, but were now coming to see that it offered them nothing but subjugation and impoverishment in return. In Zululand, the outward signs of white rule were still few and far between, but there, instead, the contrast was greater in comparison with the prestige and independence the Zulu had enjoyed less than a generation before. Whereas in Natal Africans were exasperated by the prolonged reduction of their power and wealth, in Zululand bitterness was engendered by the sudden fall from grace. Both groups – including many in Natal who had not only never been part of the Zulu kingdom, but who had sometimes actively fought against it – came to regard the Zulu kingdom as a source of nostalgic pride, a golden era of strength and plenty, a time before the advent of the white man and all the misery he had brought with him.

Against this background of discontent, the Natal authorities in August 1905 introduced a poll tax of £1, to be paid by every African male. The Natal government was suffering from the effects of the recent Anglo-Boer War, and the imposition of a fresh tax on the African population seemed to offer an easy solution. Yet for most African groups, it was a tax too many. Some groups were already on the verge of ruin, while the tax was particularly resented by the young men whose wages would have to pay for it. Hitherto, they had been only taxed indirectly, since previous forms of revenue – notably the hut tax – had fallen primarily on wealthier homestead-heads, who had in turn deducted it from the wages sent back by their young men. Now, these same young men, who had no wives or cattle, would have to pay an extra contribution, which took no account of their junior status in African society, and which taxed them as if they were already married men. Moreover, the very use of the term poll tax was unsettling; it aroused fears that the government might one day tax other parts of the body, and even that dismemberment might follow for those who did not pay.

Popular resentment at the tax manifested itself in a wave of millennial rumours which swept through Natal and Zululand. As early as May – before the tax was introduced – a violent hailstorm which devastated the region was thought to have been conjured up by Dinuzulu, as proof that the Zulu Royal House had not lost the abilities as rain-makers with which it was traditionally credited, and as a sign that he was about to reclaim his birthright. By the end of the year it was widely rumoured that the overthrow of white supremacy would follow a pattern of sacrifice; believers were required to slaughter pigs – which had been introduced by Europeans – and white fowls, and to cast aside European utensils. Early attempts to collect the tax were greeted with sullen resentment, and many chiefs found themselves trapped by the contradictions inherent in their position, as the government called upon them to pay, but their young men refused to do so.

Violence first flared in Richmond, near Pietermaritzburg, in February 1906, when some of the followers of Chief Mveli registered their opposition to the tax by gathering in the vicinity of the collecting magistrate's post under arms. The following day a police patrol was sent to arrest the ringleaders, but the attempt was botched, and a scuffle broke out in which two policemen were speared to death. Always deeply suspicious of any signs of African protest, the Natal government reacted harshly, mobilising its troops, and declaring martial law in the affected districts. The murderers were arrested, tried and later shot, despite protests from the British government. Moreover, troops destroyed homesteads and crops, carried away cattle, and flogged Africans indiscriminately. The intention was to serve a warning to any other groups who might be inclined to resist, but historians generally agree that these demonstrations had the opposite effect. Although the military superiority of the government forces was all too obvious, many groups felt goaded beyond endurance, and preferred to fight – and in all probability, die – rather than see what little that remained to them trampled under foot. Indeed, the rebellion may have been a self-fulfilling prophecy as far as the settler community was concerned; long used to living in the midst of a potentially hostile African community, generations of settlers had long feared that an uprising was an inevitable response to their administration. Opposition to the poll tax seemed to confirm a deep-seated paranoia, and provoked a stern response; ironically, it was the very nature of that response which caused many groups to rebel.

Although the Richmond affair had been thoroughly suppressed by April, a fresh, and in many ways far more serious, outbreak then occurred which seemed to offer the terrible possibility of a movement united to restore the independence of the Zulu Royal House. The instigator of this movement was a minor chief of the amaZondi people, by the name of Bambatha kaMancinza.

The Zondi lived in the hot, dry Mpanza valley, which lies between the town of Greytown, and the old Zulu border. It is an area of spectacular beauty, of deep, stony valleys intersected by steep, high hills, but it is an impoverished landscape, with a shortage of good grazing grasses, and little water. In 1906 the Zondi people were scattered over a number of white-owned farms; as such, they were considered squatters in their own lands, and were already finding it difficult to pay the rents demanded of them, before the poll tax added to their burden.

Moreover, Bambatha was not on good terms with the local farmers. He was a young man, still only in his forties, who had become chief in 1890. Over the following decade, he had been charged many times with failing to pay rent, and with cattle theft – a charge of which he was acquitted. By 1906 he was deeply in debt, and his chiefdom, moreover, was suffering from a number of related internal disputes which had led to several serious faction-fights. He had earned the disapproval of the Greytown magistrate, and the local white press had dubbed him 'Bellicose Bambatha, the Chief of Misrule'.

The Zondi were ordered to pay their tax in Greytown on 22 February. When they assembled, however, Bambatha found that many of his young men had come armed with shields and spears, and were in defiant mood, refusing to pay. Uncertain of their reception in Greytown, Bambatha decided to remain with them, while sending into town those among his followers who were prepared to pay. Some idea of the tense atmosphere of the time can be gathered from the fact that the rumour promptly swept through Greytown that Bambatha had surrounded it with an *impi*. Fearful of the magistrate's reaction, and no doubt worried by the stories that were circulating of the fate of other groups who had refused to pay, Bambatha procrastinated, and ignored the magistrate's order that he present himself to explain his actions. By doing so, of course, he fuelled the authorities' suspicions that he had thrown in his lot with that section of the Zondi who resisted the tax, and that he was contemplating rebellion as a result. At the end of the month Bambatha was summarily dismissed as chief, his position being given instead to his uncle, Magwababa, until Bambatha's younger brother, Funizwe, came of age. That Magwababa accepted the chieftainship under such circumstances says much about both the different perceptions held by older and younger generations, and the divisions which had been engendered among the Zondi.

205

It seems unlikely that Bambatha had committed himself to any such cause at that stage. His own statements clearly suggest that he knew any sort of armed resistance was hopeless, yet the alternative course, of surrendering both himself and his young men up to the vengeance of the authorities, must have seemed equally disastrous. As one African witness perceptively put it, Bambatha was motivated primarily by desperation:

> He went to extremes because he was tied hand and foot by the network of troubles in which he found himself. He then strayed off in revolt. He was very much like a beast which on being stabbed rushes about in despair, charges backwards and forwards and, it may be, kills someone that happens to be in his path.

Significantly, Bambatha turned to Dinuzulu for help. The Zondi had never been part of the Zulu kingdom, but, like many of the groups living across the border, they were linked by ties of friendship or marriage to those who were. Moreover, Bambatha, like so many others, clearly saw Dinuzulu as an alternative – and much more sympathetic – source of authority to the white government. Whatever the limitations placed upon him, Dinuzulu was the living representative of the heroic tradition of the Royal House, the successor to Shaka and Dingane, and the very son of Cetshwayo. In the middle of March, Bambatha slipped away from the Mpanza valley, and made his way to oSuthu.

Quite what happened then was the subject of much speculation after the rebellion was over. According to Dinuzulu, he advised Bambatha to pay the poll tax, and to urge his followers to sit quietly. Certainly, Dinuzulu fiercely denied ever having encouraged the rebellion, and consistently urged those chiefs who appealed to him to submit to the government's authority. Publicly, at least, he could do little else, as his role was under close scrutiny, and he knew all too well the folly of taking up arms against the white man. Yet he must inevitably have sympathised with Bambatha's plight, and it is possible that he was waiting to see how the rebellion developed before committing himself. Certainly, many Zulu chiefs later admitted that they would have followed him if he had publicly declared for the rebellion; it is surely significant under those circumstances, however, that he did not. Nevertheless, he offered to look after Bambatha's wife and children at uSuthu while the chief's difficulties lasted.

Moreover, when Bambatha returned to the Mpanza valley at the end of the month, he was accompanied by one Cakijana kaGezindaka, who was widely believed to be one of Dinuzulu's *izinduna*. Cakijana was an extremely shrewd man who pursued very much his own agenda over the following months, but his presence added credence to Bambatha's claim that in fact he had the full

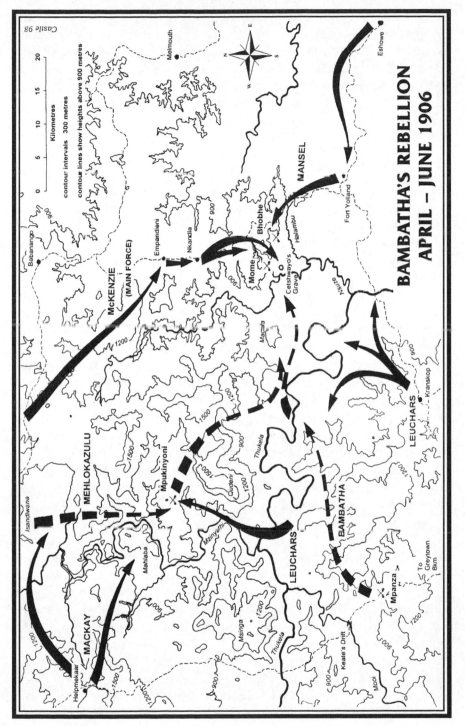

support of Dinuzulu. Bambatha claimed to be in possession of *intelezi* medicine, given to him by Dinuzulu, which would render his warriors invulnerable in any subsequent fighting, and Bambatha further identified himself with the Royal House by adopting Dinuzulu's war-cry – 'uSuthu!' – and the *tshokobezi* badge (a white cowtail worn upright in the head-dress, or attached to regalia about the shoulders or arms) by which the uSuthu had identified themselves in the 1880s. Dinuzulu was later adamant that he had never given permission for these symbols to be used by Bambatha.

Nevertheless, encouraged by the evidence of royal support, Bambatha's supporters were clearly prepared to take up arms on his behalf, declaring 'the Chief should not be shot as a buck [nor] as a beast nor an ox driven to the slaughter-house'. No sooner had he returned to the Mpanza, therefore, than Bambatha promptly attacked Magwababa. Magwababa was jostled and insulted, and bound with hide ropes, and Bambatha taunted him with the revealing words, 'Where are your white friends now? We acknowledge not a Natal king, but a black one.'

When garbled news of the assault on Magwababa reached Greytown, the magistrate set out the following morning to investigate, accompanied by a small police escort. The party had ridden some way along the road through the Mpanza valley when a group of Bambatha's followers, all apparently armed for war, appeared ahead of them, and opened fire. The fire was ineffectual, but enough to cause the magistrate's party to seek out the safety of a police post at Keate's Drift, a few miles away.

This was the moment when Bambatha actually took the irreversible step of taking up armed rebellion against the government. One can only speculate on his reasons; no doubt he realised that the attack on Magwababa, a government appointee, would lead to his arrest anyway, and, with so little to lose, he might as well die fighting. No doubt, too, the support of Dinuzulu – real or imagined – provided an illusion of comfort.

While most of the troubles in 1906 were characterised by a purely local character – indeed, a marked inability on the part of rebel leaders to work together – Bambatha actively tried to broaden the support for the rebellion, and to form a combined army of resistance. For this reason, Bambatha is widely regarded as one of the first heroes of the modern liberation struggle in South Africa. Although he consciously tried to secure the support of specifically Zulu chiefs, he was not himself a part of the Zulu warrior tradition. Historically, the Zondi were not part of the Zulu kingdom, and unlike the principal Zulu chiefs who supported the rebellion – Mehlokazulu kaSihayo and Sigananda kaSokufa – Bambatha had no history of involvement with the Zulu royal *amabutho*. Whereas they were men of an older generation, who had known the full glory of the independent Zulu state, and had never been truly reconciled to white rule, Bambatha was a product of colonialism, who had never known anything else, but who had come to reject it, and to try to overthrow it. In this respect he foreshadowed a later generation of 'freedom fighters', and his outlook was very different from that of his allies; while he perhaps lacked a certain grandeur which distinguished many of the survivors of the old order north of the Thukela, he was more flexible in his outlook, and this is reflected in his military tactics. In short, whereas Mehlokazulu and Sigananda were part of a redundant elite, Bambatha was an outsider, a man of no great importance in the eyes of the Zulu kingdom who, ironically, came to be seen as the leader of the last forlorn attempt to resurrect that kingdom. It is perhaps entirely appropriate that the 1906 disturbances as a whole should be largely remembered as the Bambatha Rebellion.

When news of the attack on the magistrate's party reached Greytown, 150 Natal Mounted Police under Lieutenant Colonel Mansel rode out to relieve the garrison at Keate's Drift. The column passed through the Mpanza valley without incident, and since the police post seemed to be under no threat, it was decided to leave the garrison in place. Three white ladies – wives of local farmers – had taken refuge at the post, however, and Mansel decided to return with them to Greytown, despite the fact that it was now late afternoon. The column covered the distance from Keate's Drift to the Mpanza without incident, but stopped for a short rest at a deserted hotel by the road.

The last stretch of the road through the valley ran through a patch of particularly dense bush. When the column set off again, an advance guard was thrown out in front, but it proved impossible to post flankers on either side. The road ran along the side of a hill called Hlenyane, passing a large boulder which lay close to the track on the right-hand side. It was by that time quite dark, and due to the thickness of the bush, almost impossible to see anything more than a yard or two from the road. As the advance guard passed the boulder, there was a sudden shout of 'oSuthu!', a splutter of shots, and about 150 warriors rushed out from the bush around the boulder to attack.

The rebels were commanded by Bambatha in person. According to local tradition, he had watched the column on the outward journey, and, when it stopped at the hotel on the way back, had decided to attack it. His warriors were carefully hidden on either side of the boulder, while he himself is said to have been sitting on top, carrying a double-barrelled shotgun. The advance guard of the police column passed by only a few yards away, before Bambatha opened fire. This was the signal for the attack, and his men sprang forward, rushing in among the police party before they could be checked. Rather than attack the riders, the rebels stabbed or shot the horses, adding to the confusion, and lunging at the riders as they fell. Most of the police casualties were inflicted in the first few minutes, before the advance guard managed to rally and open a heavy fire on the rebels, prior to retiring steadily on the main body. Hearing the sound of shooting, the main body rushed forward, dismounted, and fired steadily into the bush on either side of the track. The rebels promptly disappeared into the darkness, wriggling along on their bellies to avoid the police fire.

The entire incident lasted no more than ten minutes, but four policemen were killed and four more wounded. The column closed up and headed for Greytown as quickly as possible; in the confusion, the body of one man, Sergeant Brown, was left on the field. It was found the following day, disembowelled and mutilated; Bambatha's war-doctor, Malaza, had removed Brown's top lip – which boasted a fine moustache – and right forearm to make *intelezi* medicine.

The action at Mpanza precipitated the main outbreak of the rebellion. Although only a handful of policemen had been killed, the death of any white official at African hands caused huge concern in the white community, preying as it did on deep-seated insecurities. Outlying farmers fled into Greytown, and the town went into laager, while the authorities rushed troops to the area.

For Bambatha, the attack had been a striking success. Only three of his warriors had been wounded, and this was taken as sure proof that the protective medicines he claimed to have brought from Dinuzulu were extremely effective. Moreover, the body parts removed from Sergeant Brown were sure to add to Bambatha's *itonya* – the mysterious spiritual force which ensured him superiority over his enemy. Nevertheless, Bambatha was not fool enough to think these would protect him from the wrath of the authorities, and soon after the attack he and his warriors abandoned the Mpanza, moving northwest, towards the border with Zululand.

The rebels crossed the Thukela into the territory of the Ntuli people, who had a long history of loyalty to the Zulu Royal House. In theory, the colonial authorities expected any chief through whose territory the rebels passed to arrest and surrender them; Bambatha, however, making good use of Dinuzulu's name, and the success of his *intelezi* medicines, managed to persuade a section of the Ntuli, under Mangathi kaGodide, to support him. From there, with his adherents, Bambatha moved eastwards, towards the Nkandla forest.

The Nkandla had long been regarded as a place of refuge in Zululand – Cetshwayo had hidden there after his defeat by Zibhebhu in 1883 – but it held particular attractions for Bambatha. The Nkandla was the territory of the amaCube people, who were ruled over by Chief Sigananda kaSokufa, now in his nineties and held in great respect throughout the country. In his youth Sigananda had fled Zululand after arousing Mpande's ire, and had been given sanctuary among the Zondi by Bambatha's grandfather; Bambatha therefore hoped to be sympathetically received among the Cube. Moreover, the grave of King Cetshwayo also lay in Cube territory, and it was to prove a potent rallying point for the rebel forces.

The Cube, too, should have surrendered Bambatha, but they were disillusioned after nearly twenty years of colonial rule, and many among them had refused to pay the poll tax. Bambatha argued vehemently that his aim was to restore the authority of the Zulu kings, and Sigananda, whose father had been a friend of Shaka, and who had himself served in Dingane's *amabutho*, was persuaded. Once it became known that Sigananda had joined the rebels, there was a very real danger that the rising would spread throughout Zululand. Many chiefs who were tempted to join asked Dinuzulu for his advice; ironically, in the light of subsequent events, Dinuzulu told them firmly to remain loyal.

The colonial response was to attempt to contain Bambatha in the Nkandla, and to intimidate any chief who might contemplate joining him. The Natal militia units were hastily mustered, and supported by volunteer units raised in both Natal and the Transvaal. Anti-rebel sentiment was running high in the white community, and there was no shortage of recruits. Troops and police units were rushed into Zululand to form a Zululand Field Force, under the command of Colonel Duncan McKenzie, an experienced officer whose tough methods had already earned him the praise-name 'Shaka' among the Africans.

McKenzie's main force concentrated at Dundee, in northern Natal, and moved south towards the Thukela. At least one wavering chief along the route – Mehlokazulu kaSihayo – was so intimidated by the troops' approach they he decided to join the rebels. Another Natal force was established at Fort Yolland, which lay between the Nkandla and Eshowe to the east, while smaller forces were established below the Thukela to the south. McKenzie's plan was that these forces should gradually converge on the rebel stronghold.

Yet the Nkandla was difficult terrain for European troops. It consisted of patches of dense primordial forest, spread over a succession of steep, twisting ridges and plunging valleys. While the rebels could move through the forests without detection, the colonial troops were hampered by wheeled transport and by poor intelligence. Moreover, Bambatha deliberately sought to avoid open confrontation with large concentrations of white troops. Whereas Mehlokazulu's followers adopted strictly traditional tactics at the battle of Mpukinyoni at the end of May 1906 – when troops attempted to head off Mehlokazulu's move to the Nkandla – Bambatha made no attempt to attack either troops or white civilians, but instead contented himself with keeping on the move, rallying support, and only fighting when cornered. In action, his men avoided mass attacks in the open, but tried to ambush their enemy from cover.

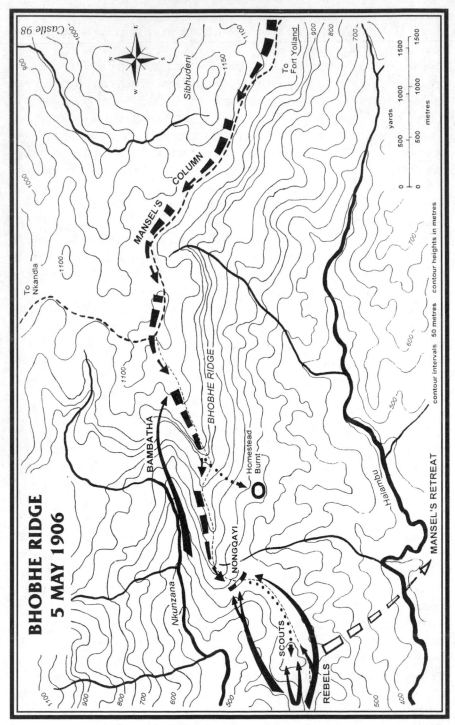

BHOBHE RIDGE
5 MAY 1906

By the beginning of May, the cordon was beginning to close in on the rebels. On 5 May Lieutenant Colonel Mansel marched out from Fort Yolland with a mixed force, consisting of 410 white troops (principally Durban Light Infantry), 86 Zululand Police (Nongqayi), and 400 auxiliaries. Mansel does not appear to have had any firm objectives, beyond reconnoitring the country towards Cetshwayo's grave. After a hot, tiring march across difficult terrain, Mansel's column had straggled over several miles of road, and as it passed through the outlying areas of the Nkandla forest, it came under sporadic sniper fire. The road ran past the head of a high, narrow ridge, known as Bhobhe, which fell away steeply to the left in the direction of Cetshwayo's grave, and Mansel ordered his column off the road, and down the ridge. A party of mounted DLI were in the lead, followed by the Nongqayi on foot. The head of the column had descended about half-way down the ridge when suddenly some 300 rebels sprang up from the cover of an overgrown field about 100 yards to the right. They shouted the war-cry 'uSuthu!', and came forward at a run, with their shields held up in front of their faces, convinced that Bambatha's *intelezi* charms would ward off the white men's bullets. The DLI scouts dismounted to return the fire, then fell back on the Nongqayi, further up the ridge. Several horses were startled by the noise, and refused to let their riders mount, and these were forced to run back on foot, in some cases just a few yards ahead of the rebels. The Nongqayi formed a front to the right of the road, and opened a heavy fire on the rebels, who nonetheless pushed forward with great determination, and at least one was killed by the bayonet. By this time, however, elements from the rest of the column were pushing down the slope to support the Nongqayi. Although the rebel attack now extended across the road, the rebels could not withstand the heavy fire to which they were exposed, and began to fall back.

Once the first attack had been repulsed, Mansel regrouped his column, and pressed further down the spur. The rearguard were still descending the high slopes below the road, however, when another rebel *impi* came into sight, advancing up from a valley on the right. This was commanded by Bambatha himself, mounted on horseback. Almost certainly, Bambatha had planned to attack the vanguard and rearguard simultaneously, but owing to the difficult ground, and the fact that Mansel's column was so extended, he had not been able to reach the rearguard in time. As his men pressed up the slope, they came under brisk fire from the troops above them, and abandoned their attack without attempting to charge. Small groups of rebels continued to shadow the column as it descended the ridge, however, and on several occasions came close enough to force the rearguard to halt and fire on them. Nevertheless, the column reached the foot of the ridge safely, and turned back towards Fort Yolland. The rebels shadowed them for several miles, but despite the onset of nightfall, did not press their attack again.

Although the action at Bhobhe was unsatisfactory to Mansel, it was a bitter disappointment to the rebels. Bambatha had planned to trap the troops in very difficult terrain, but had proved unable to execute the plan properly, and about 60 warriors had been killed. The rebel commanders blamed one another for the failure, with Bambatha accusing Sigananda's followers – who had made the initial attack – of incompetence, while the Cube pointedly asked why Bambatha had failed to press home his own attack. More serious, however, was the realisation that Bambatha's *itonya* had deserted him; that his much-vaunted *intelezi* medicines had clearly failed to ward off the soldiers' bullets. The spectacle of Bambatha being publicly berated by women who had lost menfolk in the attack opened cracks in the rebel coalition, and they immediately dispersed. Sigananda and his followers hid out in the bush near the Mome gorge – their traditional stronghold – while Bambatha retired west to Macala mountain.

Over the next three weeks, McKenzie's troops converged on Cetshwayo's grave, and from there made a number of sweeps through the Nkandla, destroying Sigananda's deserted homestead, and trying to pin down the rebel forces. This resulted in a number of skirmishes, and the death of up to 60 rebels, but did not prove decisive. On 3 June about 150 rebels – mostly Sigananda's followers – were killed in a stiff action at Manzipambana in the Nkandla, but Sigananda remained in hiding, while the whereabouts of Bambatha were unknown. Moreover, on 17 May some of McKenzie's troops, burning grass near their camp at Cetshwayo's grave, accidentally set fire to the thicket which marked the site of the grave itself. Although McKenzie was adamant that this was an accident, it was a deeply offensive act to most Zulu, and probably helped to spread popular sympathy for the revolt.

Nevertheless, the rebel leaders were becoming concerned at the lack of widespread support for the rising. Although Mehlokazulu was on the point of joining the rebel cause, few other chiefs had done so, and on 20 May Bambatha and Mangathi rode to the oSuthu homestead to try to persuade Dinuzulu to commit himself publicly to their cause. Dinuzulu, wisely, wanted to remain aloof; while privately he may have sympathised, he no doubt saw that the rebels had little chance of achieving a military success, and his response was blunt. 'If you desire to fight', he was reported as saying, 'go and do so, it is not my doing. Go and join Mehlokazulu, I hear he has joined the rebels.'

Discouraged, Bambatha and Mangathi returned to Macala, where they had left their *impi*. By this time, Mehlokazulu and his followers were in the vicinity, and the two forces combined amounted to 23 companies – between 1200 and

1500 men. This was the largest force so far assembled by the rebels, and despite their recent successes, it posed a very real threat to the colonial forces. Mehlokazulu, because of his formidable reputation as a warrior, assumed overall command, and it was decided to move the force from Macala to the Nkandla. Despite McKenzie's activities in the region, it was felt that the Mome gorge was such a strong natural defensive position that it remained the most secure base for the rebel army.

The rebels moved out from Macala on the 9th, and reached the mouth of the Mome late that afternoon. Mangathi was anxious that they should proceed into the gorge itself, but Mehlokazulu was tired, and scoffed at reports that there were troops in the vicinity. While Mangathi wisely took several companies of his own followers into the gorge, Mehlokazulu and Bambatha camped at the mouth.

This was a fatal mistake. While European commentators have blamed subsequent events on Mehlokazulu's over-confidence, many Zulu understood that this was final proof that Bambatha's *itonya* had deserted him. The rebels seemed blind to any danger, even when a herdboy reported the sound of muffled cannon-wheels in the darkness. Moreover, a heavy mist hung over the rebel camp when dawn broke on the 10th, obscuring the fact that McKenzie's troops had, indeed, surrounded the gorge during the night. Mehlokazulu and Bambatha sent out scouts to investigate the rumours of troop movements, and they hurried back to report that the enemy were in position around three sides of the gorge mouth; the gorge itself offered the only possibility of flight. Bambatha and Mehlokazulu assembled their men, forming them into a circle, an *umkhumbi*, to receive instructions. At that point, if further proof that their luck had deserted them were needed, the mist lifted, and, clustered together as they were, they were suddenly fully exposed to the troops.

The battle of Mome gorge was lost within the first few minutes. No sooner did they spot the rebel concentration than the colonial forces opened heavy machine-gun and shellfire on it. As shot and shell rained down on them, a few *izinduna* kept their heads, and tried to direct their men to the attack, but their formations were soon broken up, and the rest fled in panic through the mouth of the gorge. Bambatha himself, in this crucial moment of his greatest military test, apparently lost control, and fled with his men. No sooner had they entered the gorge, however, than they found the upper reaches were also surrounded by troops under McKenzie's personal control. The gorge became a death-trap, and over most of that day the troops lining the heights simply shot down the rebels at their leisure. Over 600 rebels were killed, including Mehlokazulu, and the heart was cut out of the rebellion in Zululand.

Once the battle was over, the authorities became anxious to know what had happened to Bambatha himself. The chief's fame had grown to the extent that it was necessary to prove without doubt that he was dead. Five days after the battle, one of Bambatha's personal attendants surrendered to the troops, and offered to lead them to Bambatha's body. A party under the command of Sergeant Calverley of the Zululand Mounted Rifles, and including two men from Bambatha's chiefdom who knew him well, descended into the gorge, where the rebel dead were still lying thickly on the ground, many of them already in an advanced state of decay. Bambatha's servant took them to the body of a man, wearing a white shirt, who was lying on the banks of the Mome stream, a few hundred yards from the entrance. During the battle this man had been spotted walking up the stream, unarmed, by two auxiliaries, one of whom was in front of him, the other behind. The rebel spotted the man ahead of him, and made for the river bank, only to have the man behind rush forward and stab him in the back. The rebel fell, but was still alive, and as the auxiliary tried to pull out his spear, he found that it had bent in the man's body, and would not come loose. While the two were struggling, the other auxiliary rushed over and also tried to stab him, but the rebel grabbed the blade with both hands. While all three were tussling, a Nongqayi came past, and shot the rebel through the head. Since at that stage there was no interest in his identity, the body was left where it fell.

By the time Calverley saw it, it was already beginning to decompose, and the head was badly disfigured by the rifle-shot. Nevertheless, Bambatha's men claimed to identify the body from various distinguishing features, including scars on the face, a gap between the front teeth, and a slight beard under the chin. Since it was impractical to remove the entire body from the gorge, Calverley cut off the head, and took it back to camp. Here it was placed under guard in the care of the medical department. According to official sources, it was only shown to a small number of officials and *izinduna* as proof of Bambatha's death, before it was returned to the gorge to be buried near the body. The existence of several photographs which show troops posing with it in triumph suggest, however, that the respect due to the remains of a chief was forgotten in the euphoria of the moment.

There is, indeed, some doubt that it was ever Bambatha's head. Rumours began to circulate soon after the rebellion that Bambatha was not dead, but had escaped the massacre, and gone into hiding. Certainly, Bambatha's widow, Seyikiwe, did not go into mourning, as custom dictated she should. Moreover, in recent times, the descendants of both Sigananda's people are adamant that Bambatha survived the massacre. While the grave of Mehlokazulu remains a landmark in the Mome gorge, the Cube still deny the existence of Bambatha's grave. Moreover, the Zondi insist that the authorities were deliberately duped by Bambatha's followers, who had directed that one of the chief's attendants identify the body of a man who resembled him, and then conspired to support his claim. Certainly, none of the white officers who saw the head had ever met Bambatha in life. According to this view of events, Bambatha escaped to Mozambique, where he lived for a few years in exile. He later returned to Zulu-land, where Seyikiwe joined him, and he lived out the rest of his life in obscu-rity, under an assumed name.

It is perhaps a suitably mysterious end for a man who had been among the least likely champions of the old Zulu order.

The battle of the Mome gorge did not end the rising, but it did quash the movement in Zululand. A week later a fresh outbreak broke out among groups living on the southern bank of the Thukela, near the coast. This rising remained largely local in character, however, and the leaders made little attempt to form a united army of resistance. Indeed, they had little chance to do so, for the full weight of the authorities descended upon them, and the rising was ruthlessly suppressed. By the time the rebellion was finally declared over, over 4000 rebels had been killed, 7000 had been imprisoned, and hundreds flogged. Hundreds of homesteads had been destroyed, and thou-sands of head of cattle confiscated. As one African survivor commented, 'Happy are those who fought and are dead.' By contrast, a total of 24 white troops had died during the rebellion, not all of them as a result of enemy action.

Bambatha's rebellion proved to be the last attempt by adherents of the Zulu kingdom to restore their position through military means. If nothing else, it had proved that the heroic tradition of waging warfare with shields and spears was hopelessly out of date in a world of magazine rifles and Maxim guns. Nevertheless, the spirit of Bambatha has survived into recent times, in more senses than one. Bambatha's image had a contemporary appeal to those who struggled to keep African rights – and the tradition of the Zulu king – alive throughout the subsequent decades, when the reality of military defeat and white rule had created for most Africans a very different world from that of Shaka, Cetshwayo or even Dinuzulu.

And there are said to be ghosts, too, in the Mome gorge, which is still a remote and mysterious spot. They were first encountered a few years after the battle, and they looked like ordinary men. Except that they had no mouths, and could not speak; instead, they moaned, a soft, terrible noise, that spoke for the sufferings of the long-dead warriors, and their dispos-sessed descendants.

FURTHER READING

Binns, C.T., *The Last Zulu King; The Life and Death of Cetshwayo* (London, 1963)

Binns, C.T., *Dinuzulu; The Death of the House of Shaka* (London, 1968)

Bulpin, T.V., *Shaka's Country* (Cape Town, 1952)

Castle, Ian, and Knight, Ian, *Fearful Hard Times; The Siege and Relief of Eshowe, 1879.* (London, 1994).

Emery, Frank, *The Red Soldier; Letters from the Zulu War, 1879* (London, 1977)

Gibson, J.Y., *The Story of the Zulus,* (London, 1911)

Knight, Ian, *Great Zulu Battles 1838-1906* (London, 1998)

Knight, Ian, *Brave Men's Blood; The Epic of the Zulu War* (London, 1990).

Knight, Ian, *Zulu; The Battles of Isandlwana and Rorke's Drift, 22/23rd January 1879* (London, 1992)

Knight, Ian, *Nothing Remains But To Fight; The Defence of Rorke's Drift, 1879* (London, 1993).

Knight, Ian *The Anatomy of the Zulu Army; From Shaka to Cetshwayo* (London, 1994).

Knight, Ian, *The Zulus* (London, 1989).

Knight, Ian, *British Forces in Zululand, 1879* (London, 1991)

Knight, Ian, *Zulu, 1816-1906* (London, 1995)

Knight, Ian, *Rorke's Drift; Pinned Like Rats in a Trap* (London, 1995).

Knight, Ian, and Castle, Ian, *Zulu War 1879; Twilight of a Warrior Nation* (London, 1992)

Knight, Ian, and Castle, Ian, *The Zulu War; Then and Now* (London, 1994)

Laband, John, Rope of Sand; *The Rise and Fall of the Zulu Kingdom in the Nineteenth Century* (Johannesburg, 1995; also published London, 1997, under the title *The Fall of the Zulu Nation*).

Laband, John, *Kingdom in Crisis; The Zulu response to the British invasion of 1879* (Manchester and New York, 1992)

Laband, John, and Knight, Ian, *The War Correspondents; The Anglo-Zulu War* (Gloucestershire, 1996).

Laband, John, *The Battle of Ulundi* (Pietermaritzburg and Ulundi, 1988)

Laband, John, *Fight Us In The Open; The Anglo-Zulu War Through Zulu Eyes* (Pietermaritzburg and Ulundi, 1985)

Laband, John, and Matthews, Jeff, *Isandlwana* (Pietermaritzburg and Ulundi, 1992)

Laband, John, and Wright, John, *King Cetshwayo kaMpande* (Pietermaritzburg and Ulundi, 1980)

Laband, John, and Thompson, Paul, *Field Guide to the War in Zululand the Defence of Natal* (Pietermaritzburg, revised edition, 1987)

Laband, John, and Thompson, Paul, *Kingdom and Colony at War; Sixteen Studies on the Anglo-Zulu War of 1879* (Pietermaritzburg and Constantia, 1990)

Lock, Ron, *Blood on the Painted Mountain; Zulu Victory and Defeat, Hlobane and Khambula* (London, 1995)

Lugg, H.C., *Historic Natal and Zululand* (Pietermaritzburg 1949)

Mitford, B., *Through The Zulu Country; It's Battlefields and its People* (London, 1883)

Marks, Shula, *Reluctant Rebellion; The 1906-08 Disturbances in Natal* (Oxford, 1970).

Stuart, James, *A History of the Zulu Rebellion, 1906* (London, 1913).

Taylor, Stephen, *Shaka's Children; A History of the Zulu People* (London, 1994).

Webb, C. de B., and Wright, J.B. (eds), *The James Stuart Archive of Recorded Oral Evidence Relating to the Zulu and Neighbouring Peoples* (Four Vols, Pietermaritzburg and Durban, 1976,

INDEX